@abigfuckingbully

@abigfuckingbully

© 2019 by Atticus Davis
This edition © Heavy Athletics

All rights reserved.

Printed in the United States of America

No part of this book may be reproduced or transmitted in any form or by any means, electronic or mechanical, including photocopying, recording, or by any information storage and retrieval system, without permission in writing from the copyright owner.

This is a work of fiction. Names, characters, places, and incidents either are the product of the author's imagination or are use fictitiously, and any resemblance to any actual persons, living or dead, events, or locales, is entirely coincidental.

Book design by Atticus Davis
Cover art by Atticus Davis

@abigfuckingbully

@abigfuckingbully

NOTHING BUT GOD

.I

IN A FIT

My determination to leave the village is in direct proportion to the feelings of futility it bred. Santa Clara's a town that, had it not been making trickle down money from its urban hubs, could easily be mistaken as Salem as much as it was seen from outsiders as a signpost of prosperity. We knew it wasn't: witnessing out a 9x9 gridded window, from across the lot, a burglary, where a hooded figure darted into a cage-link door and ran across the only light on in the invaded house. He ran out, with something in his hand. A thin dripping trail of blood, snailing behind him.
    An invalid picking a fight in the complex parking lot.
    Enough domestic disputes—the sirens running up and down our streets like jockey's, like race dogs, like vermin look for heads to break, lead pipes to busy themselves chewing, Karen Drive was a place regularly combed by police.
    The S.W.A.T. team was called in once for a suicide attempt gone hostage situation. Where some Marilyn Manson fan pressed a gun to his mother's head swearing, 'I'll kill her for fuck's sake, I'll pull this trigger if these cops don't fucking leave. Just let me do it in peace." The entire block and myself rubbernecking, watching without enough fear, like it was daytime drama.
    On Independence Day a gunshot I whispered to myself, like a mantra, was 'only a firework.' Out of my window I stared at the lights swelling into the scene. All I could see was a pair of Jordan's soaked in blood poking out from behind the tires of a cable van across the street. Safe in here, you think to yourself. It has nothing to do with you. It was just a man with a heater on a bicycle, left out for too long. Are we lonely out here?
At a certain point a even a pig's baton is touch.
    Living in the suburbs but never really invited.
    The corner next to the record player, with a joint and an introvert: my neighborhood.
The pretty girls would sometimes stop in for the novelty, giving you rides for artisanal coffee at the outdoor mall. You never went anywhere without them and that's when I started to get sick of myself, when I hated every woman I got to know who paid attention.
    Animals go blind living in the dark for so long.

@abigfuckingbully

My car broke down and I was sleeping in it for the week I was waiting move in. I stayed in the area I first parked in, paranoid because it was stuffed like a piñata with what I belonged to—my hereditament: clothes, a mattress, and my house, a car. Offered seamless transfer to one of my job's original retail locations.

I met him at a Starbucks®, the cheapest coffee shop I could choose populated enough to avoid my own murder, which seemed a sensible concern after my ex- girlfriend's classmate was raped and murdered meeting with the infamous Craigslist Killer. I sensed he was insane but like many determined people, I ignored my instincts. The science minded are the most vulnerable to lapses in logic. A mind's contents: the weakest thing you can rely on. The projection of your own equality into the world is not insurance from a snake eats snake reality. I was either going to be hung up, decapitated on the fence of nearby development, body winding down cage-wire like a gnarled root of a nearby tree, or going to have a room in Santa Monica.

He sat in front of me awkwardly wearing a yellowed white -t under a heather grey zip up hoodie. His appearance was disheveled; he had beady eyes, thick black hair, and 5 O'clock shadow—kept asking for the deposit.

"I want to see the room first."

He shadowed me to an ATM where I pulled the money and flashed it. Then I followed him to the complex and was told to wait outside. There was a conflict inside, a yelling fit, with me embarrassed, flushed, and nauseated. I summoned all of myself and dragged myself by the collar to the front door, hammering on it. The ex-tenant of my room was answering the door. The master tenant pushed forward, past him. Off more drugs than he was on, I imagine, he swore to me everything was fine. I spent the night inside of his room, him telling me, calmly, "Sorry, he's just...frustrated. He's supposed to be out of his room already. He should be gone by tomorrow."

Nerve-burnt, totally alone, and without refuge, I accepted the cartoon's offer of spending the night but couldn't sleep. My instincts, which I consciously push aside, allowed me to tap into a determination for safety that kept me wired until 4 a.m. Stupidly, I watched Blade Runner in its entirety. I finally fell asleep, waking at 6:47 a.m. From a nightmare of an Asian Lieutenant strangling me. I moaned into the room, it was empty now.

■

Scouring Craigslist® was an act of desperation. There had been warnings posted:

BEWARE! ROOM SCAM, SANTA MONICA!

Do not trust room listing for room on Wilshire. I responded and arranged to supply deposit when I found out there was no room available. The room was occupied! Then never saw him again!!!!!!

    I went back to my car to wait and confront the thief.
    I called the police and waited for news. Staying in the area a few days before he was scheduled to start working again. I got a message from the master-tenant who assured me 'the situation is fine, it's only a matter of time.' The police told me the same thing. Unless I could prove anything was stolen, there was a breach of contract, or if there was a disturbance at the house.
    I was spending time in places with free Wi-Fi where there's always a hissing espresso machine prodding me into tears before the next game plan. Fighting hard for the safety of anonymity "Nothing to see here..." as I cried in coffee shops.
    It's the suburban fear that keeps their children suburban, poverty and psychopathology are the mainstays of the city. Debauchery, open mindedness, and excitement were side effects. The cities were okay to build yourself up in but no place to stay any longer than you needed. It was the threat of a child learning too quickly and in learning too quickly is estranged from the world it inhabited.
    Curiosity is perversion; anyone displaying too much emotion is a threat. Curiosity is an interest, interest a vulnerability, vulnerability like walking in on a roach crawling out of your drain. After the lights turn on and the screams have finished tripping in waves across the porcelain, you put him out like a cigarette.
    You could be him—scuttling back into the sink. Get what you want when they throw their fit, know they could spend their lives terrorized by your existence...but adapting to your surroundings too much was considered maladaptive itself. In a world so transposable, inconsistency was adaption.

■

The sun's purple over my rightful complex. I notice a letter tucked under my windshield wiper, and begin slipping a phallic forefinger into the soft lips of the envelope when red and blue lights were barking in my periphery. The siren sounded in chopped taps as it drove into the driveway almost up the stairs. A shouting match that slowly came into ear's focus. He was there, holding a mattress over his head, prepared to throw it over the balcony if the tenant stayed any longer. He'd promised.
    "Goddamn it! You fucking creep—I just moved in here!"
    The police leapt out of the car and walked up the stairs. The white man with his hands around his belt, pulling up his pants, his elbows bent at a 15° angle. Leading the patrol with his puffed up chest followed by a black woman with a short braided hairstyle and baton out, clapping it, classically, into the palm of her free hand.
    "What's the problem here?"
    The white cop shouted to interrupt the fit by threat of force alone.

Authority is a threat by force. The man threw the mattress off of the balcony and the black cop kept her gun on him. They rushed up the stairs to finally detain the delusional pathy. What about being sheltered too long can drive a man into the determination it takes to stay locked away all day in his room, away from the work, away from the sun, away from the fair?

We're satellites inspecting one another; constantly praying we can make contact. Communication is so high risk we have a barrier at all times. We don't like hands on interactions, we imagine the heat and pressure to be enough to burn our skin, so feeling itself, heat and pressure, human touch is alien. The police are social lubricant; they acted as a physical manifestation of the modern world's practical material mindset.

The pigs grabbed him and dragged him down the steps, he was laid out like a carpet being slid to the bottom, where then, like a blow up clown, he was beat into submission, fists raining down on him, with a pigs baton following as an accented up beat. He was gurgling blood, slowly pushed up and out by a spasming tongue, loose teeth spiraling in and out of the mess in his mouth.

I watched it all, running immediately to offer a concerned testimony. I felt I was watching my life in perfect cell division, repeating it, squared after. Existence in the Nth, functioning on artificial intelligence, intelligence itself. The suburbs are following me, my suburban is showing, this was a mistake.

■

I turn on the radio, leaning back in my seat listening to the slow churning beat until my vision blurred and the tears stream across my eyes. Vacantly burning for vacancy while burning inside sunbeams. The sky was red again, my vision red, the sound closing in on me, all around me a crushing presence, the present. The positive would say plans change and to keep moving forward. Even though my Shakespearean fate is screaming for me to submit to the weight of homelessness, no matter how safe I really am in reality.

I closed my eyes, which coughed up their last bouts, tears sputtering, like the death rattle of my Saab, I heard it die, turned the key and heard it momentarily be resurrected. My initiation—my primal rite. It was all as black as life before birth, its gestation the big bang—everything stems from this moment.

.II

FATHER FIGURE

Trapped in Barstow, California for the next hour, he was thinking of his arrival, somewhere else. Trying to focus on staying in the lines, he thought of the last time he had seen his son, the feeling he hadn't seen him since 'staying in the lines' was advice he'd given him. That's how Taylor always imagined his children. The divorcee hadn't seen his children in three years even though he lived in the same state now. His eyes on the road were both vacant and burning. Taylor's son once dated a girl Taylor was convinced was a heroin addict, a woman he strongly disapproved of, she had the same exact look he has on now. It's the same look though, it's like the trainwreck of a heart—something gasping it's last breath, stuttering it's fucked death rattle, before flying off the rails in silence and slow motion. It was the only water running; the head was empty except for traffic lights:

Scrolling through Google image results for 'waif,' like through a Viewmaster®, his mind held up to traffic. The 3D Rolodex® for a reminder, both of how he felt and how he couldn't admit to himself, but knew, that his children felt. His heart was burping up emotions but it stopped pushing blood years ago—it was an ant race of shifting lint through his arteries.

■

He was out of the shower now, staring at a hotel bible in a half-pulled drawer buttoning a striped shirt up. It wasn't that he couldn't imagine a different way of dress; it was that Taylor's life was full of Sunday's bests three times a week. Taylor had age on him; at 52 it wasn't enough to topple a deep youthfulness. His Grandfather left him a receding hairline, as baldness skips a generation.

He looked from The Bible to the dresser mirror and stretched his neck, exposing himself to himself. Grey chest hairs reminding him ironically of youth. Leaving the top two buttons loose he picked up a golden chain from next to the hotel Bible and placed it around his neck, framed perfectly. A cross dangled.

He picked up the Bible, such an ancient tool of wisdom where all points were a point of entry. This mimicked man's stance at our point in the food chain, tertiary predators who can access the food web at any point—the most enduring and highly evolved predator. Tarot Card readings where Luck was God's will. He opened The Book.

16 So, because you are lukewarm—neither hot nor cold—I am about to spit you out of my mouth.

He closed The Good Book, touching his pendant, his forefingers scanning its rocky surface. The emaciated body of Christ running into his fingerprints. He opened the drawer and neatly tucked the Bible in. Then he moved to the his bedside, sitting with perfect posture. He lifted the phone and started dialing a number. The phone rang, Taylor was nervous. The phone rang again. Taylor opened his vacant palm as if there was something to read. The phone fed his ear a computerized ring. Then a silence, almost with a click.

"We're sorry—"

His son's voice came through the static, "Jordan Stookey."

"—is not currently available, leave a message after the tone. To leave a call back number press 9."

A sustained beep sounded and Taylor could now feel the pressure of him on air. He was good at writing letters; he always wanted to be a writer.

"Hey, Jordan," he started, with the weight of disappointment in his voice, pressing into the receiving parties receiver. A whisper of what it could be—

"I'm in Los Angeles, and I've got some time to see you, my son. I'm heading to an event later, so call me when you get this. I love you. I'm so proud of you, Jordan."

He put the phone down after a second of breath. He laid himself down on a completely untouched bed. The accents, different shades of browns, framed the sheet in a different way. Each line an opportunity to see it's blank beige in a new way. He leaned into the headboard, both hands behind his head. Then he turned off the light. The blinds already closed still leaked a small trace around Taylor. His chest rose and sank. He closed his eyes.

■

The blood rose to his face when he heard the phone grating against it's casing, it growled until Taylor found his eyes rolling back from out of their sleep and he reached for the phone.

"Hey, dad."

Like he was eating, "H—ello."

"How are you?"

"I'm good! I'm in the Los Angeles area, I was wondering if you wanted to meet up."

"Yeah, sure. I can show you around Santa Monica. Where are you?"

"I'm closer to downtown."

"Alright, I'll get ready now—it'll probably be an hour."

"Okay. That sounds great."

"Alright, see you soon, dad."
"Love you, Jordan."
There was a pause.
"Love you too. See you."
The phone clicked.
Taylor put down his receiver.

.III

UNCOMMON UNION

"You're driving now?"

My father had never seen me in the driver's seat before. He had never taught any of his children to drive so it was magic he could be given a tour of a town he knew for so long. My eldest brother was born in San Diego and Los Angeles was an area so full of life and culture; he couldn't help but stay for weeks at a time. For being bred in the sticks, dad had a cultural understanding deeper than some of the most educated urban-blooded peoples. Maybe it was the Frank Sinatra he had been exposed to opening his eyes to a world of lights, brooding with potential that both attracted and frightened him. In this weird way, he was a star-struck hopeful.

His upbringing had given him beauty—the gifts that only nature can nurture in man. It's stillness as vast as traffic jams in Los Angeles, blackouts in Oakland, the satisfaction of feelings of belonging in a place so new and unnatural to you that you thrive in it. Some of us, in sink or swim, always swim, while the passivity that comfort breeds makes even the fiercest minds go soft—clay in the hands of context. Loveless labors made daily that by sheer force bore the spirit into absolute submission. Deserts where even the most stimulated—the most introverted—are sawed through like butter.

"It's great to see you...my son." he smiles and a puts a hand on my shoulder, adding comically a dramatic my son but mostly out of an sincere guilt and insecurity, a reminder that I'm, still, his son.

I smile.

"It's great to see you too, it's been a long time."

A motor was lulling.

"What're you doing down here?"

"Oh—I'm here for work, building the business."

I'd been distanced for so long the phrased triggered no recall.

"With the Tribune?"

"No this is a separate thing, it's an event. I was wondering if you wanted to come with me."

I was stone faced, looking away and when turning forward, smiled.

"What is it?"

"It's some speakers from around the country. I'd really like it if you came."

.

Brevity was pressing hard enough to press sweat through my collar.

"Maybe...what is it?

What do you want to do right now?"

"Show me around—it's your neck of the woods. What would you want to do right now if you could do anything you wanted to?"

The sun cleared even the South's infamous and suffocating smog. It was cut through, clearing way to a sapphire blue, tickled by the feathers of tall palms, the frame of any sight. You could only look up. In so many cities you felt consumed by your sight, weighted by greys in complexes and businesses burying you to only feel concrete and your eyes, the pressure to watch with a fearful eye counting cracks in pavement, as if open eyes and awareness weren't only impossible but uninteresting. Cities claustrophobic, heated, air like the breath of its occupants. Death in every bored conversation—everything sounds like a mutter, bodies dragging themselves back-shuffle into the safety of chain link front gates. Door knobs handled by so many before so nothing was old enough or new enough. You could never break a space in or feel the history of it before you.

What was it that brought so many people to the same crowded spaces? It wasn't the immigrants that came with gifts to offer it, wasn't the shining promise of commerce—it was a myth built on the rusted bones of predecessors, the myth passed on in whispers, part by commercialized local histories and part by the settlers, the new money sucked all of the primordial talent up and is pissing it's remnants all over territories new money live in. Centuries ago it was acceptable but here and now it was the glue of a myth, passed on from the suburban satellites of interest and like a dime bag, hand to hand in a cycle making every major city something like Hollywood.

The hotbed San Francisco used to be, its political and artistic history was gone. The women who made it were buried. They could not afford to be buried there anymore. Sid Vicious, arrested for public intoxication said it all, his hypocrisy as a pillar of punk:

"You can't arrest me! I'm a fucking rock star!"

In the end even the infamous are seeking fame. Recognition in a society where on some fundamental level, the most immediate, it did not exist. In the end everyone just wanted to be an icon in a world of symbols—even if it meant being a rune, a hieroglyph—anything but nothing. Anything but what we are right now. A goal so huge and unattainable it seemed specific without a specific plan, just need. That's what brings us together—need. No one doesn't have it.

"We can go the Boardwalk and then Venice and check out the shops. Whatever you want. What're you feeling like?"

"Are you hungry at all?"

"Yeah, you want to get some Pho?"

"Pho?"

"It's...a Vietnamese style soup."

"Jordan, do you remember when you were really little and I took you with me on a trip from San Diego to San Francisco. You were probably, 8."

I remember it, vividly, as the youngest and least traumatized by childhood. Repression was never a necessary survival skill. I had always been the

12

most proud of the pride and my rebelliousness left me unbroken through all the attempts at caging me in God the Father's discipline. As family keeper, I remembered with both eyes the most vital parts of us. I gave them all of my attention. Seeing more good than bad naturally I was hero to my four brothers who in childhood severely rejected me as an other. My annoying, clingy, tendencies drove them away. After seceding, the family motto was, W.W.J.D., 'What would Jordan do?'

"Yeah I remember. I found the journals you kept before we left for California."

"I wish I would've kept those, I think I threw a lot of that out..."

"It even had drawings I did in the car."

"It was so long ago." he said.

"So, you're hungry?"

■

I stopped in a well-lit parking lot we had to pay for in West Hollywood. Dad got out of passenger's side and I followed after, leading him down to an animated Pho bowl pouring itself out in neon. It was packed so I asked the waitress for a time.

"For two? About 15 minutes."

"Lucky..."

Outside the weather simulating a damp room. Dad was sweating, the sunburn in his face had time to calm, he was still swollen, but better.

"So what's it like to finally be out of your mom's place?"

Dad was rubbing everyone the wrong way with a speech about how 'the boys needed to earn their own keep now' that we were older, last time he visited California, before his life-affirming move of familial desperation. Wondering what 'the boys' were still doing living with their mother, though at the time to oldest was 20. Dad was a strong believer in the myth that everyone got what they deserved, and that there was no explanation except for lack of willpower for a lack of anything you needed. Both financial and psychological bootstrapping were his core beliefs, as an in denial, at risk, schizophrenic, and ex-alcoholic. His children who had failed to meet the standard disappointed him.

Good intentions: really just another way to conquer. Dad never made a full child support payment since the divorce, and Mom, used to doing everything herself, felt hopeless, taking no legal action. Her helplessness was the rich girl syndrome found in Nihilistic women who see no better future and who's longing to help themselves, undermined, turned into sympathy for others. Literally translated—pathetic. Mom was well cared for in her youth, in better conditions than she'd ever had in America. Feeling sorry for others whether or not they can afford it. Helplessness and a dream deferred made men iron fists of authority, domestic fascists, and women: paper millionaires, golden ring prostitutes, or philanthropists.

    Dad's failures were both as a human and man. He had somehow failed to keep the woman of his dreams with his plan of burdening her with children and his moral rigidity offered a weapon against his children who out of laziness he also felt he needed to control. He couldn't be too involved as he was already so wrapped up in his empty aspirations for a generic success.

But with me, he was bored enough of it to pick up again, and in me tried to find the children he'd abandoned. He had left them and now he could do them the favor, coming back to save them from their fatherlessness.

    He would write me letters of apology but we never answered his phone calls and all his letters were the same, except they took twice as much effort to complete. He took every chance he had to instill his values because if he didn't have paper, if he couldn't have publication, he would live on in his genes forever. But no one's genes are theirs anymore, in fact, the amalgamate belongs to no one. A child is brand new, it hasn't previously existed in this combination before, and the benefit of sexual reproduction is that, unlike plants, there is so little of us in something made up of so much of us. The apple doesn't fall far from tree, but people eat apples and their lungs don't shit oxygen.

    I was careful to answer the loaded question, smiling in disbelief.

    "Well, it only took me three years dad."

■

We made it to a table, following the empty, shaking skirt, to glasses half-filled with condensing ice water. She guided us to our respective seats with an outstretched arm that whipped at its fingertips and lit our chairs. Planting us, tucking ourselves excitedly into the edges of a chair. Once we fit, the waitress handed us the main menu and the drink menu, a menu Dad handled with a tearful respect, his hesitation reminiscent of the weight of a Bible. It filled his palm like a scale and it slowly dropped to the table.

    Opening my menu while the sound of hooves clicking trailed away into a swinging door, behind it, cracking glass. There were televisions in the corners of the room, all muted but almost as bright as the tropical aquarium lights. I sat in the booth side, looking at a small plate perfectly blank on the black marbled desk, with green and mild greys swirling in itself, the murk of a simulated naturalness. Past my hands that seem more brown than ever in this light and up into my father's face, unavailable.

    The memory of throwing ice down dad's t-shirt, tucked in, during a drive down from Michigan back to Indiana; he was selling something then too. Or shouting at him in front of a television, across the cottages mangy, spotted carpet in between the ends of the ratty futon. Accents of gnarled, splintering, wooden walls. Shouting as loud as I could to wake up this 6 foot tall, tank of a man from his blue-light high, stoned after the hours of just as vacant factory work. It wasn't his fault.

Dad kept a tin tub of Bag Balm®, whose tagline, "every farmer's friend," was a medicated hand balm for the strongest and most damaged hands. Farmers after hours of milking cows end to end would have calluses for palms, a new hardened skin would create a permanent pair of gardening gloves for hands. He was never all there. It was how I imagine Jericho, if I yelled loud enough I could break down the walls but after Dad snapped out of it, I felt the little 70 year old wooden casing that kept them together in one place. It would all fall, leaving the sides blown out and roof sunken in. Like years of tears no one was willing to shed had left them waterlogged. Like our lives had sat out, stagnant for too long, the way a carton of milk's sides start to bulge in a hot car.

"Dad!

Dad. Dad. Dad. Dad."

He snapped out of it again but didn't look away. He made a sound like a chopped hiss before saying, slowly in his wooden voice,

"This Boston Bombing stuff...it's just...sick."

"What happened?"

"These...terrorists, right here in America, decided they were going to bomb the finish line at the Boston Marathon."

"Oh, I thought that was unmotivated."

"No, it was Terrorists. They said they were reacting to America's presence in Afghanistan."

"I don't blame them," I said flippantly, not realizing that what would get me out of the conversation with most friends was dragging me into conflict with my father.

He knew they dressed different in California, he didn't really think that anyone he liked could have a different opinion than him, or a different sexuality, or different politics. If he thought about all the varying existences he would live his life trembling at just the thought of his own being, existing among so many others, uncontrollable and out of reach.

"You don't blame them?"

"It's stupid to use symbolic gestures in a group of two to attempt to make a major defense of Islam—specifically in a nation as apathetic as ours."

"It's disgusting. It doesn't make any sense, murdering innocent people."

"—no one's innocent here really."

This quickly turned to harsh territory. I was in church again.

"If you're not born again, then you're not saved. There was only one Jesus, and if he's not your savior..."

"You're saying if you don't believe in a Christian God, then you're going to hell. What about people who have never, ever, heard of God? People existed before God."

"No one's existed before God."

"So the Native Americans are in hell but George Bush is going to heaven?"

He paused for a long time before answering me, dead in my eyes.
"Yes."

The waitress fluttered over. Her nails were done in three different pastels on white or black, commanding all attention, her hands clipped to her checks like a throne's backing. Her black hair down to her ass, falling over her shoulders like water. She slanted her thin hips and a slender neck, and a smile grew from her dimpled cheeks, shooting a glow into my eyes waiting to ask him the question.

Dad in a nervous preoccupation took initiative, to distract himself from the sermon he'd given me. A compensational confidence for his shaken stance.

"I'll have lemonade to start." he ordered before the woman could ask. She wrote it down without looking, her eyes at me asking silently.

"I'll have a Thai Iced Tea, please."

The woman smiled and turned, almost into herself, as she disappeared behind the kitchen divide, always partially visible for being such an unnaturally tall woman.

I was face down in my palm, the other hand running laps through my hair. For a few seconds dad seemed forgivable but I saw nothing in him I recall in myself. I was not even tied genetically, literally I was, but I inherited my mother solely. Staring at this aging, white man, who may as well be a brother separated at birth. This stranger, this greying portrait...he couldn't be real. There was nothing but the impressionist finger painting of the man that had raised me.

Virtue calmed the spitting hatred in me that no man should have for a father. I wanted his mind to stop reeling and so landed on pity time and time again, but pity doesn't make a person, it barely makes a feeling. It's the atoms before they have a place. Pity is a place where nothing can be built and so a quiet resentment fills the blanks, and it chalks it up to God, or what space was before we were in it. Years had passed and the old man was the smear I remember him as.

The waitress came back with a smile bigger than before, which forced our table to shrink. Humming orders happily, dad's for the equivalent of a Chicken Noodle Soup and an order with pig's feet, for me, for the fuck of it. We ate in silence.

∎

He asked to go to a record store, the go-to option for the easily entertained. Luckily, even if I'd been jaywalking with my city legs for a year now, I was born in Indiana, the only of the brothers to be a red blooded Hoosier, an Oaky at heart. We never complained about the quiet.

I rummaged through pop for a classic, Mariah Carey, and started examining the back. Mariah Carey was almost naked, he seemed nervous. Feeling a strong guilt, flooding his hands, when I passed it to him, he was almost

shaking.
"That's such a great album. Mariah Carey is incredible."
"She sure is. Also very naked on this album."
"Well, she's beautiful."

"...have you made a lot of friends here?"
A question that lingered too long to be about 'friends.' I avoided talking about my love-life with my fundamentalist father. In phone conversations with my mom he'd scold her for not keeping a closer eye on the oldest one, who had a sexual appetite. A father is heavily invested in his son's sex life so feels responsible for it. Less puritanical families would have opened the lines even vaguely about the brooding sexual life that youth starts to sputter up, like jism but out of a pot rim, drips down into a mess that for all good reasons can't be ignored.

"Oh yeah. It's crazy how lucky I've been meeting people over here considering how horrible the move was. My roommate is one of my best friends and we really click."

"What does he do?"
"He's a sushi chef."
He flipped through another row of records.
"Where are you working right now?"
"Same job, near the boardwalk."
"How you likin' it?"
"It's good. I like it."
"You going to school?"
"Yeah, I'm taking voice lessons."
"Your cousin Katherine was taking voice classes for a while. Your Grandma's always been practicing in a choir. That's great, Jordan. I'd like to hear some of that. I miss singing, even for church. It's such a good feeling."

"I've met most of my friends through my voice class, it's helped me out a lot, I've got a great teacher. I can tell the difference."

"I used to remember taking piano lessons from this big, German, woman, 'zaftig' you could say," he laughed at his own joke, "and I hated it. I never kept up with piano after I got into high school. I regret it more than anything. I should have stuck with it..."

He let out a sigh. Nothing more concrete than regret. I smiled, it wasn't what I felt but it seemed the only appropriate response, silence. It seemed like after that the atmosphere had died without a rattle and couldn't be summoned up again. With age was there a certain sensibility lost? The faculty to know when to be happy for someone else and not compare it to anyone's accomplishments. Parents, they seemed so full of sighs, constantly racking their minds wondering what happened like they never had any chance at all. It was that being an old fart wasn't a metaphor, they had resigned in every in so many senses. They were passing through their lives like gas, loosely to and through to the end. In their fiercest attempt to preserve their ego they cushion themselves

from the blow of failure and in that, all of life's opportunity for success.
 I tucked a James Blake album in my armpit.
 "I'm ready."
 He put down the Mariah Carey album and tried to snap out of it. Looking up, lost, and readjusting to the space around him. He followed beside me and put a hand on my shoulder, he brought me to his side with a firm, punctuated, loving grip and walked forward as if leading a procession, his unlived years behind him like a battalion made prisoners of war. The air died as his hung head and pair of sunken shoulders slinked through the doorway. The sun was hidden somewhere now. The air was slightly cooler.

■

Despite better sense I was pulling into the convention center, a smaller boardroom sized event inside of an enormous four star hotel. Parking was designated, I filled my space like water poured into a drinking glass—choreographed dance before choreographed dance.
 He stood tall and pulled himself out of the car, with a pride I had only seen before a church sermon, with his briefcase in hand like it was a bible—his word lived in a box, behind a combination lock. Just the right pressure and opposable thumbs can unlock certain freedom. I was chaperoning a dance for my own son now. Fearing what I discover he really does.
 People were funneling through the double doors. I joined the mass, side by side with him. From a steady satellite to a binary in the steady influx. Shoulders brushed against us, in time. White faces lifted up and dad gave a polite greeting. Southern hospitality from a man who'd just moved to and from Tennessee.
 He was afraid of his interests, his ambitions, he only trusted drudgery—he only believed in hard work and bloodshed as a means of freedom. To be interested, to be immersed was too high risk. Believing martyrdom the only virtue and all pleasure sin he could never embrace himself, his faculties.
 He tortured himself, to feel a pain he believed was always for a reason, he could not control pain, he could control how it was interpreted. It was inevitable, it was a constant—what varied is whether he interpreted it as senseless or success. The sting of sweat in his eyes reminded him he was alive. When in a dead world, a world that traded passions for passivity, he was like them, living.
 Shoulders brushed him again, it was Sam and Midori, long time friends who'd made it independently. Sam gave me a firm handshake, while giving dad a quick pat on the back. Sam and Taylor had contracted Syphilis together in the Navy. That felt like connection to them.
 "Sam—nice to finally meet you, Jordan. Taylor talks so much about you."
 "And how you're quite the ladies' man," chimed Midori, "being such a

handsome boy."

"Thank you." I laughed nervously.

"Are you ready for this?" said Sam.

"I can't wait." said Taylor.

"We'll see you in there."

They passed in and found another group they recognized near the open seats they were approaching. They were Diamond, you could tell from their suits.

"How're you feeling, Jordan?"

"Good—what are we doing here?"

"You'll find out, just wait."

We walked into the room, nothing but purple and gold, like they'd made everything down to seat cushions out of recycled Crown Royal® bags. The chairs had white accents and there was a faint paisley pattern in the carpets, with flowers to break up the monotony, all shades of purple in the rug but the flower's bulbs. It was arranged like a theater, the chairs in a semi-circle, split down the aisles, leading up a small staircase where solid velvet covered it, like thick shining moss. Then, the lights, an altar, a microphone, and a pull down screen.

I had seen this before but it felt as if it were the first time. This was a temple, another place of worship with the perfect amount of men and women filling seats. The ministers were filling their seats, behind the pulpit. They weren't just suits that fill any small town church arena—these aren't your average hope peddling goons, these are power players. In mind, body, and spirit, immaculate presentation. The grey hair and hard bodies, a vampiric youth proving you could live like this forever too. Carey Bartleman, an ex-televangelist filling the seat furthest stage right.

People are so dependent on vision, so much evolution is based on having the perfect distance from a perfect star, and that the select range of light making it through our perfect atmosphere was neither too imperceptible nor too harsh. We are not to look to directly at what gives us life. It blinds you—worship your origins and don't look too close.

I find myself staring into a stage light a crew member's testing. It flickers, my vision a flashbulb floating under closed eyelids and then dying. I reoriented myself. I saw my father inspecting a seat cushion from directly in front of it, before politely taking his place, Taylor dusting the seat of his pants the way a woman would keep her skirt together. He was comfortable but anticipating the presentation and my reaction with nervousness. The anxiety tucked like his hand in between his crossed legs.

He always crossed his legs like a woman, which I found strange, not just because I imagined it's painful but because he was such a man, always self-aware in his masculinity.

The best Christians are narcissists.

Narcissism was believed, by Freud, to be a result of an over policed child. One scolded too often for tripping over themselves or eating their dinner gracelessly. High strung children adapt to the conditions of always feeling watched, to the point where they can only watch themselves.

    The cyclical thinking leads to a cyclical psychology, bound to be unwound and only with the most conscious efforts could you disarm a spring this tightly coiled. Like a rusting piano string, the narcissist is a long and loveless labor. Only the most detached and patient love could set him straight, in tune for himself and with others, to be hammered at, harped on...he thinks. The narcissist is impatient and hates to talk. He bangs his head on the wall and sees progress as the brick's red fading or wood displaying his relief his only consultation. His reality is a mirror and women as mirrors and his life is a manipulation of others. His moral system mechanic. Taylor was in every sense a narcissist. The narcissist was bound to and by himself. He ended up taking more than he gave. He saw himself as he saw others seeing him but didn't ever really.

    The crowd calmed, the pulpit filled, throne after throne, and even though it was silent the crowd's anticipation felt the way a creaking door sounds, a stutter before sound begins.

"Good evening," said Carey, rising from the furthest right chair, taking a confident walk to the altar.

    "Ladies and gentleman, I want to thank you for coming here tonight. It's amazing to see so many men and women congregated with the focus to free themselves from the bond of serving others senselessly. Amucorp® has been a business that has helped men and women help themselves for decades now. You're the reason and the cause of that growth.
You can't get what you want working for another person—a life in service of another is wasteful. Is it truly mutually beneficial? In order to truly free yourself from toil, you must start your own business—Amucorp® helps you do it. Who's making the real money when it comes to a business? It's those who are the originators. But you don't have to be alone to be the originator, you need help, you need investors, a pool of others from which you can start.

    The worker, he works thinking he's getting what he wants, he thinks he is going to move up, rise through the ranks, and be noticed by those on top. The worker sees his efforts as statements to those above him in the workplace. He went to college, he wrote the papers, and he followed the rules. He wants what's rightfully his. The businessman sees things differently. Think of the world's most innovative minds—Benjamin Franklin. Never set foot into a classroom and yet he's one of the most well-known American minds. A pillar of our history.

    My father used to tell me: 'A' students work for 'B' students and 'B' students work for 'C' students. You know who survives in this society? No—anyone can survive. Do you know who thrives in the society? Those who go out and get it. Those who seize opportunities. Those who take the initiative—those who build the framework that others follow."

    Taylor was furiously scribbling in a notebook he'd silently taken from out of his suitcase. I watched, starting to feel my face heating, I was slowly getting red. Some noise in me, vague and formless sought a shape, but only sank into an inky anxiety. My father, in the same place I'd seen him 10 years ago. A decade had passed and I was beginning to think it wasn't a second that'd passed but with the sermon running on I noticed my father had physically embodied his changes. His body had lost color, it'd lost life, it was dying in front of my eyes with the same power that a will to live had in a person. My father had lived protecting himself. As if perseverance itself was to be valued, chasing ideals with no grounds in reality. Achieving any one specific goal would ruin the chase.

The problem was that he, like so many other men, had lived without sharing the child, the source of all life. The spirit's fuel is that which gives, like a tree gives it's exhale your inhale, it depends on being expressed. The only evidence that you ever existed on this planet is what you've given. It's only a song when you sing it.

His ambition stemmed from a fear of being swallowed by his desires again because the time when your one true love seems to slip away into murky doubt or the illusion of a concrete danger are the most crushing to feel. Birth and kidney stones don't compare to the feeling of being left and the only feeling worse than being left alone is having driven someone away. But like the myth promises, the only time your wealth can leave you is if you want it to. Life feels important only when you have some other place to be.

Taylor's most promising venture was wealth and making it as a means of escape. The feeling of need and want themselves making him weak. When he was younger he would write letters to his brother while on trips out. His time in the Navy was long and distant. He would come back once a season and be on the sea again. What exactly he was doing no one would know except his brother. He never talked about it to his wife or kids. The reason Mom found herself with a bad case of the clap after dad's trip to the Philippines. He, like so many famous writers before he decided he wanted to be one. His career highlight a rejection letter from National Lampoon telling him to keep sending work, it wasn't bad, it just wasn't a good fit for this issue.

Music started playing and he looked to me, clearly uncomfortable during the talk, startled, bordering on disturbed now. First an American flag fading in from black, the extreme close up being pulled out. A horn slowly gushing up with the beating of wind on cheap, heavy, fiber, slapping metallic chattering from the rivets.

Amucorp® appeared straight in the frame.

From the worker, to the soldier, to the wife, an entire family, shots of an American neighborhood and a church steeple, and the gates of heaven opening into a bald eagle. The exhausted imagery all added up to feed the marks of the American playground that a responsible adulthood provides. You could be what you wanted. It wasn't about buying what you're selling, living what you want. It was about finding a comfortable middle ground for exchange. Life's a compromise, regardless of how it compromises you.

The hallucinogens were run down and they started watching an interview with an ex-military. He was older now, 31, but he'd made it. He was tired after the military of putting his college education, something he'd risked his life for in the service of his favorite nation in the world—America, in service of massive organizations he felt completely out of control of. America, the only country he'd spent more time living in than killing in, which is what informed his opinion of his nation, like every other stubborn nationalist, was a nation that had apparently promised him something.

I couldn't help but wonder what exactly America had promised him. The American was so infatuated by a nation that it would choose to be tricked by its non-specifications. Who was this America? Where the fuck was its mouth? Who was it talking; it reminded me of a burning bush. The explanations based off of some interpretation as fact.

The soldier wasn't turning his back on his nation, he just believed there was a more satisfying direct, proactive way to satisfy his financial needs and that would mean, naturally, a more labor free and satisfying life. Pushing work onto another and wearing a cross was the main project. It faded and the lights blossomed back in. Taylor was readjusting himself, picking at the jean near his crotch as casually as you could pick, trying to be quick.

The suits picked themselves up and shuffled. The legs they wanted to stretch, were in quiet. We are all respectful out of reverence just for respect. Another speaker came forward, the next in the row of chairs. Sweating, my jaws tightened like a car jack, like a bad case of lockjaw. I felt present, visible in the light, the way a sick girl at a party hangs around for too long and the night is just waiting to smell the vomit, the room was its own feeling of missing something and being sure of it and how to fix it.

I looked at my father for a moment, who I knew was proud but I didn't feel anything near pride. Holding onto my shoulder blindly, he turned to me with a beaming smile that I wished I could have remembered outside of any room. Outside of a church, outside of a congregation, outside of a car, away from the past. I felt longing and pathetic.

"God bless us. We're so blessed to be able to be together like this. Building the business, our own. We don't have to answer to anyone else but ourselves..."

Exploring himself after child rearing became too real. He was a man, he had a right to. How'd he have so much money to just pick up and drive from Tennessee to California to Santa Monica to Idaho? I was witness to the mid-life crisis. Internalizing, fully and finally, I was orphaned.

I was on a baseball team once but don't remember it. I felt alone most of the time, my whole life was batting practice. A strange adult man in the same outfit as me, feeding a machine its ammo, swing after swing on an overcast evening, hoping to make it to make him proud. I could have lived my life being bought hot dogs at neighbor's sporting events.

"Living for ourselves," the voice blared, in that dramatic southerner's oratorical drawl, where even the sounds alone made you feel proud, "is the best gift we have to give to others. We are the salt of the earth; we are our only gift to give!"

The audience broke into applause, shouting one man screamed, 'Amen!' It was an event being there together, cheering, the way you would at a ball game. My stomach sank. I panned the room and like a breeze through dandelions, bobbed through their movements, joining the applause like I knew I never could.

■

Passing back out of the double doors we met with Sam and Midori again, both newly smug, refreshed by absolute reinforcement of their preexisting biases. The only thing worse than a religion based on original sin and the constant guilt that drives you to adopt unrealistic goals and an infinite inferiority complex, is a spiritual retreat with the generic feel good embrace, warming you with the feeling of total acceptance of everything you've ever done, are doing, and will do. The horoscope-inclusive attitude dangerously close to a Klan rally.

That's when an enormous white hand planted itself into my left shoulder. I shot up, startled. Sam was ready to say goodbye, he'd arranged a ride back home with another acquaintance in advanced, which was Sam's polite way of saying he'd the time and money to stay a few days extra in Santa Monica.

"It's always good to see you Taylor, coming with you to these events always strengthens my resolve. You'll go sapphire soon enough, Taylor. Don't worry. That's why you're here."

"Thanks, Sam." he smiled.

Sam and Midori power-walked away into the milling heat of hopefuls and he turned to find me.

I filled my place, playing my part, subordinate but care-giving, supportive-lead I turned the key, muttering, sighing as privately as I could. Dad had lived years this way, a wet nosed salesman, where the goods and services were as good as an alms bowl. A beggar without a robe, a monk without a tower, he was like a drunken Noah, where, after ruthlessly disgracing the name, and betraying his kin, they did the Christian thing. Turning another cheek and sending the crowds away, tucking in their red faced father. The family had its own demands but its laws were greater, it was its obedience forever.

.III

BUCKET LIST

On entrance to the hotel room, he placed his briefcase against the bed's headboard. A click and the handle dropped, like a deflated actor after the take. He started undressing at the collar button, after reaching the television in the end of the room; he turned towards me, standing in the entrance.

"That was fun, wasn't it?" he asked, knowing it wasn't.

It was rhetorical. He stood, dazed, in the mirror. The silence was the dusty glare filling with an incomprehensible guilt. I found a place and laid out on the bed. The perfectly matching color scheme reminiscent of a teenage blog's margins. The power of design, the subtleties of accents as a foundation. He had completely undressed himself in my periphery until crossing my line of vision. A man, more alien to me than ever, a great ape in a gold chain. His body covered in an almost fur thick mane of hair. The closet door, two sliding panels, also mirrors. My father's shriveled and aged cock disappearing as he pulled the door open for a hanger. It had been normal to me for years.

I can only try to piece him together. Who he was. Not dress, not a history came to converge to make the person I had learned half my life from. Tethered now to a man I'd never really met. The closest to family history was a conversation about grandpa being an immigrant. His religion had left a man in denial, blind to years of his own existence—banished as sin, deleted from memory. A passionless man made up of passionless ritual. Without words he closed the closet doors and walked without thought into the tiled bathroom. Gears squeaked, values sputtered, water ran through walls and finally the peaceful muted hissing of water. He was humming the tune of Frank Sinatra's, 'I Did It My Way.'

I noticed the briefcase next to me, unlocked, a dark slit down the glittering brass lining of its fastening, peaking out. Curiosity called me to open it and I couldn't deny myself. I picked it up, held together on one side, and slid it over my chest. Opening it, slowly, quietly, it was popped open, exposed like a dumb clam. My soft hands blindly burying themselves in the contents and pushed around until I was clenching a year-thick planner.

Randomly, flipping past some sparsely filled dates, until, suddenly, the weight carrying my fingers momentum stopped on a list. Pages flicked into their places, splayed, reading:

BEFORE I GO:

—————————SAVE THE BOYS
~~BUY A HOUSE~~

- ~~FIND A PLACE TO BURY MOM~~
- ~~PERFORM A STAND UP SET~~
- ~~WRITE A BOOK~~
- ~~VISIT JAPAN~~
- ~~MOVE TO SAN FRANCISCO~~
- ~~GO BACK TO CHURCH~~
- ~~GET MARRIED~~
- ~~RETIRE IN ROANOKE, IN~~

In all caps. My heart skipped a beat while my stomach ran up and down my throat. I threw the day planner into the suitcase, and the suitcase across the clean but clearly worn hotel room rug. You cannot wash the use out of a place. Even when it's invisible it's permanent. It has a taste. Collecting my things, catching myself in the mirror, in front of me. Grabbing my phone from the table, I noticed a half open drawer with a leather jacket exposed. A piece of red ribbon poking its forked tongue through between the pages, where I opened it, containing the passage:

30 I and my Father are one.
31 Then the Jews took up stones again to stone him.
32 Jesus answered them, Many good works have I shewed you from my Father; for which of those works do ye stone me?

I slammed the book shut. I was swallowing the heat down my throat. Hands were nothing but pressure, tectonic plates waiting to slip. Eyes watered. Third breath the catalyst to a high-heat pitch of the book straight into the glass. It's iced-explosion in glittering cuts. I tore the front off the book and with a pen; ham-fisted something barely legible across the top. The inside of the underside of a turtle-blank slate. Tearing at the door handle and finally, stepping out of the hotel room, crying, into the patient womb of an elevator. Its doors closing like curtains. It's ringing...

■

The water sealed up. The shift through walls finished snaking. The bathroom door handle closer to a dorm stall than a 4 star hotel. Exiting the steam and walking, shamelessly, into the cold room.
"Jordan?"
He looked across the floor, following the train of paper to a desk buried in glass. A mess of diamond bright shards, salting the wood. He stepped lightly but couldn't avoid the coals of splintered glass in his feet. He bled from his feet like Christ would have. He looked through the pile, and pushed a flat palm across the torn jacket, reading:

SAVE YOURSELF

      He slid his hand to the gold cross on his neck, twisting it, pulling his prayer like a rosary through his fingers. Telling himself with every stroke he was a good person, his son was backsliding. He needed his help and his father's love and Christ's love. When a father's love would have done. There was no mirror, finally, to absorb him in. The theories were an absent reflection. It was blood and debris. He looked up, craning his neck all the way to the ceiling.

@abigfuckingbully

@abigfuckingbully

IVORY ELEPHANT

If I was a proud South Indian family, beautiful, and born in the remnants of the caste system, I probably wouldn't give my daughter away to the rail thin, white bread, village idiot. Even if I am mixed. They had their reasons and I'd gotten lucky, Amy was 5' 11" and a potential model. She was a straight-A Psych student. Loud, funny, smart, but sometimes belligerent. The downside was the public humiliation I regularly suffered. Amy and I had been seeing each other since before the beginning of summer. It was a long romantic meeting. I met her equally tall, bratty, and beautiful counterpart, Nancy—Amy's family friend—first. We crossed paths at a show. A mutual friend with a psychotic monomaniacal inferiority complex, a Leo himself, like both Nancy and Amy were, was going to use every social advantage he had to increase sexual access. His interest in niche-culture: *punk rock* was a much narrower mating pool to select from. Rejection *feels* lower-risk when the potential mates have been whittled to nothing. Being seen playing an instrument gave him an evolutionary advantage above most others, one he had in no other venue. Whose function was a persecution mania that left sex tucked into the same shredder that Our Father the Martyr would have pushed it through. Even though in public he would get dirty looks, when he was leaning in the hallway entrances, his arm straight out, watching his mouth move but too far to hear what was coming out, 90% of the women longing for touch were stroking themselves in a life-deferring whisper to another easily policed goth. They wear unlovable costume to make sure that someone shallow isn't making contact; only others who had been hardened by a false sense of marginalization could walk the hot coals. Of course the buffer itself is an expression of how susceptible they are to judgment. What are we but all our projections?

We're there, on the periphery, because we knew the guy from college, and we were all studying liberal arts. Which made sense but was still looked down on here? There's no winning. Nancy wasn't paying me any attention.

Nancy remembered me from the last party I'd seen her at, my drunken 6' 3" English friend, Andy, coming on too strong, but still, was probably hooked on some other better dressed, less punk kid there anyways. She was talking to our circle and, still, ignoring me. My feelings were it was the same tactic men were taught to use to drive women wild. Ungendered because everyone hates being ignored. It worked. After I met Amy, I was still obsessed with Nancy. I was developing a sexually submissive fetish all of these personality types satisfied perfectly. They represented power in both posture, height, and manner. Authoritative parents that made authoritative women who didn't wear bras when they wore lace and drove Bimmer's and *never-mind* anything. If a boy was hanging around them for more than a few hours they knew they were as lucky as village idiot because they had the awful habit of wearing down their nerves and putting them in *their place* as a sort of replacement.

Nancy passes me up at the show. It has my mind wandering...Nancy walking to a bench, the back seat of Buick, white leather hanging on for life, outside the venue, The Smile Factory. She stops to talk to someone sitting next to a short Chinese girl with straight cut bangs and a thick gauge septum piercing, hood of her black pullover up. I like girls who look like that, look like they were waiting to get into fights. They flicked their cigarettes like you were underneath them, your face was an ashtray, and even if neither of you have a fetish, you were licking her boots.

As she walks off, the girl uncovered was just the opposite, though she had the same nose piercing. Shining like gold underneath the campus lamp was a girl so long she barely fit on the couch. She was tripping almost everyone who was trying to get by. She excused herself every time, laughing. She wore a thick knit cardigan, with a tie at the waist. Llamas were knit, pixelated into the design. The bottom quarter a solid brown stripe for accent. She was wearing a blue velvet mini and white sandals to match. I made direct eye contact with her. We both didn't pause. I heard the next band at sound check and she put out a cigarette in the sole of her paper thin sandals; blowing the smoke out of the corner of her mouth. She got up and I followed the mass of people, passing the couch like you would a confession booth. Looking directly to my right at just how eaten and empty it was. You lose something when you catch a look and then they disappear, you bottom out from this amazing high, you hate every person who is just a back of a head to you.

They start playing and the room heats up like a toaster oven. Bodies were throwing themselves around even though Rank/Xerox was playing that same night and was going to wipe them out. They showed support, they were paying it forward. The set ended with only the guitarist and singer chorusing out. He knelt down to a cassette recorder, more than thirty years old, it had this beautiful warm sound, and it gave a humanity to Siri reading a poem. Once the feedback purred out the bodies filed out.

The exact same people went to the exact same places, in the exact same formations. Like we were all actors in a play. Here to satisfy a need by satisfying others needs. Stonehenge was a long and grueling religious ritual, men died for it. I feel that, even more than it's significance to their God, its significance was to give themselves significance. It made a population of men and women immortal throughout time. Erecting natural technologies for the greater purpose of humanity's progress. I think that even on the most microscopic levels, this is what human communities are doing. I tried to forget long enough to muster the courage to talk to Amy, whose name I didn't know yet. While Nancy was walking off to a record store nearby to smoke a cigarette with a much taller, richer, white boy.

My approach has always been the same approach, one without filter or buffer or aims even. Breaking the ice was a lot like breaking an arm for me, you will be blindsided, you will have to decide quickly whether I'm a threat or not, you will have to be instinctual and animalistic. Part of it was clearly my resentment for the allotted gender specific actions in dating rituals. I am always the one to initiate any talking although so many women are really initiating, shooting a glance, white eyes with wide smiles full of white teeth, the clear green light for a conversation. I hate doing this. I was never taught how to do this so my style was that of a caveman, as refined and subtle as a fire bomb. How I ever ended up on a date was beyond me. Every attempt I have ever made was a complete blind fire: run your mouth until they want you to shut up, listen until they are tired of talking.

"Hey, what's your name?"

Startled she stared for a second, a second pair of eyes synchronized.

"Amy," she shot a long thin hand full of long thin fingers covered in rings into my hand.

"Amy? My name's Josh."

"Nice to meet you," she giggled at me.

"What?"

"What do you mean, what? Nothing, what."

"Who are you here to see?"

"Well,"

"—Ben invited us." the girl to her right interjected.

Fuck. I have this habit of ignoring everyone besides the girl I want to talk to in social situations. This was another social grave I've habitually started digging. I was completely blindsided now. It was not that she was unfriendly just that I was up for review by another person. I was wearing corduroy shorts that were mid-thigh and a grey hoody almost the exact same color. Nothing more exciting than a bicyclist in uniform!

"Oh, you both know Ben, or…"

"Yeah, I went to school with him." said the other girl.

"What's your name?" I repeated.

"Jaclyn."

"Nice to meet you, Jaclyn."

She laughed.

And when I heard her laugh I realized that I'd met this girl before. I'd already embarrassed myself in front of these women before and neither party was given a name. Amy, here, was wearing a gigantic red bow in her hair, it stuck up like she was Kiki from the Studio Ghibli film. Jaclyn here, made fun of me while I was dancing at her 21st birthday party, the DJ was naked, I was dancing alone and the only other person on this flat, sweat soaked wood paneling was a woman spread eagle on a table near the couches. I was wiggling my arms more like a bird and I was dancing terribly. Uncharacteristically bad.

We had seen each other but didn't know each other and they didn't seem to remember. I have that face, that flat, white, face.

"So how do you know Ben?" she asked.

"He has film classes with my brother. He lives in our neighborhood."

"Oh that's cool. Ben…"

"What'd you think of his band?"

"Very Ben." said Amy.

I laughed.

Amy lit a cigarette. Jaclyn was looking down at Amy in disbelief. Amy smiled after a brief glance at her, and continued putting her cigarettes away smiling. Then she looked back at me. She put the box into her purse and put the strap over her head. She stood up and Jaclyn sat. The next band started playing, the sound beating against the windows. The ambience of a wood chipper. I had lost concentration and couldn't remember what we were talking about.

31

"I think we're going to go." said Amy.

"Yeah..." said Jaclyn.

"Oh, okay. Do you go to a lot of shows?"

"Not really. We both live in Santa Cruz."

"Together?"

"No, even though we're best friends, no."

"I like your white sandals."

She was beaming. "Thanks!" She blushed.

"It was nice talking to you. Maybe we can hang out sometime."

"Yeah, sure."

"What's your phone number?"

      Here was the exchange, two people almost exactly the same height, speaking entirely different languages, with entirely different perceptions, sharing each other's phone numbers, both looking down, around, she's smoking a cigarette acting like it couldn't have gone worse, knowing this couldn't have gone better, both dying to hang out with each other but appearing cool and collected. She gave me a weak wave and walked into darkness.

                                      ⁂

      She was at a party Ben was throwing at his house in the Sunset. That same year I'd had Anne take me home from another one of Ben's parties. Even though the kitchen smelled like B.O. from house shows and cigarettes, and cat-shit from the litter of kittens he'd been too busy to get rid of, Ben's house had so many positive associations. Eventually me and Amy would spend New Year's Eve there, in separate rooms after she asked me if it was okay if she did cocaine at this party—but right now was my chance to harness those positive energies, so after a three day wait, I texted her. She seemed hard to convince, even through text, playing hard to get but I told her that I thought she was beautiful and I just got a 35mm camera with a zoom lens and that we should take pictures. She made a joke about me being a pervert and then agreed. Which genuinely bothered me, something about disowning your own desire to participate and shoving it off on perversion startled me. This was a wall I'd run into for my whole life though, it should have been expected but I am a choice amnesiac, it is my coping mechanism so that I'm not as judgmental as my father.

She asked me what about her made me want to take pictures of her. I told her she looked like someone who should be recorded, whose personality shines through something as dead as print. She was playing hard to get, which I both liked and hated. Eventually this text message conversation devolved into a sext message conversation and the first time I ever texted Amy was the first time I ever had sex with her. How it happened, I can't explain in specifics. It had been an entire year, since Anne, that I had sex. But me and Amy were close after.

She finally agreed to a date. There was no talking in between then and now except to make arrangements; rightfully. There's no use for it. What else could you think of to talk about after that? Shocked by excitement, paralyzed both in the sedative after effects and by the anticipation, we decided not to stain a perfect silence. She picked me up at 7 and there was no plan. We were going to hang out at Nicky's house, a real low pressure thing. I can't remember anything we talked on the way but I remember we were listening to Pinback and we both really got on about 'P.K. Offline,' which made me fucking ecstatic.

We parked in the gravel outside of the apartments, Mountain View, California. They were higher in the hills than I'd expected. What the cost of living was for an apartment like this, I couldn't guess. Why someone who could live up here would pay rent also confused me. Mountain View is a good place to live if you're middle aged and working a tech job. It was not as good of a place if you were young and an aspiring artist.

We got to the apartment door and knocked. We were expected but the door always stayed locked. I was nerve wracked already trying to remain composed for Amy and the feelings of being scrutinized through a peephole were driving me near a panic attack, which I later would find out Amy regularly had in youth. I couldn't imagine such a hard girl; she even had a scar down her forehead, breathing into a paper bag to calm herself. Nicky opened the door.

"Oh my god, hey girl!"

"Nicky!"

They hugged each other around the neck. I stood perfectly still. I have a bad habit of making the other person I'm meeting introduce themselves first, an international 'fuck you' in total disinterest. I wasn't disinterested though, I was just nervous. Amy had a bottle of wine stashed in her purse and pulled it out, coddling it like a child and passing it on.

"This is Josh."

"This your new thing?" she laughed. Looking at Amy and shaking my hand.

"*Shut* the fuck up!"

"I'm Nicky."

Nicky was almost a redhead. Her arms were tight and thick, soft and tanned. She had a smoky voice that began gravely because of all the cigarettes she smoked. She was putting one in her mouth now.

"Come in."

She shot her arm back while the other both lit and protected the flame of her cigarette.

"Can I have a cigarette?"

"Amy!" a voice from on the porch shouted, "Get out here, please."

Nicky was in the kitchen to the left of us now, slipping by me, concerned with the etiquette of taking my shoes off. Amy ignored Nicky, opening a drawer and getting a wine opener from the drawer, shouting without looking at Amy, who she thought she was pointing at, "Take your fucking shoes off. Take them off. Take off your *shoes* I know you're wearing your *shoes*..."

"I will." She fanned her arms out and did a Lucille Ball style march in heels over towards Sam.

I walked through, after Nicky, to the back porch, the only place anyone was allowed to smoke, which meant it had that dead asbestos smell staining it as well. It reminds you of pets. There was a pet; it was a microscopic Chihuahua yapping in the center of these three women now all reuniting.

"What are you doing this summer?"

Nicky was struggling with cutting the wax.

"Hey do you want to..." she handed me the bottle.

" For sure." I grabbed the wine and stopped listening, focusing all efforts into opening it.

Sam still hadn't introduced herself. She stole Nicky's seat, a fold out rainbow beach chair, and was taking a huge drag. She turned up one corner like a sailor and made that stupid scrunched cigarette face I loved to watch them all do. I shot out my bottle steadying hand for a moment and gave the biggest smile I could. She shook it.

"Sam, nice to meet you...where are you from? How do you know Amy?"

"I'm from Santa Clara. Indiana originally."

"What do you do, here?"

"Well I work and I write."

"Ohh. You write? What do you write?"

"Sometimes stories, sometimes music, sometimes poetry."

"Where do you work?"

"Right now, I'm working...retail. I work at AA."

"Jesus, it's like everyone I meet works there."

"It's an easy job to get."

I'd finished the wax and was starting the corkscrew.

"So how long have you been working there?"

"Maybe a year."

"Do you like it?"

"Well, it's easy to steal from."

"Is that how you met Amy?"

"No. Why? She used to work there?" I smiled.

"Yeah, obviously, look at everything she's wearing." she laughed.

"We met at Ben's show." Amy interrupted.

"Stop asking so many questions, he just got here." said Nicky.

"I wouldn't mind reading your stuff." Nicky said.

The cork popped out. They all three put their cigarettes out. Nicky into the ashtray, Amy on the sole of her heel, and Sam straight into the ground, the pimpled, metallic, balcony.

Nicky grabbed the bottle from me before I could untwist my legs and she started grabbing glasses. Sam took a seat around a piece of a polished tree trunk for a table. Amy and I sat behind it, on a blue velvet couch. Amy was wearing a floral print, spandex, dress, in two shades of brown. Shining in the light along with everything else. An ex-boyfriend had made the table by hand, Nicky would tell us. There were holes where knots used to be but none big enough to fit a cup. Nicky would say putting down the glasses, pouring each one out and handing them one by one to each of us, Amy last. They got caught up and I drank my wine like it was water, nervously and quickly—how I do anything related to eating with anyone else. "Sam's from Israel." Amy said. "Oh yeah?" I tried. Amy pat me on the back really hard, asked if I was already slurring and I closed my eyes laughing like an idiot. Everyone else joined in, they loved me.

※

We were all wasted by now. Nicky had invited her boyfriend, the owner of a hummus company, who had ripped the Om patterned blanket off the wall, making a bad joke, and was now staring at an unfinished painting pressed against the wall. It was a nude in smears of a long haired woman.

"I like this one." he said.

"Those are Amy's tits! One's bigger than the other..."

Sam had been stood up by her boyfriend who just couldn't make it. She drove home drunk and alone.

"I'm tired, I have work really early in the morning."

"Okay, you should get some sleep. Is it okay if we stay out here?"

"Yeah...do you need anything?" She smiled.

"We'll be in there." Nicky pointed to her bedroom door with her thumb.

Amy got up and followed Nicky. The boyfriend was getting water, "Goodnight. Nicesmeetinggyou!"

"Goodnight."

Amy came out as the boyfriend went in.

"Are you tired at all?" She asked.

That classic question—*are you tired?* Are we both fully committed to this or are you going to half-ass on me? You're not going to throw up are you? You're not going to pass out in the middle and I'll be fucking your corpse, will I?

"No. I'm not tired."

"Here," she put her legs over mine and leaned over me to pour another glass a wine.

"Drink thiss." she said. So earnestly. That earnest that's only possible when you're that drunk. Sedated into vulnerability, we didn't even notice. No one minds when they're fucked up too but otherwise life was a lot like a prison in that no one was to show any weakness. Worse if you were on a date.

I took a sip and lifted it up with a mocking eyebrow lift then put it back on the table.

"What...re you doing?"

"I don't want to fucking drink this."

"So what do you want to do?"

I put my arm over her and squeezed her closer. She was looking at me, the pressure already increasing because we're centimeters from each other's faces, the full survey, chin to forehead, enough to count the freckles was made. I put her thick, straight, jet-black, hair back behind her ear, which revealed a black pearl earring. I looked her in her enormous eyes, almost circles like I was on a date with Sailor Mercury, and kissed her.

Her lips were perfectly shaped, top and bottom fit perfectly into each other, they were soft and muscular at the same time, they looked carved from ebony, they looked like polished stone and felt like marshmallow, we were melting now.

A palm pressed into my chest, while fingers started combing through my hair. I felt down her back, a slick polyester feeling after her stone smooth skin, exposed in the perfect 'U' at the shoulders, the way you can feel what's under the fabric the same way you would without it is the most exciting part. Her arms stayed planted while my hands found the niche, the soft electric part of a girl just above her hip bones, just before the cute cuts at the bottom of a stomach, the way thighs as big as this feel, scarred with a new tattoo, vertical an indicator of dead center of the outside of her.

"What's that say?"

"It's a Tibetan prayer."

We started kissing again. I got to the hem of the dress while her long fingers found my pants button, like it was something you could press and have undone, not something you untie more. They say the skin on your lips is about as sensitive as your fingers. Twitching highs, like some draining burn up you, like Big Red. I lifted up the bottom half. We were awkwardly shifting. I had to take the lead, it was implicit. We moved ourselves both parallel, managing to fit two long, broad bodies, down this couch. In so many way we looked alike. We could have been brother and sister. I'd never met a girl I felt was as American as this. She stopped me as I got under, palming an ass that fit perfectly into my hands.

"I'm not a slut. I don't want you to think that."

"Jesus...No, what the fuck? I'm not a slut either."

"I like you."

"I wouldn't be here if I didn't."

"You're such a slut!" she laughed.

There was a Pendleton blanket draped over the couch. She pulled it over us. I could have fallen in love with her that moment if I wasn't as motivated. If I would have taken my time and noticed every little thing. I thought I was supposed to consume her, to take her as quickly and aggressively as possible. *This is it...make it count!*

I peeled her dress off and kissed her once before looking at her.

"Nickyyyyy..." she moaned. "I forgot, I needed a...rubber."

The door opened and Nicky stumbled, wearing nothing either, and threw it at us.

"Fuck."

We both laughed.

We were both glowing and panting.

"There's no way we're both going to fit on this."

"Yes, exsactly." Amy said. "That's why you're sleeping on the floor."

I looked at her from where I was, already laying out, like a drunken Noah except shameless. She shot up like a bird and then leaned on one arm looking at me, looking at her.

"You're really affectionate." she said.

I looked back, very seriously, waiting for the follow up.

"Is it weird that I liked to be choked sometimes?" and then she flopped back onto the bed practically into a fetal position.

"You're such a slut." she kept chuckling.

We didn't turn off the light before we went to sleep.

Meeting her friends was so much easier than I had expected. Regardless of the shamelessness I'd made a great impression on Sam and Nicky. They knew I was a great guy, what they were basing it on I had no idea, but I felt the same way about them. The more you get to know someone the more that changes.

I kept my head down, even when they would both hurl insults at me about being a hipster. Such a dirty fucking word. I had taken less offense to cracker before that word and I never understood why, what would make someone say that to me.

Amy was living in a huge house in Santa Cruz. She had a job, sort of, and an internship, which didn't pay so I'm not sure how she could afford it. Except when you're driving around in a luxury car with a stereo system you're sure was not included you just have to chalk it up to well-planned children and better planned parenthood.

I met her roommates one by one; everyone looked and dressed like they were actors in a film. We were immediately thrown into their exciting life of non-stop social interactions and loose plans for drink and sex. The beach was first and closest. Everyone in the house got in the car, singing bad pop songs genuinely and asking if anyone had pot with him.

"Wow. The beach without pot, you idiots!" I shouted.

They all laughed.

"Pot? We're on a beach trip with my fucking dad right now."

They laughed harder.

We got there, I was holding a cooler and wondering how to gauge Amy's comfort with public displays of affection. I had already been mocked for wearing a striped shirt: *'junior'* and *'Frenchy'*. The beers were cracked open and drained almost instantly. Hands nabbing in the red chest before Amy could get the blanket off. Luckily Carlos brought a camera because my light meter on my 35mm was broken.

"I like you." Carlos said, "Just don't break her heart okay, or I'll kill you. I've known Amy since I was, like, a freshman. We're blood, practically. She's been with a lot of really fucked up guys, you're not like them. So just don't fuck it up or I'll kill you, okay?"

"Carlos!" Taylor had the same cut as Carlos. He was a blonde wavy haired Grecian looking man; he looked like a statuette, a James Dean type. I couldn't help telling him, part of me was genuinely really attracted to him, if I was ever committed to finally exploring my sexuality, this would be the man I would want to do it with. He had a Herculean chin dimple.

"Relax, he's cool. You're going to scare him away!" he slapped Carlos across his arm. Carlos was wearing torn jean shorts and a faded vintage Ocean Pacific tank with a beige accent for the lining. He had a cropped worker's cut that he never took the time to slick back, so it stuck up like a pomp. He was big, he could have kicked my ass but they all seemed gentle and giving. They wanted me to take group photos with them. I wish that I could have built relationships like this with people. I'd never been a part of a large group.

"Now get over there, right in the middle, you and Amy."

We all lined up with each other, Amy was wearing bright red short shorts, and a yellow, red, blue, swimsuit with a floral design tucked into it. I grabbed the leg she threw over me and smiled as wide as I could. Photos are hard for me, I usually weakly imitate what I think others will read as a smile, but I was happy then. My teeth were showing, the gap in the middle fully exposed.

"Josh, no, you're so stiff, like this." Amy pushed me in place, and we smiled.

Carlos would show us his photos later, they were good, they had life I sometimes feel I never have in them. They breathed like Amy.

A few weeks later, I got to know the rest of the roommates during a costume party. Amy pulled up to her house where Carlos, dressed like Donnie Darko on Halloween was jamming a cigarette into the porch's ashtray, an oversized, emptied can of diced tomatoes, the label completely removed. Tyler was leaning in the hallway dressed in a white suit and a Michael Jackson costume, which, even though he was blonde, fit him perfectly. We all fell in after Beetlejuice, who yelled into the house where Aubrey dressed as a cartoon of a hillbilly, a picnic print button up tied into a bandeau, her boyfriend who didn't dress in costume, like me, and Emily the 'house bitch' Amy would tell me, dressed like Jasmine from Aladdin. See through pants and everything, regardless of 'that cottage cheese ass…'

Bottles were grabbed out of the back trunk and we waddled our way to the biggest house in all of Santa Cruz. It was perfectly kept, the bushes were as tall as the great wall, and masses of people were flowing in and out. The sketchiest of characters in the drug laced, new aging, surrealist yuppie, college fraternity, wannabe hobo punk mix of Santa Cruz. Like paint could vomit people vomiting down sets of stairs. And they were all beautiful in that way, that they could all, together, fit in the same house, be in the same room, dance to the same music, kiss in the same halls, fuck on the same beds, sweat into the same wooden banisters, slide drunken across slate outside. There circles were not friendly but the head of their bodies made night air happy. You don't have to be happy to be surrounded by them and to love their light. It's the clarity of alone with oxygen that makes your thoughts clear if you want to dilute life in their particular waste.

We were all standing in front of the house, people pouring in, people pouring out, maybe we wanted someone to tell us that it was going to be okay. There's nothing to be afraid of. There is liquor inside so the worst that happens is you all embarrass yourselves and you have an excuse. The best is a night you forget you loved forever. I started moving up, no consulting the group, it was now or never, or I was going to start thinking about people's height, dick size, why I didn't go to college. Pushing forward, with the force of a shark, the necessity of forward motion, less human than them even. I wasn't dressed up, except for a blue gingham button up, a haircut from Sam, and Amy's red lipstick, planted perfectly on my left cheek. I wasn't allowed to talk to too many other women, so stay with the group, is the impression I got. She was a very jealous person though she would never just say that. I can't count the fights I'd gotten into with Amy that would be solved if she would just admit she was jealous. I was jealous.

  She mouthed something and then her mouth disappeared at my ear.

  "—Sam..." I caught.

  Then Amy walked off fixing her skirt up the staircase. She had a 40oz. in her purse that the other hand was starting to dig up. Tyler and Carlos looked around, not annoyed, just unprepared for the life in here. They needed to find the kitchen. They were in the mood to sit on a sink and down and whiskey. That sounded good to me. I told them I'd meet up with them, with no plans to. I sat, took in the first room for a minute, waiting for Amy, who I know would show me around. The Victorian house, the Victorian staircase, the beautiful banister, the drunks leaning in velvet arm chairs with taxidermied boar's heads above them, handmade tapestry, quilts, Persian rugs, winding lighting fixtures, bored stoner's pushing stupid hats down other girl's heads. Computer lights, blue lights from mixing equipment, the needle was spinning lit in orange down the hallway. Two arcs before the dance floor. We watched bodies sweating incessantly, humming, feet hitting, limbs in strobe, hair bobbing, swaying, splashing into other bodies. It was real—this was not a place for modesty. Cut a rug. What rug? Oh you mean this, under my feet, that's about to drop out at any second? Amy tapped me on the shoulder, I started following her, we passed a girl in jean shortalls with My Little Pony purple hair and too much mascara, in a good way. Amy looked back and saw us smiling at each other. She pulled my arm harder.

  In the kitchen, girls were circling the island. Yolandi Visser was taking a shot and screaming, '*Fuck you! Fuck you for doing this to...*' she choked on her spit, cracking up, the biggest, reddest, drunkest smile, full of the biggest, whitest, teeth '*me! I'm so fucked! Oh! Amy!*" Her inflection shot up at the end, spiking, blissed out. Like something that had it's back stroked blindly and was going to be there to rub up on for a while.

Jaclyn's hair was cut perfectly. So tightly shaved down. Bleach blonde. She was wearing a cropped tank, white. White shorts, and some Reeboks.

"Okay, okay, here's your shot glass."

They readjust themselves, nestled close to each other. They both looked at me briefly, I was already sweating that, 'guy who doesn't like to drink,' stink but they passed me a shot glass and I was as enthusiastic as anyone.

"How's this game work?"

"Give me your hands. All of you."

I gave my hands to a stranger to my right, a rail thin girl with a Portuguese nose.

"Down by the banks of the Hanky Panky,

Where the bull frogs jump from bank to banky,

With a hip, hop, hippity, hop,

Leap off a lily pad and go KERPLOP!"

"Oh my god, I'm never going to get to drink. He's so bad..." said Amy.

She looked at Jaclyn, looking at me, laughing.

I laughed and took a shot.

"Here, pass the whiskey." I said.

"Yes! Yes! Yes!" said Jaclyn.

I took another for good measure.

Wasted, I asked where Sam was. Amy was smiling, smoking a cigarette inside on a couch in the corner of the dance floor. Where I would have been, during Jaclyn's birthday. The beat was chewing on my neck and wanted to drag me in. I moved my knee and politely bobbed my head.

"Anyone have any pot?" I asked. "It's hard to dance without pot."

"I don't smoke pot, Josh. Ask Jaclyn."

"Where's Sam?" I asked.

She stared at me. She took a drag and her tiny stomach bulged out of her skin tight dress. Her breasts hidden in a short silken blazer, black and white vertical stripes. She was looking down at herself, sweeping something off, maybe ash.

"I don't know, Josh." she said lazily.

I walked over to the outside edges and start moving in. You start with a modest shake. Something in the background. Wait for the heavy parts, freak out during the heavy parts, feel your shoulders from your feet, your neck is practically head banging, shake like you're praying in tongues, try to sweat God out, try to meet another body for anonymity. And she was there. She didn't care who I was, she never looked up. We were torsos; we were limbs, were lovers for a second. Her hips found this way of moving around me, an orbit; I was lost in this universe. Red lights/black lights/white polka dots/flesh/legs/tits/wrinkles/drum tight skin/dots/red lights/black lights/white polka dots/flesh/legs/tits...and then she looked up and smiled. A brunette. Enormous eyes. Small body. Rail thin even. She was smoking a joint.

"Can I?"

She couldn't hear me.

"CAN I?" I screamed into her ear.

"Yeah! Yeah, yeah..." she faded.

I plucked the joint from her tiny glossed but unpainted nails. I touched to her mouth and part of me wished it was her mouth but I drank the smoke instead of her sweet spit. I know it was sweet. You can tell. As sweet as her.

Sam cut in, the strobe blackened, and white cut over the girl I was with. She was dressed like a doctor. She always wanted to want to be a doctor for her parents. Her white lab coat was like a red flag, 'toro, toro you bastard' the girl I like is right *behind you* Sam. She took the joint out of my hand without asking and then mouthed something. When she saw my blank face she screamed it:

"Hi Josh!" such a proud smile.

I smiled back.

"Where's Amy?"

Amy walked over and pulled us out of the pit. One of each of our arms in one of each of her hands. The girl stopped dead and was shouting something through to us. Sam took the joint and she wasn't mad enough to do anything about it. Out of the frying pan into the filter.

::

We all moved outside, drunk, and freezing, letting the sweat cool from our backs. Amy to my right, kneeling, sat against her own legs, leaning on her side, into her hand. The pavement was perfect. There was a tree caged in next to us. 'Beautiful,' Sam said. 'Yup!' someone yelled.

It felt like a real meeting. Carlos to Amy's right. Taylor to his right. Aubrey to his right. Her annoying boyfriend to her right.

"I mean, it's a good album…"

Jaclyn to his right, looking a little lost. Company had come through, people that used to work with Amy: Cam from a popular punk band, he wasn't playing with them at the time was out with his girlfriend and An Australian with an oversized designer tank, looked like his friend had come from L.A. and I was playing it cool. They obviously all want to fuck Amy, I thought, paranoid. It's okay though, I have done this many times. Apathy works like a charm.

"Nicky's apartment has a pool you know."

"Sounds great!" he said in a thick Australian accent. His ironic mustache, his rugged beauty, his tan, his jewelry, and the survey of sexual behavior I'd read, about how Australians will dick anything.

"There's a pool so much closer, my friend has a place." said Jaclyn. "It's so easy to hop the fence, open the hatch from inside." She lit a cigarette.

"Me and Trish are outta here. Nice seeing you Amy," and they hugged a solid hug. Then Trish. Cam waved and walked on. It was just us now.

I couldn't hear anything the friend of the Australian was saying. But we were going.

"So we're going skinny, then, yeah?" the Australian jeered.

Bastard. Bastard. Bastard. Bastard.

"It's been awhile since I've last seen you." the friend said. His name was James. Or Jake. I forget but he would eventually be my manager within the year transferring into our store and making my life hell. He was tall, thick, and baby faced with a muscular body. Freckled with a tinge of red in his hair. A charmingly Parisian demeanor though he wasn't from there. He oozed sex and at the same time seemed absent.

I stood up first, knowing it was inevitable. I dusted my ass off and Amy looked for my hand. I looked down and reached her. She wrapped her arm around me, near my hip. Carlos and Taylor stared up. They wiggled their cigarettes into the corner of their faces after a drag and popped up one after the other. Jaclyn waddled last, feeling discouraged. Sam was squeezing her way through us closer to the Australian despite having a boyfriend. Taylor started singing something with a voice as big as his body. And I turned around walking, funny to be leading this many new faces. They didn't think anything of it. One by one they put their cigarettes out into the smooth bark of the trapped tree.

"Feel like me...Feel like me..." Taylor's voice faded. By the time we got into the pool we were all naked. Everyone was beautiful naked. Everyone could look at each other now, in full. And Amy smiled at me, while she was listening to a dirty joke from the Australian. I wasn't envious naked.

※

The next morning we woke up early, Amy had to visit her family for a few days and I was given a ride back into my neighborhood. As we were pulling up to the train station, I had work, she looked at me seriously, straight into my face and finally as we stopped dead she said, "I love you."

I love you.

I was not expecting, I love you. I didn't know what to say. I didn't love her yet. Maybe I did love her and I just couldn't say it yet. Saying it would mean that I'm as tied to her as she is to me. I love you is a game of pinochle and she has the upper thumb now because she initiated. I am completely blindsided. I am looking at her completely blankly while I think all of this. I dread the response I'm preparing either way. Consciously facing it, 'I don't know if I love you yet.' Consciously facing it with the weaker hunch, 'I love you but I can't admit that yet.' Consciously facing it, 'I don't love you.' Consciously facing it, 'You don't know that yet.'

"I love you too." I said and grabbed my things. I needed to catch a train. I couldn't talk about it and so I said it. It felt like it had weakened her because of how weak it was when it hit air. It was unconvinced and that much more unconvincing. I wanted to sit in the car and feel ashamed of myself for her but I was too distracted. I lacked the focus; I was in flight, and ready to feel my mind scatter on entry to the doors of my retail job in Palo Alto. Years of psychological prep for this, I couldn't blow it now. I was going to be normal; I was going to reclaim my life, my independence. Every day counted. It didn't matter as much as she mattered to me but I wouldn't have said it this way then.

She could sense the hesitance. She drove away after a confusing kiss, smiling a broken smile, even though her white teeth were showing. A wave. From 0-60 in less than 6 seconds.

⁂

The sun goes down and she's texting me to come outside. 'I don't know what door it is.' I run out of my complex, rushing down stairs like I was jumping rope, and swing into her car. I kiss her. She puts on the gas and turns up the volume for this song. I'm not into it but I'm into right now. I love that she loves it. One of the most underestimated skills in sustaining a long term relationship: liking that they like it.

We're getting nearer to her house. Up a winding road into a suburb I've never even tried to go to before in San Jose. A neighboring city. The lights are always shining on the cathedrals, up at a cross; it's back shadow stark and uncompromising. Like God's judgment.

She pulls into the church parking lot suddenly. She unbuckles her seatbelt and crawls over the center divide. She pushes her mouth into mine and she's tasting me. The way she always smelled like perfume made her pulling up her skirt in passenger's side so romantic. It wasn't just an animalistic fuck. When she pulled me out and into her in passenger's side she was giving me something. It was an anointing. Years I had spent inside of these buildings and now, outside, in her car, I could submit to something entirely different. Something real, like love you could touch. She grabbed the back of my neck and pushed my head into her chest. She fucked me slow and hard until I couldn't anymore. She smelled like blush but was washing me in rose oil. She pulled off and planted a kiss on my forehead. Turned on a light, fixed herself in the rearview, and started the engine. Whipping out of church and back onto the road where in 3 blocks we were home.

⁂

    I was sweating bullets trying to stand up straight at the door. I've always hated meeting other people's parents. At my house we were trusted enough to have made proper decisions about who we were investing time with. As rigid and disciplinary as my father was there was one aspect of your life that you had full control of: friendship. A blind eye was turned or maybe he was blind the entire time. No one was judged walking into our house which is uncharacteristic. Of course I never brought a woman over in my entire time in Indiana.

    Other people's parents were never as forgiving. The eyes that parents have, combing through the weak for their children. The questions about career plans and colleges. Grades. Parental relationships. Hobbies. Another interview. More eyes watching. More people smiling and listening and then turning their backs for a vicious critique. I had dressed as I always dress, nicely, articulately, without drawing attention to myself. Parents would love it.

They didn't greet us at the door. I walked in, over the welcome mat, over the small, shimmering, rugs. On the couch as I turned back after shutting the door, I saw him. Amy's father. He was tall, not skinny, not too fat, clean shaven, a black cropped haircut. Blue Ralph Lauren button down with orange embroidered player on the right breast. He shook my hand and asked, 'You're here for the party? Glad to have you.'

    "This is my friend, Josh." she said.

Friend.

"Nice to meet you." I said. He gave a stern pat on my back and let us pass through.

He sat down immediately again, no lights on by him, just a drum Amy told me he never practiced. We walked into the kitchen all the liquor was lined up perfectly, open across the island. No one inside but voices outside.

Walking through the living room, three steps from the level of the kitchen to the floor. The glass door, present, as everything else in this house. To our right before we walked out was a glass shelving filled with accomplishments. Portraits of Amy graduating high school, turning the tassel, tossing the hats. Amy played sports she never told me about like soccer. I wonder how long it took her legs to end up as skinny as they are now.

She pulled open the screen door. The backyard was filled with familiar faces. All of her Santa Cruz roommates were watching the house. She had left the party to come get me. We all hugged and gathered. Medina was coming through to meet me. She was the guest of honor who instantly saw I was holding nothing and filled my palm with a red Dixie cup she poured something into. She was holding the bottle but the label had been ripped off. Then she asked, everyone in a circle around her for some coke and grabbed it rudely making a fake smile and poured it laughing into my drink. Now we were all square.

There were only a few characters I had never met before. Two girls whose names I never remembered, one had hoop earrings and dyed black hair, she was wearing boots with tassels on the zippers.

"Those are four hundred dollars." Amy would tell me later.

The other girl was wearing black sandals and kept looking down her own shirt to make sure everything was in place. The guy, was,

"Dino." he said in a thick accent. "So you're Amy's new boyfriend?" he smiled, slow, and labored. He wasn't only drunk. His cigarette smoke was blowing all over me. "I haven't seen Amy in such a long time. This is my sister Medina, did you meet her yet?" He called her over with one hand movement. She came closer to him.

"What?"

He pointed a whole hand towards me.

"Yeah, I already met him." and she went back.

"How long have you been seeing Amy?"

"Since the beginning of the summer."

I didn't know what to say.

I went inside after downing the little in my cup.

I found Amy grabbing ice out of the fridge and I asked for some.

She stood next to me while I found a place on a raised chair in front of the island. I grabbed her hip and she pulled an arm around my head where she pulled me in and planted a kiss on a cowlick I can never get rid of.

"What's up with Dino?" I asked.

She looked up.

"What do you mean?"

"Like, what's his deal."

"He's my ex-boyfriend. He's like a total e-tard. I can't tell you how sorry I am that I dated him but he's Medina's sister so, try to chill out."

My arm was still around her hip and her arm was around my shoulder when we both looked up at the approaching footsteps. Two sets. Mom and Dad were standing directly in front of us. They were still smiling and mirroring the position we were in, Dad with an arm around the shoulder, Mom with a hand around the hip. They asked a question in Tamil and my stomach sank. My face was the way it always was: stone.

They said, "Have a nice night!" in English and the room's air cleared up. The front door opened and shut. I filled my ice filled cup with whiskey and I got up.

"What'd they say?"

"They asked me why I was touching you like that and then I told them you were gay and that you always do this." she laughed.

"Oh." I didn't think any more of it.

We passed through the kitchen into the living room. We walked down the three steps. I stopped at the threshold again, this time noticing an entire shelf granting space to an ivory elephant. I had always heard that they were carved out of one single piece. They were filled with holes filled with elephants filled with holes. They never stopped sprouting each other, dividing themselves in the stone, like cells. Like each new animal was trapped in the one before it.

    I walked out into the backyard. Dino was there. He offered Amy a cigarette and they started to catch up. Rehashing the camping trip to Yosemite and all the great times they had. He had finished half a cigarette before the end of the story. I drank faster. She looked into his eyes, and I was watching hers, light up, bulbs, the way you do when chemicals are telling your lies to everyone for you. The same feeling of turning your eyes down from someone your body and blood has noticed, someone whose beauty you have consumed in seconds, the slight embarrassment, whether made up modesty or a real guilt keeps you from acting on the full smile you know you want to give but can't bear the consequence of.

    She still wanted to fuck the chain smoking Bosnian. In the backyard of her house, a mini-mansion, with a fountain just past the grass in the yard. It had it's own lights. Even by middle class living standards there was both the absolute sense of entrapment and her house was both it and one-upping it. I couldn't focus on any one conversation. Now we were all drinking prosecco. My color faded. My will died as I raised my glass to cheer Medina on. We were wearing designer shoes or some shit. I was invisible now.

    She's boy crazy, I thought, jealous. Filled with this new unlovable Self. It didn't matter where he was from in Europe; all American girls were this Eurocentric. They're not stupid, they're bored. The American machismo that fascinates them soon bores them. The mysterious quiet drug addict was a fascinating new breed. I wonder what exciting new trip I provide. Looking to men who their fathers would hate, becoming the source of their pain, part of them knowing by their choices, certain they'll hate these very men later. We sit down, on the steps before the concrete in the backyard. They offer me a cigarette that I impolitely decline. My hands lose strength across her shoulder. I feel like the neighbors, bothered, poking my head into the conversation to hear, acting like I disapprove, dying to talk to her the same way. They made sure to tell us to throw our beer cans out. I have loosened. I sag. My embrace is the touch of a sopping wet towel. The yard is our beach, my filthy truth is the filth, like these cold, lifeless, voices, washing over everything I've broken down to this point.

@abigfuckingbully

@abigfuckingbully

SOMEWHERE IN HUMBOLDT A TRASH FIRE IS BURNING

Heather's mother was on again about how important it is that Heather and Ruby get along. The tiring broken record of perfectly strung clinical logic, wound too tight, strangling itself on the air as soon as it came out, unconvinced of itself. It was too early; there would be no sit down discussion. Just out of the shower, her black curls loose and unwound over her face and both hands completely cupping it. She had crashed the car this morning, just before work. She walked the two and a half miles after going through the professional motions of announcing and pitching personal disaster as alarming enough to be excusable.

"We're only human," the bloated voice would worm through. Every doctor was familiar with how humans are treated. Statistical checklists, quickly analyzed, harshly judged before truly tried, hours they read mouths moving and could on really hear answers to the prescribed question. Information slowly loses its importance. Besides, who's on trial? Guilty until proven innocent—we were all hiding from ourselves, that's why they hired her. Her job was like any other but she was a professional, she put herself on that pedestal to give herself the burden of helping others. With no umbrella for the walk she was now raining in the living room, talking in an exhausted voice, like a screw turned too many times, stripped of it's hysteria.

"Heather, you've got to learn to get along with your sister. She's a part of this family and in the end, we're all we've got."

"No, it's all I've ever had."

"And you just want to up and leave that, like we've given you nothing."

"I don't owe this family anything."

"No—you don't. Neither did your father. Neither did I."

"I'm not Ruby. I never want to be, Ruby. Stay in this shit hole for another three years so I can be ignored shouldering the Good family cross?"

Her mother paused.

"You're doing it to yourself. You do all this for yourself. The selfless psychologist, taking a pay cut to counsel fuck ups relapsing, forever, at a discount."

"Heather—you need to talk to your father."

"No. You need to talk to him. You blame him for this."

"Heather!"

"Do you blame him for being a cripple, mom? You're crippled—by your own self obsession. You chose to marry him. In sickness and in health. Are you sorry you married a fuck up? He'd love to hear it from you Katherine."

Heather's mother stared. Heather's voice like timber falling as her will collapsed. Her own study, again, counting the rings, remembering her age.

"You can't leave. That has nothing to do with me. Take control of your own life and stop grasping at mine."

Katherine dropped her head as if she were a tinker toy and sat still. The words ringing out endlessly through the house, out of the kitchen as Heather stomped back into her room to get her bags. Her mother was crying louder now, her tears running with the rest of her mother's rain. All her mother could see now was the inside of her hands, black, except for the kitchen light, leaking a glowing pink from between the two halves cupped. A shadow eclipsed it. The door slammed.

INFIDEL

Heather waved Carter back to the table from his place at the bar. Like the bartender said, "it's a full house tonight." "Over here," she was saying. Carter found the raised hand and read the muted mouth. He sat down, carefully placing the champagne glasses at their respective seats.

"This is amazing!" Heather said.

"In Humboldt!" said Carter.

"How did you

find out about this place?"

"Jeannie told me about it."

Heather's smile flinched.

They turned their heads to a low set stage in the corner of the room. A six piece Jazz band playing—the swimming rhythms nearly swallowed by a crazed drummer, never losing focus for a second. The bass like the hum of a deep forest, silence inverted, sweetly oozing into the ears. The horns announcing to God their human happening, the sound of a cicada sustained to a swarm of locusts, a black rain soaring over the band. The guitar washing over the ears in waves beating into the shores, into canals, crescendos ending in decrescendos ending in crescendos, hypnotizing Heather and Carter, until, as if a cleaver were taken to the sound, a staccato sealed it.

The waiter broke through their fixed stare at the band. Words were shot, they dribbled 'Thank you's and took their menus, doe eyed but smiling. They turned their heads down.

"I haven't seen Jeannie in a while." said Heather.

"She's not coming." said Carter.

Heather looked up from her menu, straight into Carter's face.

"Of course."

Carter looked back down at his menu and spoke quietly, "She couldn't get the time off."

He wiped the lower half of his face with one hand and opened his eyes wider. He shivered.

Heather looked up.

"You knew she wasn't going to."

Her eyes narrowed, as if her line of sight were a beam and closing the aperture would increase the thrust of static, sending the noise of her nerve-wracked body into the lake-calm mind of Carter. He turned his head up, lead by his right ear, his face a pendulum strung by the neck, eye contact lagged until it clicked like two magnets.

"I miss her."

Heather felt a small impact; a piece of her was chipped off with the words. She took it in stride, her face

Still except for the micro expressions, still nothing revealed. The discomfort started stinging, like a bit lip, a cut you didn't know you had, a chipped tooth. Her emotions humming like feedback, laced in her words.

"I miss her too." Heather said.

They stared at each other again. The

waiter stepped in front and center of them. They were on both ends of the booth's crescent and looked up at him.

"What can I get you two beautiful people tonight?"

Heather hesitated. Carter turned his head to the menu a made a low noise.

"Uh...um.." Heather looked at Carter.

"We'll have the special," they both said at once, laughing.

"Great choice," the waiter said. He was busy scribbling. "Would you like anything else to drink? A sparkling water? Someone here owes someone a coke, I think."

"Yeah, a sparkling water would be great." Heather said, still giggling.

"You

two are dressed up. What's the occasion?"

"It's our anniversary," Carter said.

"Two year anniversary." Heather said.

"That's beautiful...I can tell you two are really in love." The waiter said. He was collecting the menus.

"People are jealous when they see that kind of love. They're going to try and break it up. I know you'd never let them." He winked and slanted a hip, then turned and walked away.

■

Carter was moving hesitantly, deciding whether or not he wanted to dance under the oppressive red lighting. Heather, Jeannie, Ben, Adam, James, Missy, Monique, and Isabelle, had all made it to the celebration. No one else was expected. Years in Humboldt would lead you to a million outings, a million opportunities to meet your lazy town, it was either the pot smog hanging over the entire suburb that made nightlife forced and desperate or the people were desperate and making a pot smog— but this was it.

Every party was the same sodden hope, that this would be the day, a life changing moment where you would shake hands with a character who has the power to change your life, leading you into the drama this town's always needed, without the same necessary tools. The savory smell of weed, the sour smell of whiskey, the stale smell of cigarettes. You think to yourself, 'I should be grateful for being so spoiled by Sunny California,' but it's not enough. Your mind knows the truth behind that half hearted smile and it makes you feel worse to face the empty sprawling roads dead ending in oil caked stoops, the mouth of cramped houses. It's hard to imagine what it's like with a desire to be sober. Feeling like a tourist in your own America. The social conventions as strong as religious doctrines. Keeps pushing for that individual freedom and depressed as ever look for another bottle to leech off of. You wonder,

'Am I an American? Did I come from this place? This state, this county, this town, this country?' Everyone else seems content with the expectations, maybe it's because it's they can easily meet them. You feel selfish for dreaming of being in another place, they make you feel selfish. They tell themselves they want to be here, when making the best of it becomes the best thing to do. Cognitive dissonance

 all sutured for those lacking the will, funds, or talent. All healed up. It was time to leave, and these were the ones they could account for, these were the people they could count on, friends—whether by chance or chains—friends.

■

The bar was playing club hits, ass shakers, but they congregated next to a perfectly suitable tall round table. They stood to drink. Jeannie was taking a sip of a whiskey sour, daintily, and dancing by herself. She paused in front of Heather, while the rest of the group was busy in their own splintered conversations.

"So are you both going to Europe, still?" said Jeannie.

"We'll manage without you, Jeannie." Heather looked at Jeannie and laughed. "Of course we're going, you were never really going."

"I was going, okay—I couldn't get the time off."

"You had a year!"

"You're right, I don't know. I just want to save my money."

"For

what?"

"Shut up!"

Heather laughed.

"Have you decided where yet?" said Jeannie.

"We're going to the Catacombs in France."

"Jesus."

"It's amazing. I've never seen anything built like that. Natural architecture."

"Do they consider mass graves 'architecture,' Heather?"

∎

"You're leaving tomorrow, night." said Adam.

"To France."

"You bastard!" said Adam.

"Another trip to Europe. Maybe you're last." said Ben.

"The catacombs are beautiful," said Missy, "I was horrified when I went. My little sister wouldn't go in."

"Please get me something," said Monique.

Monique's face lit up like her pocket, a quiet vibrating. She started pinching at her phone from the pocket of her jeans. Adam, turning his neck away from a distracted Monique, pushed a gentle fist into Carter's arm, almost whispering,

"I'm jealous of you, Carter."

Carter laughed and put an arm around Adam, whose soft-spoken voice was totally unfit for his huggable bear sized, Grecian body. No one could feel the importance of all of them together under the bodily heat of red lamps, they all looked to each other. The circle drew closer. The separate conversations osmosed into one again as Adam searched for an escape from Monique. The support of others in conversation can easily divide the pressure that would reveal one as disinterested. The mundane could be an important conversation as a group. As long as they were talking no one was too hurt or bored. The chances increase that someone's interested or, if not, that the topic would change.

"We're going to miss you Carter...Heather." said James, looking at each.

"We'll be back in Humboldt," said Carter.

Heather laid her forearm across her stomach and scratched the opposite, nervously. The trip hadn't even started but it was already starting with its end.

"To be alive," James said, raising his glass, "and in love, to celebrate the dead."

Everyone raised their chilled glasses and with the perfect pressure met in the center. They all tipped their glasses back and drank. Missy cut her sip short, noticeably shooting a look beyond James's shoulder.

"What?" asked James.

Missy's eyes followed a blonde haired boy from one end of her sight, to the other, her eyes moving like a kit-cat clock. Jeannie's eyes followed Missy's and then the blonde's. James felt a heat fill the bottom half of his eyes. He swallowed it down and kept it in his stomach, like whiskey, where it kicked like a baby.

"Why don't you talk to him?" Ben asked.

"I do." said Missy. Her eyes from Ben, to James, then into her glass.

"If you don't I will." said Jeannie, smiling behind the mouth of her beer glass.

Missy looked at Jeannie. Her hair stood on end, inside she hissed, but she sat still playing it cool. She looked longingly at the boy opportunely alone.

"His name is Geoffrey."

"I won't need an opener then, thanks."

Jeannie slammed her beer down. By the time Missy had looked away, Jeannie was at home in the place Missy's eyes had just left. She returned them and watched. Instantly Geoffrey was off to buy Jeannie a beer.

"Stupid, bitch." Missy murmured.

James, smiled a quiet smile, something about his eyes gave it away.

"You're not going to talk to him—" Ben said.

"Shut up, Ben!"

Everyone paused. The atmosphere had a pin-sized hole draining it.

"Why the Catacombs?" Monique asked.

"It's like the caves of Lascaux but with more stinky corpses."

"—it's not a tourist trap. It's beautiful. Perfectly constructed from the bones of a forgotten mass."

"Sounds horrifying." said James.

"It's a little scary but too frequented to have anything haunting it." said Carter.

"You sure?" said Ben.

He took a sip from his glass and raised his eyebrows. He scanned the circle and then choked on his drink. When he was done coughing and drying off, he gurgled with an ice cube dribbling in his mouth.

"Where's Missy?"

"—Oh no..." said Heather.

She dropped her drink down fast onto the table and quickly rushed out of the laughing circle. Her head poked up like a bird searching for Missy. She ran to the bathroom.

■

She entered slowly. The perfect hall—to the left sinks and mirrors, to the right, asphalt colored stalls after asphalt colored stalls. A cleanliness atypical of a bars bathroom, the only graffiti some weakly scraped scribbles in glass. She walked forward, her head perfectly aligned for her eye to frame each stall separately as she passed. Only one was sealed. She knocked. The metal echoed. Heather's knuckles were red. She knocked again. The door unlatched and slowly sucked in against the wall. The shrill crying shot like a laser into

Heather's ears. Her face was burning just under the skin, it contorted into one enormous frown and she fell over Missy like a blanket, hugging her.

"Jeannie. That...dumb...b-b-b-b-biiiiiiiiitch."

"I'm sorry Missy, I don't think Jeannie is trying to hurt you."

"—No! No! She is trying to hurt me." Her lips were jutting out like a cup holder in a car. Her face was soaking wet, she covered it with her hands and then let them drop to her sides, her palms scrunched up like a bug-sprayed spider. Heather was bending over in front of her rubbing the outsides of Missy's arms over and over.

"Oh, Missy."

She sat in Missy's lap and hugged her. Missy gently pushed Heather's strong loving grip away.

"I'm okay, I'm okay now."

Missy squeezed out past a confused Heather, who sat down on the seat watching Missy. Heather heard the door open. Missy was face to face with Jeannie after pushing the swinging door. Missy stared at Jeannie and Jeannie smiled. Missy's face contorted and she looked at the ground and jabbed a shoulder into Jeannie's side, vulnerable ribs exposed while Jeannie politely held the door open, Jeannie's hand above Missy's head.

"Jeannie, what the fuck is your problem? You knew Missy was going to flip out. You went over there to taunt her, you kissed him right in front of her."

"She's not going to—I have a right to."

"Jesus, you're a pushy bitch. This is the last night I'm going to see these people and you decide to get drunk and push Missy around, trying to fuck some guy you didn't even know existed until ten minutes ago."

"You just hate how assertive I am. Missy is over reacting." She smiled.

Heather was frozen. Her anger had hit the same wall her argument had.

"It's what you guys love about me!"

"Yeah and most of the time what I hate about you."

"I have a right—"

"Yeah, Jeannie! You have a fucking right. I have a right—but it's not always right to use it."

Heather's face was barely an inch away. Jeannie was quiet. She moved a hand onto Heather's hip. Heather softened, her back straightened and her face left. Then they returned a little closer till their hips touched.

"You love me." Jeannie laughed.

Heather separated and tried to wipe away the anger with her hand.

"I'm sorry, okay? Tonight's the last night I can see you before you go, are you coming over?" said Jeannie.

"Yeah, sure."

■

They walked from the quiet anonymity by the noisy bar seats back to their seats with the group.

"Missy had to leave." said Ben, nervously.

"Oh, that sucks," said Jeannie. Passive aggressively playing dumb.

"I think I'm going to head out too. I've got to wake up really early tomorrow." said James.

"Yeah, me too." said Ben.

"Okay..." said Monique. "How about one more round before we end the night?"

They ordered. They gathered in their original circle. They raised their glasses.

"What do we drink to?"

"—Fuck it."

They all finished their drinks in one slow gulp.

"Here! Here!" laughed Jeannie.

■

They drunkenly stumbled into the house. Jeannie after heather, falling up the narrow stairway. The heat was instantly groping the both of them and the yellow light added to a whiskey-gut stagger.

"Fuck..."

"Food!—" yelled Heather.

Jeannie veered right after the end of the banister and Heather ran into the kitchen. Jeannie opened the door to her room and turned on the light. She flung her purse against the farthest wall as hard as she could.

"What was that?!" Heather yelled down the hall..

Jeannie turned the light off and poked her head and back out of her room.

"You bitch, are you looking through my fridge without me?"

Jeannie marched down the corridor, past roommates terrible coffee shop worthy artwork, somewhere between comedy and street art, into the kitchen. It was a genre perfected by the locale. Humboldt must have entirely been swallowed by an enormous pot cloud. It's residents trapped in a contact high of lazy hallucination. A painting of a hot dog had a venue here. Jeannie snapped out of it. A spoon hit her in the temple and

Heather howled with laughter.

"Stop staring at that trash and feed me."

Jeannie looked around the corner and into the fridge where only Heather's back half could be seen. Jeannie's eyes crawled up Heather's calves, around her ass and stopped at the dimple peeking out from in-between the lifted hem of her shirt and the sinking waist of her Jeans. Heather put both arms on the sides of the open fridge and pulled herself out like a squirrel with her head trapped in a tree knot. The 5' 8" woman stood all the way up patting her hands clean. She stared at Jeannie staring.

"There's nothing in here."

She slowly closed the fridge and quickly opened the freezer. She pulled out a half eaten carton of raspberry gelato and slammed the freezer closed.

"Ladies night!" Heather mockingly sang.

"It's not even mine...don't fucking eat it."

Heather stared and then smiling pulled the lid off the tub.

Jeannie struggled to pick up the spoon Heather threw while Heather grabbed a spoon all too comfortably from the drawer. They both sat at the ends of the table, pushed against the far side of the kitchen, at the same time.

"Is Carter mad at me?" said Jeannie.

"He's always mad at you, but he still loves you."

"How was the anniversary? It's been a whole year. Are you bored, yet?" said Jeannie.

Heather dropped her head and stared down her carton.

"It was good..."

"Oh my God—Heather I was just joking."

"It's been good. It does feel a year older."

"You guys seem really happy, together."

"I'm happy, it just is harder to trust someone you've known that long. There's so much to lose and people drop out under the pressure."

"What do you mean?"

"I don't...know if he's been with anyone else."

"Carter wouldn't."

"He loves me but he's constantly fighting me. About small shit. Pushing me into corners about things."

"He's afraid you'll leave him."

"I can't appreciate what's here, he's always saying."

"What's his plan? Stay in Humboldt? Forever?"

"He hates it."

"That's why he tells you that. He's talking to himself.

He's giving you his own advice."

Heather got up, half listening. Jeannie reached across the table and grabbed the carton.

"Do you have anything else to drink?"

She opened the freezer again with an amazing sobriety, cutting for a moment through drunken heat. Jeannie got up.

"Only in my room. One second."

She turned quickly and went back into the dark hallway, leaving the ice cream to melt.

"I want to lay down..."

Heather struggled to follow. Jeannie was scrambling under her desk for a bottle. Heather fell hard against the mattress. She started digging through Jeannie's nightstand. Had she been sober, she would remember it was wrong to do it. Maybe sober she would do it anyway, she doesn't know if it's bad or not that she finds making decisions based on morals a hassle. Liquid courage makes her feel her record allows a few arbitrary abandonments of judgment. Heather leaned up as she breached the point of debate. She turned the night stand's lamp on. The sound of bottles clinking together stopped and Jeannie completely focused on unscrewing the cap of her rum, hopped on the bed, sending a slow wave to Heather through the bedding like water under a ship.

"It's so good."

Jeannie stopped, she looked over at Heather, her hands filled with paper.

"What are you doing?"

Heather looked apologetically into Jeannie's face.

"Oh." She laughed and laid out straight at the edge of the bed. She lifted a handful of paper.

"I'm reading the postcards I sent you."

"I have every, single, one."

Jeannie smiled and moved closer to Heather, she was cross-legged facing Heather. Jeannie grabbed the postcards quickly shuffling through them. She stopped on a postcard from The Louvre in France. It had a portrait of Lee Miller on it:

Dear Jeannie,

Paris is exactly how I left it. Feeling lost in the busyness and pigeon shit. It's cold and all the leaves are gold and red. With the little French Carter and me know we're getting through meals but it's impossible to make friends. We're here for us anyways—we're tourists—but Parisians don't appreciate the effort.

Spent last night in the countryside illegally camping on the edge of a small farmer's plot. Nothing beats camping out in the complete open. We were barely hidden by empty corn stalks and a tree. Waiting for Greece.

xOxO Heather

Heather laughed, blushing, drunk, and embarrassed.

"Stop!" Heather said.

"This is crazy…"

"So long ago."

"No—that you still have every one."

"What do you mean? Lose a postcard from, Heather?"

Jeannie moved closer to Heather and laid arm to arm with her. She took a sip of rum and passed it to Heather, who staring into the wall took it without looking. A minute of total silence passed. Jeannie noticed a bracelet on Heather's wrist she hadn't noticed before, it was Cartier.

"Where'd you get that bracelet?" asked Jeannie.

Heather looked down.

"It's for our anniversary."

"It's Cartier."

Heather was silent again. Heather kept reading. Jeannie laid her head back and combed her hand through her hair.

"Are you tired?" asked Jeannie.

Heather turned her head towards Jeannie, the rest of her totally stationary.

"No, not really."

Heather's arm broke out into a wave of goosebumps. She salivated. She swallowed.

"Why?"

"No reason." said Jeannie. "It's cold, though. I want to get under this." She dropped her hand palm first into the blankets.

"Okay." Heather said.

Heather hopped onto her feet from the bed and started unbuttoning her shirt while Jeannie got up and turned around to pull the blankets back. Jeannie remained clothed, flipping through the leftover postcards when she settled in the sheets. She stopped to watch Heather undress. Heather untied her shoes and pried them off. Then, leaning over she peeled her pants away in one swift downward motion, like a magician. One leg up and out followed by the other. She turned around.

"What?" said Heather.

"Nothing."

Heather smiled a quick smile and crawled into bed. Jeannie tossed the postcards off the bed. Her teeth were chattering, she turned on her side. Heather pulled up the blankets.

"How is it so cold in here?" Heather said.

"I know." said Jeannie.

Jeannie scoot over to Heather and wrapped her legs around Heather's, laying her head in Heather's chest. Heather's blood started to rush through her body. Her heart was pounding. Her legs felt a soft electricity flutter through. She reminded herself to breathe easy.

"You're so warm." Jeannie said.

Heather laughed.

"I'm going to miss you." said Jeannie.

Heather looked down at Jeannie, whose eyes were closed.

"I'm going to miss you too." said Heather.

Jeannie looked up smiling, her eyes wide open. They looked at each other until Jeannie pushed herself into a slow kiss with Heather. Heather lifted a hand to Jeannie's cheek as their faces rose. Heather's mouth filled Jeannie's.

"Turn off the light." said Jeannie.

Heather turned off the light and crawled over Jeannie, straddling her.

"I...love you." said Jeannie.

Heather's hair fell over Jeannie, hiding them from the only moonlight left in the window.

"Don't tell Carter."

The kiss was punctuated by a lip pulling away from between Jeannie's front teeth.

"I won't."

@abigfuckingbully

@abigfuckingbully

AIN'T WORTH A DOLLAR

If she really loved me, like she just said she did, high on something (but she always had fucked up eyes, like they were always draining, out.) then she would talk to me at a time when she didn't want to cheat on her boyfriends. She's sitting in the car with her hair tied up, I forget how beautiful she is, I always think I'm going to be immune to her, to them—so she smiles this unblemished smile, that lasts one second before it collapses into this miserable, needy, fearful smile. I feel guilty for being here. She passes me a joint she neatly rolled in the parking lot of an outdoor mall. I watched her nails seal it end to end, perfectly, as the paint job. Neon pink nails on a girl as pale as a ghost but in a good way. When she was open, unguarded, and her posture was touching you, getting close to you, everything she could do for you—just by being with you, I trusted her.

Parked in front of my complex now she lit it and tilted her head back. She breathed death into the car. She slipped away somewhere else and then passed it to me.

"I'm sorry." I said. "For all the fucked up shit I said...I've thought about it for such a long time."

"It's okay. I was really fucked up too."

"I think I could feel that you liked me but the whole time you were with men that made you miserable. I felt like you chose men you knew you couldn't really be with. My brother or Jeffrey. I had to act like I fucking hated you."

I took a hit, a long drag and started choking.

"It's a spliff—you can't hit it that hard," she said laughing.

She took it back and dragged. She exhaled. I took it while coughing and regained myself. I took a small hit and passed it back. She was touching her ponytail, high and prized, giving me her full attention, finally. She'd never done it before. I wonder if this is a pattern for me or for her. She could give those eyes she's giving me now to anyone. She was always accusing me of it. She was always saying, 'You say that to every girl.' Which always made me angry. It's why I don't give anything to anyone anymore. 'Yup, this is all bullshit. I just run my mouth like this so you'll pay attention. I'm not even here. See-through, clear as this windshield, Mia. Just listen—I'm a fucking radio show, I'm not even a real person. Fuck you...fuck you...fuck you...this is how I talk! This is who I am. You don't believe it. Pearls before swine. So If I have to, I'll keep chewing it, cud, fourth stomach it, swallow. Baa, baa, just a sheep. Lead me on.' Everyone is so affected. Can't believe that you would give them that kind of love.

"I remember the night my brother left your Range Rover and it was just you and me in your car, and you told me I would be a better boyfriend. I remember you slid your hand over mine and you leaned all the way into back seat to give me a kiss." Her face was fat and colorful then. "You were always looking for *me* to talk about *them*."

I looked down—embarrassed by the effort I was putting in. It's easier to be quiet or lie about your feelings because some feelings are soft feelings and a lot of soft feelings turn into toxic thoughts later. I look up. Her eyes are watering. I'm guessing more from me than from the drugs.

"I love you too. I guess I—"

Her phone was ringing. Everything turned into her bag vibrating. She started digging ferociously through her bag, hungry animals don't look scared though.

"Hello?"
"*Where are you?*" the voice weakly aired itself out into her car.
"I'm out right now."
"*You're out? It's almost one. Where are you?*"
"I'm sorry. I lost track of time, I haven't seen Josh in a long time. I just want to—"
"*You're with, Josh? What the hell are you doing over there? With Josh.*"
"I'm..."
She kept going. Again, witness to the end of a relationship she should have never been in. Creative men—the novelty fades fast. Jealous and poking his Napoleonic dick into our night. Conquering her at every angle. Ten steps ahead of us. She was shouting now.

"Find somewhere else to stay! Because you're fucking scaring me. Seriously. I will wake up my dad and have him find you and kick you out of my house. So get the fuck out of there now, Andrew. Get the fuck out, now. Right now."

   "*Don't do that. You don't need to do that. You need to come home now.*"

   "Shut the fuck up! I'm calling my dad. Find somewhere else to stay. Okay?"

She hung up. She looked over to me and she started crying.

"He's such a bastard."

I opened the car door and got up silently. Sealing her into the car, with her tears, walking away a headless torso from the frame of the passenger's window. Jogging up the steps sweating into sense again.

@abigfuckingbully

@abigfuckingbully

I NEVER DID ENOUGH DRUGS

I mostly told her to stop doing drugs around me because I knew that she would stop being around me. When I wanted her she was unavailable and vice versa. She was a stronger person when she was with other men—men she could ignore and fantasize about men who were not those men.

One night, she was chain smoking on a miniature park bridge telling me what her parents thought she was good for, which was nothing. She could have gone to college at UCLA but she decided not to mostly to spite her parents. Now she's dated 6 different employees from the same Whole Foods and wants to be a different person. She was talking about regret for the next 20 minutes before I stopped her and asked her if she could see the ducks perched on the rocks across from us.

"We're being too loud." I said. "we woke them up," half kidding.

They looked half perched and half ready to fight, feathers ruffled, quacking funny.

"Huh." She said disinterested. Clearly she needed to talk more.

"You can feel bad about it if you want or you can move forward. I think you mostly just ask too many questions."

"I don't need an answer—I haven't asked anything."

"You're asking without asking," I said.

She put the cigarette out into the banister of wood.

I stopped dating girls who smoked cigarettes a year ago as a general rule.
And women with tattoos of people they know, especially if they are on calves. Partly because I always think of a girl I knew when I see them and partly because I know that tattoos are for sentimental people. Sentimental people are compensating for all the feelings they don't really have about very many things.

I walked away, across the rocks in a simulated river in a simulated city, Los Angeles, and walked to the swing set.

She eventually followed.

She stared at me as I started to swing. I couldn't fully extend my legs to pump because I was too tall, these were for the kiddies. I started feeling everything rushing to my stomach and out of my head and then back in. I started feeling everything coming to a point in my head where I loved everything. I started giggling like I was on laughing gas and closing my eyes. I spun and felt a high better than drinking and it was probably seventy but the air brushing across my face reminded me of a winter in Indiana and I felt happy, which is worth noting because I never feel happy enough myself to just say it like that.

She started swinging and said,
"You don't get out much do you?"
I looked at her and laughed.
"I never did enough drugs."

She laughed angry.

"Just for a few seconds swing."

She flicked her cigarette where a kid was going to fall on their ass on the rubbery part of the playground.

"Jesus..." I said.

Then she started swinging and stopped talking.

Scenes I'm Outside Of

On a night out I pass you outside of a bar, Anne, in the cheap tin furniture with friends who all don't give a fuck. You're tall, protective gay friend is there when I pass. You and I make eye contact. It was your wine colored lipstick I noticed. And how you can wear hoops like that. You hesitate to greet me so I thieve the initiative: seeking balance for an angular adrenaline count. Riding the high with an approach straight into your table. Two or three other girls, and the blonde one, Debbie, are staring, annoyed.

"Anne." I say smiling a glass smile. But it shines like some eyes do. I lean into the grating, cocky, and brush my hair to the side of my face. Because I know, right now, you're remembering me 4 years ago at Ben's New Year's Party, drunkenly announcing into your stomach, is face level when I sit and you stand, your floral patterned crop top, boxy—modern—square—like you are, built by hand like you aren't. Your touch was fucking me up more than the screwdriver's I was drinking, and your perfume more than your touch—but I wasn't drinking screwdrivers because you walked me to the liquor store with you and bought me a 24oz Sierra Nevada I was too young to buy. That's what I was drinking. Right now you're remembering my pathetic, "You chose me?!" red faced into your stomach. Or how we used your Jewish friend's bed...

But then I'm a man now and you want to fuck me like anyone else you'd want to fuck. And you can't tell if I want you to because I'm standing up military, and my hands are in the pockets of my sun bleached jacket, the corduroy white at the elbows, buttoned to my neck, collar up.

"You never wrote me back. Why not?"
and you're looking nervously straight up at me from the opposite side of the table. Wracked, you'll tell me you didn't have the time. I'll lean into the table, across the table, over the center and ask you, never breaking eye contact:

"Do you think I'm crazy? Or a pervert? Or something...? Like you think I want something from you? Your money, maybe—here."

I'll walk to your side, you staring into me still and suddenly lift you like we're married, push the seat out with one foot, you in my arms, fill your

77

seat, and sit you on my lap. Brush some hair out of your mouth.

"I can love you like every man you've had wished he could."

I'd take your face in my hand, your jaw in my palm like a wineglass, and close my eyes and take your mouth. And you fill me up bittersweet. And I'd lift you back up, and pull the chair in with one foot, with you still in my arms, like we're getting divorced, and drop you back into your seat like you were someone else's woman anyways and walk off. Turn my head both ways before jogging across the street, curled locks bobbing, me smiling wide and your heart sinking, taking a loser's walk, and each step a beat of your heart, while my pride makes a joke of the jokes you make me. And your dumb ass friends would start talking, laughing, and asking you 'what the fuck that was,' and for once you'd remember me the way I remember you most nights.

Nature

"I'm scared of the ocean." I said, looking mostly into darkness at the irony of a glowing cherry bobbing through space. She walked closer to me and gruffly plucked the cigarette out of her own mouth and blew down.
"You're a pussy is what you're telling me."
"I'm not a pussy! The ocean's God!"
She stuck the nub of her cigarette back into her lips and untied her shoes, almost falling over in the sand. Here from years of change. I had no evidence that the 'what goes around, comes around' concept of karma actually existed, but in birth in birth-and -death, you find sand. Sand is the result of broken down stone. Same as cliffs eaten by the salted teeth of waves. Eventually sand would die, to be born a different sediment, hardened, back into stone—the resurrection. Everything on earth works by itself. It feeds itself. It recycles itself. It shifts its contents into perfect balance, one wave at a time. Animals like us would evolve eventually to gaze not at the navel but into the womb.
    She was running down the beach now, just past the line drawn where the tide would crawl up. I watched her walk in, towards the horizon, where I stopped to stare at what wanted to be a reflection of the moon over the water. It's light rippling over, the way T.V. static moves, waves plucking their heads up to catch coast, breaking in series, whiter and larger, emerging from each other, multiplying like cells, dying on impact.
    I untied my shoes just to barely let what I expect to be freezing cold water by September under my toes. It's warm—it's easy. I feel myself anchoring in even as waves eat sand out from under my feet, the shape left, smeared like oil pastel of a print.
Looking out again, a girl turned, smiling my direction, letting waves beat at her legs. I smiled, feeling salted air across my face, peeling away pretense.
    I'd once read that looking at the horizon was a dopamine release, physiologically proven now, not just a natural fact from the experience of crushing absolutely all remnants of the urban perspective through sight alone, that a life alone might be 100 years, outlived by some tortoises—outlived by all roaches. Our problems are small—the mind makes itself bigger. But we've built cities as replacements in hopes we might feel the same. Those cities filled with readers interested in the incentive of looking at a horizon. The opportunities we

have to debunk every natural wonder in hopes of it revealing its truth, so that later we can bottle the feeling. So that later we can sell it back to you.

      I stared, straight on, at the hard line. The details blurring, into murky midnight blues. The rushing feeling of the sound of waves filling you. In sequence, surrounding, one ripple after another, the hands of wind sounding out, like one long breath. I don't swim, all life comes from the sea—the sea is God, he giveth, he taketh away.

@abigfuckingbully

It Takes One To Own One

I notice a poem in my feed—formatted like a regular poem, accompanied by a picture of her, Molly. I'm reading it the way I always read poetry on the internet, it's limitless potential, it's legitimizing of everything ready-made as art, something to be immediately distrustful of. I find my hair on end by the final line. It's impact tugging on my mind to remind me to get a handle. Molly—lives in Los Angeles. I'm living in Los Angeles, now.

I'm clicking the heart, I'm clicking the plus, I'm taking down her name, and I'm sending her a message. I'm overstepping my boundaries. I'm Gchatting her. I'm convincing her to read my work—I'm convincing myself based off of this one piece this is a potential working relationship. She's convincing too. We're exchanging poetry and fiction, photos, phone numbers, and Snapchats until we meet this weekend for coffee a block from my house. I'm really this lucky. I just moved to Los Angeles and I'm making friends. I've never had real artists as friends. I'm always hiding myself from them, even my girlfriend was an artist. Jealous and arrogant like me. She wants me to fail like her parents made her feel she did. If she can't—no one will. But not this time. I'll show them—myself again...no compromises.

Saturday—11:30am into a notebook.

■

I'm walking a block down from my house to a coffee shop I started frequenting, partly by accident, partly by convenience. I'm already talking to the barista, which I worry, about sleeping with, she has purple hair, smokes cigarettes, and I'm already breaking a few of my own rules. I'm looking around to make sure she's not here this morning. It's a bad look, the curled hair of a dyed blonde Jewish girl might make a purple haired Turk that much more attracted. I'd be caught in the middle of a coffee, overdressed for 11am and completely disoriented. I'm always overdressed—boots before winter seems embarrassingly L.A.

I see her blonde hair glowing in the sun. I can't decide if she's pretty or not. Ice blue eyes, blonde hair, big face. Usually it's exciting but my mind's with me—noticing the little things. Like her hunch and how both her hands are on her cup when she takes a sip, the way you would from a tit, or a gerbil feeds. I sit in front of her, small, shaking body, her hand leaves the coffee cup, as if disconnected from the rest of her body—mechanically moving curls, greasy from unwash, out of her forehead. Her beanie dangling—derelict, from the very end of her head, Los Angeles Autumn, just too cold. (I am burning and I'm five minutes out.)

"Hey Molly."
She smiled and curled her loose strands.
"Have you been here long?" I asked.
"Just got here."
I'm staring.
She's blinking.
"I'm gonna get a coffee."

I'm always taking a piss, or 'getting more water,' or 'getting some coffee' to give myself a 15 second breather. I know how I am with patience. I'm easily caught up in the talk, the point of losing all composure. Too much of myself to distract me from it. I threw all quarters on the table for a small coffee and came back, slowly, focused because I'm clumsy. The joke is I'm always spilling my coffee on myself when I'm out. My hands independent of me protecting me from future ulcers. No milk, just honey.

I sat back down.
"Tell me about this script."
"I'm stuck. Don't know what to do with it."
She took a sip. I couldn't yet.
We sat until I could take a sip.
She stared, took a sip. I took a sip and stared.
"You should watch movies. That always helps."
"Yeah…"
I could feel my day sinking.

■

Marilyn Monroe's grave was around Westwood, near UCLA, where Molly and I are going. She swears she isn't rich but if you drink out of a matching set of glasses and you go to UCLA I have a hard time believing that. She was playing it down, classic Rich- Girl-Wannabe-Down-Syndrome. Anytime they're sharing they can act like you're robbing them.

We talked about popular writers, publishing credits, and our contemporaries and competitors…then were distracted.
"Marilyn—seems…overvalued." I said.
"She's a tragic figure."
"She's a kind of Manic Pixie Dream Girl but actually Bipolar."
"I'm Bi-Polar. It's fatal attraction."
"That's how I feel.
Maybe that's my attraction to relationship stories."
She asked her first question:
"What's your last relationship like?"

"I'm attracted to girls who act like they don't give a fuck about anything but they're all...hollowed out, every time."

She looked at me and then looked straightforward. Waddling on, her feet almost looked broken, the way she moved. As if her flip-flops were flippers. A march but lazy like Shaggy, where the knees went up high and the feet were whipped by the knees and the toes whipped by the ankles out.

"We're lost." she said at the end of a street. There was a mass grave, white crosses everywhere, but nobody famous. What an honor to be of service: to anyone you would be nothing but a white strike in a green field.

Light was blinding, bouncing off one.

"What are your relationships like?" I asked.

The story she sent me was about fucking an Englishman at a party up a tree. She let his come run down her leg. Relationship was a strong word.

"My ex-boyfriend was a Neo Nazi. He said he liked to date Jewish girls because he knew he was better than them."

[What the fuck?] I'm looking.

"Jesus..." at her. She's looking back at me.

"Why'd you date him, then?"

"I didn't know..." she looked and looked away.

■

Her apartment's empty. She just moved in. The living room is an entertainment center, with a black, slightly glossed, wooden desk in front of a black pleather couch, with fake Indian Pendleton blankets over the top. I'm making myself at home, immediately, by marching into the lit side of the kitchen, where I pass the big glasses and instead am choosing which colored circle I want on my cup. This half pastel blue and brown circle is cute—
so then I cut open the faucet and water splashes everywhere. It doesn't need to be full blast but it's all or nothing for this idiot.

I'm getting water all over the front of the same button up I'd been wearing 'out' for the last two weeks. It's Marc-by-Marc Jacobs—second hand from a boutique in Austin, Texas. I used to say it as a joke but it's old now and I mostly say it seriously. The waterfalls straight into my belly, practically all at the same time and the glass is slamming against the counter. The way quarters sound when they're trying to stop spinning—the I drop onto the couch like the caveman I came to be loved as. I'm a beautiful lipstick Lesbian on the inside, it's rarely appreciated. On with the charade.

Molly's bending over the sink. Her red chiffon, which she yanked a little too high, on purpose—the hem playing peek-a-boo like a bullfighter and showing me a tempting white ass. The more it's hidden and revealed, the less and tempting. Until I feel I understand what silently is understood when two writers, *who just want to be successful* get together understand—the competition, like bones and steel, beat for beat we're sharpening up our interpersonal skills with a good, mindless, fuck.

It's me projecting:

If I'm tempted, I fill myself with the dominance drugs and walk like a hustler—that I could have any woman I wanted. That women would pay for this love. Confidence is delusion, practice splintering off, shedding a little reality into your world. It would be wrong of me in one place to believe she wants—but right now, instinctually, I felt it was for me.

She walks out of the kitchen and starts digging through a cardboard box: 'OFFICE SUPPLIES,' across the side in Sharpie. A computer monitor balancing level with her, one of two chairs thoughtfully placed facing each other, thoughtlessly placed inches from each other. No legroom.

I put mine up but then her hands were dropping a hammer and a golden nail in my hand. She was holding, 'The Aristocats,' LP in her hand. Los Angeles loves T.V.s. But I love Aristocats too. We walked to the wall behind the T.V. She was tiptoeing now. Her skirt showing, herself bare assed, her legs. Floral panties?

"Can you help me out with this?"

[I'm a man.] [So I do it.]

I measured it, and struck, slowly but forcefully, into the wall. Tearing pieces up around the entry. She managed the record into a frame and I tried to calm myself. I could smell her. Girl smells. Fruit scented lotion smells.

If I wanted to remain new to town and make a connection with another active writer in this desert: Los Angeles, where the only ones I knew were my brother and Anne. Still ignoring me.
I had to restrain myself.

My biggest problem is that I love to bite girls asses. Hard. I like to leave my mark on them in love and resentment. For all the games I've had to play to get a chance to give you my love—and now this pretty, plain-laid, part of you—so much volume. You walk on those legs, you live on that ass. Where the strength is—I give my love and hate.

I stop thinking about it.
Molly is just a friend.
Don't blow it you arrogant,
pig headed, horny, mother fuck.
Even if her walk is fucked up—I still have the strongest urges.

Finally,
the record was dangling. Slightly crooked from a halfhearted calculation. It would bother both of us, quietly, the way a booger no one but you knows is there. The way an underwhelming but never overtly negative social interactions makes you feel naked for the rest of a party.

We sat quietly, until she left the room.

Her roommate shuffled in awkwardly and I introduced myself calmly to preempt the obviousness of a pretty boy caveman and everything I could represent and everything I was feeling. And now I'm learning anxiety is the best drug for bravery.

Molly came back in with a miniature DVD player and a Red Envelope she ripped open with her teeth. It was *Fat Girl:*

In one scene a 13 year old, fat, French girl, in competition to lose her virginity first, loses. She, quietly, without enough complaint, watches her 16 year old sister fuck an Italian college graduate, who forces himself on her, with words as a buffer and some slight excitement, but mostly deep emotional need and her self perception as functional as a sex-object willingly given. This is all from the opposite side of her bedroom that they both share.

When Molly brings her legs up, you can see through her skirt with all the sunset light shining through. My body feels heated, my mind, as if the benz could happen to a brain and only to realize, your first sickening gasp was burning oil when you camp up from a sinking ship. I can smell that she feels the same way, the way her body leans slightly into mine as if by gravity we were being pulled together. Her eyes like the finger at the end of a pie on a windowsill in Tex Avery, me, a pot bellied kid in a striped t-shirt and flat top. Pre adolescent George Liquor American.

I choked it down, almost tearing up, my heart in an oven, my dick in a shock box, but I did it for a greater love. The chance for two artists to be artists together. Because I wondered why I didn't have any artists as friends. I'm an outsider. I'm staying outside of the outside this time. I'm turning my back and staying outdoors. It's lonely but I finish the movie without any movement forward. I felt stronger, like I'd taught her something. The air was stale with resentment. I could taste it like dirty pennies.

She got up, quietly, red faced. I was kneeling on the carpet now, screaming 'What the fuck?' because of how mind blowing the last scene was: a hatchet in a 16 year old's forehead, straight through the car windshield. The fat girls in the end—fucked, [questionable] in the grass, like the couch scene in Straw Dogs.

The chief says: *She says he didn't rape her...*

"What?" she laughs nervously.
"It's fucking with me."
"Oh. Is there anything else you want to do? Like, specifically?"
Her guard was down with the sun.
Resentment here like the moon, or her ass, while grabbing a water glass. I was tired. Hungry. I convinced her to make me a meal.
"I'm pretty hungry, actually."
"Okay...me too I guess."

The words beating against my need like the pot against iron burners. A flick of her wrist. Everything was tossed into a skillet. The eggs hatched their smell. 'Challah' sawed off in the unhappiest movements. Her body's display more and more unwelcoming. I moved to the open mouth of the kitchen, flanking its openness. Watching, bravely, as she scraped the bottom of the pan and all contents above into an unhappy scramble with a fork, my stomach turning with the sound of nails on a chalkboard. After reading the Budo, though, I could hide me weakness and I became strong in it.

I can only imagine the humiliation of crushed expectation. The few perks of being a woman include, almost totally insured, access to sex, at all times. But I didn't move to Los Angeles from the village to make the same mistakes that ran me out of the suburbs. At least it's not somebody else's girlfriend this time.

Paper plates...
She shoved one into my hand.
It looked the way she did making them.
Where I'm so unsure I'm welcome—
but I gave my biggest thank you.
We shoveled it down, her read face.
More silence.
"I've got to head out."
"I'll walk you home."

She grabbed her purse. She didn't need a jacket?
She started walking.
"Did you have a good time? I know I'm boring."
"Do you think that's why you write?"
"What do you mean?"
"It's a way of hiding from people."
"No. People just don't like me. They think I'm boring, and ugly, and talk too much..."
"Are you sure? Do you *ever* talk about *yourself*?"
"No. When people start to meet me, they hate me. They think I'm stupid...it's okay. I hate myself. I look like a gorilla..."
I've heard it before.
We were still in suburban shadows.

Los Angeles' night-lights were gaining shape and color every time I looked down the slight lilt of the hill my feet pet. Sidewalks like quiet neighborhoods you leave to get here.

This was a pitiable pity party. She wants me to compliment her. To change the level headed distance, abandon the conversation, head first at break neck into opportunity. She was going to beg...for a compliment, for company...

"You don't hate yourself. Nobody, alive, actually does. You're asking someone else to be responsible for you when you say that shit. What am I supposed to say? I don't know anything about you because like you said, you like to talk about, 'ideas.' And anything except for what *you* actually think."

"I do hate myself."
"You want to!"
She started walking faster.
At the bus stop, she made sure to stop surrounded by the most people possible.

"Well, have a goodnight. I don't know what I'm gonna do. Probably drink a bottle of whiskey to myself and pass out...are you sure you don't want to stay?"

"I'm going home."

"*Alright!*" She started walking away. Got too far for her return to be functionally dramatic.

"Okay, well, like, if you want to hang out again, text me."

She was looking over my head instead of into my eyes. She walked away, like she'd cursed me. My hair fell over me as I turned and muttered to myself. Catching eyes with an older woman at the stop. I wish I'd been out with her. She smiled and my insides wrung themselves out dry. Like jerky. I swallowed the guilt, to digest senselessness. I only said it because I had to. Because, I know what it's like, to feel like you're only as good as the ones that'll have you. It takes one to know one and I used to be you—but now, it takes one to own one, alone, totally. Own yourself or nobody will ever keep you. I'm here for you but you won't know that for another year. Winter air in autumn. It was a much longer walk than I'd expected.

@abigfuckingbully

@abigfuckingbully

MISCARRIAGE

You tie your shoes with the second loop on the inverse, for the perfect, unblemished, bunny ears. A red, cotton, windbreaker loosening, fat and filled, with October air, and a muscular contour in the absence between muscle and the lining. Your hair is still dripping wet, pieces of thickset curls unfurl themselves, like the hand of a poisoned housewife, reaching towards each visible breath's, tightening cuffs. Stained cotton colored converse. When you straighten out, you realize just where you are. You think James Dean is a played out costume but what isn't by now. You know that's a lazy excuse—

Your muscles tense as your jacket fans back into place. Jealousy fills you, the feeling of your hair on end like a cat in the neck, the sting of blood draining from the wrinkle between your eyes, when you catch a glimpse of an old high school classmate, Sandra, talking to a blonde, thick curly hair, loading into the house party. Currently Sandra is tailing behind, bobbing just slightly above a quiet few smokers on the front steps, as if politely, being expelled from the steps like a babies 'no thank you' portion.

You came alone, unusual for you. You feel too old and too young here at the same time but your presentation is always immaculate, immune. Completely untouchable, an unblemished untouchable. You summon the courage from nothing—stone cold sobriety is your choice drug. An incessant violence from absolute control presenting clear intention at all times, though ultimately disinterested. You never understood it and you can't now.

You zip your jacket to the throat and walk through, disgusted by the smokers on the first step. Beauty put to waste.

"No one should waste their beauty."

You think.

You count beer bellies on the way in. 6 like a 6 Pack. You feel yourself nervously, like a washboard, through your white t-shirt. It placates you. Only arrogance calms you. Only ego understands—how important vanity as a comfort is.

The band starts sound check. You catch eyes with a Klansmen, the one who thought that would be funny enough for offense to be overlooked. You realize a minority of people dressed up. A guy in a tiger costume by a keg, surrounded by Gen-Xers trying to keep up. Sleeveless jean jackets. Black hoodies underneath. How, for whatever reason all punks look like pained eastern Europeans, pointy faces. Droopy cheeks, beady, black, inset eyes. Freckled with shaved heads.

You pushed through everybody looking into the faces of women too eager to leave, though they fit the part, dyed blonde, manic, pierced, all of which you aren't. You make it to the opposite side of the house.

89

Further now, through Sailor Scouts, Little Red Riding Hood, Pippi Longstocking, Snow White, Hunter S. Thompson, and a 40oz to the front. With every forward movement the quiet scorn of one too bound by social constraint, still, even in beer soaked anonymity, the tribal mind of subbies who couldn't, even if they had the heart, hurt a fly.

They're mediocre musicians but they can compose. It means a lot to see an artist who's willing to put herself out there like that, more than you're actually glad to listen to them play. You watch the guitarist closely, she's beautiful. She's the best player but bores you. Her rail thin body, her plain brown hair, tied into a bun. A thin knit sweater. Men's jeans. European walking shoes. A face like a box, a voice like a priestess.

You ignore the bassist mostly, but make sure to appear to be treating them equally. She's hideous. Her face doesn't know which parts of itself to fit in. She plays bass, like she's shooting a gun. Her voice is perfect.

You fixate on the drummer, who handles the sticks like she's unsure she wants to. More focus than needed, the gap between reality and desire fill with a subtle resentment. Almost like she was handling every stroke of skin as if she needed gloves, somehow they land with confidence even though she constantly looks surprised it happens. Uncertainty in the performance excites you. Her skin is paper white. Her lips are bright red. She's rushing under her curls.

All of them together in a drug of sound. Lightly carbonated, uplifting, plinking guitar, abruptly cutting the cord and dropping an orphaned black into a mutant landscape. Cut short. Staccato. Tom Drums. Soaring guitars like saws. Cut short. Staccato. Clapping. A loud 18-year-old kid, shouting.

▲

You unzip your jacket a little. Drops of sweat, jewels in your forehead, rich with thoughts. The plot is easy. Sandra, common faced, commonplace neighborhood girl trying to get in with hip underground Riot Grrrl band.

Sandra's all wrapped up in the conversation, like the scene. Squealing at the end, like somebody pulled her French braids. You're embarrassed by her, for her. Your prize keeps you muzzled in a ball gag. You're tongue for a mind—washing over anesthetized plastic in hopes of movement—an idea, or something, to wear away at the binds by time's concerted effort. You've got it.

You drop down on one knee, a quiet, unseen, white flag. A compensating humility for your complete—insane—self-assurance. You feel the bulge of a fat rubber brick in your chucks. You loosen up the ankles and tuck in two fingers, then calmly pull a monochrome press-trigger hunting knife out. Black for a black night.

Sandra seems to be holding them up. Which is luck for you. You work through the crowd again, this time to a quiet driveway, somehow ignored by the hive, buzzing in a chorus of bubbling 40oz, the caps just snapping. It's over before it starts.

A jester and a more specific Harley Quinn are getting on about their similar costumes. Someone who didn't dress up brought a nametag to wear. Her boyfriend is Henry Miller. Your feet can tell the difference between grass, wood, and pavement. You look like you weren't looking.

Sandra—

"Hey, Sandra. It's been a while."

She looks behind her, over a shoulder, bordering on frantic.

"Nice costume." She stops.

The blonde one passes, looking nervous.

"Do you need any help loading up?" asks Sandra.

You give your hand to the drummer who followed her, finally, after squeezing herself against the side of the car, opening the door with one hand, and rolling the drum in, ignoring you, necessarily for a moment, cracking metal against glass. Whether she wants to or not, it's her job—she gives you the hand.

"Great set." You let slink.

"Thanks.

I really should get back though." she says exhausted.

"Do you need help?"

"Yeah, we could use a hand."

They're leaving.

Now with the monochrome knife you're sweating all over in your pocket, you crawl quietly to the other side of a small, square, red, vehicle, open and unprotected. Scanning across the crowd to see if anyone's near. No eyes meet. Packs of backs of heads.

You duck and press the trigger to the black blade. You drive at the end of your squat the black blade into black rubber. As much pressure as needed for a jam jar. It's hissing. You slowly stand and push the blade into place with your thumb. Square nails. You tuck it back into your pocket. You walk to the other side of the car and follow the path Sandra took. She's coming downstairs as you're on the first step. She walks down the steps carrying a bag of cymbals in one hand and a stand in the other.

You move out of her way, you push some strangers aside, kicking a 40oz along with them, again. You grab the handle of her cymbal bag to relieve her. There's a quiet reluctance but the gravity is still greater in your palm. The shoulder sinks with the weights into you. You waddle back down with them. Two other women, coming down with amps, follow them. They look like their arms are going to be pulled out as easily as a bugs. You are surprised by their speed. The trunk opens and stays open. The strings leave for their guitars. The drummer stays. No one notices the car's left side deflating.

"It was so good." Sandra says.

You turn to Sandra. She's smiling.

You're both unfamiliar by this point, a year's distance, but know the other has a role to play, what you lack , she carries confidently. What she wants to hide—how eager she is to impress strangers. Artists she'd love to know.

"How's tour been?" you ask.

Pick up Sandra's slack.

There's no way she's going to keep up the volley. She's exhausted just standing—fatigued by nerves alone. Some of us at attention like it's stigmata, perpetual surrender at a cross you wish you had the will to nail yourself to. Going nowhere—starting the volley kicking an anchor. Crash and burn early to save us all the spectacle. Fuck you, Sandra...but you pick up slack anyways.

"It's been...tough," she says, "but it's always good."

"No one was dancing." said Sandra.

"Yeah, that's common." the drummer said.

"Do you ever feel hostage in those situations?" You ask.

"Of course but you play through it. You focus on who you *are* playing to."

She smiled bored.

Letting your last words sink in...nervously she crosses her arms. She looked relieved. Her powerful arms like a Boa's flesh expanding. It was colder than anyone remembered until you notice iced smoke from her dragon-snort-sigh. Hospitable but tired. Inaccessible. They just didn't need anything from us yet.

The amps pushed through, the members like bees pollinate flower met magnetic and opened the trunk space to fill, it's mouth missing two enormous teeth, mesh on speakers, an American flag stapled into the top of one. Bull horns on another, decorations for the commemoration of the importance of art outside of ritual in the immediate but a mainstay in history, passing the torch, lighting the dimming flame in a passionless pilgrimage to burrow into hearts and minds as uncertain as you they were ever it.

Click.

And the trunk shut and so did their minds. The blonde hovering near the passengers seat shyly, trying to escape apologetically. You tell her to 'have a safe trip home,' with your whole heart, the one you don't have access to currently. The mind's in charge and so is hers...chanting, like mantra or ward in her mind, 'this little light of mine, I'm going to have to find...'

She half acknowledges you and gets in, the car starts. You realize no names have been exchanged, mutual disengagement as a socially accepted contractual agreement. One sided if she goes home with your empty compliment, stroking your ego. A cat's game if she knows just how deep it's hollowed, the sound of an oil barrel clanging through spiritual abyss. The chorus line—

The car backing out and with your perfect cut, the metal of the inside of a clunking one ton of scrap metal, hitting pavement like an aluminum knife into sandpaper. One single yelp like an animal in a fox trap, realizing too late what exactly had been broken. The car jolted, gas, brake, dip, unison scream. Hit after hit.

They turned the car off. Only you and Sandra notice muffled voice—

"—the fuck?" Like they were a whole room away. Trapped under glass. A tense aquarium. Outside surrounded. You laugh to yourself. All three clowns come teetering out. The two girls out of the car doors congregating at the front left. All cursing. You can't smile.

"What happened?" you ask.

They look up, reluctant to break their play act imitation of focus and folding, like a chair. Like their comfortable uselessness. Sighs—

and the blonde was now pulling at the handles of an amp, heated.

"Do we have a spare tire?"

"Someone really didn't like us."

"Are you fucking kidding, me?"

The bassist was blown away. Staring into the gash. The niceties that should have protected them from this venom. They scrambled to empty the trunk. Burping their rolling equipment down it's lips. Hard thoughts. More embarrassment. Bored chatter, scattering hands, metal clacking on glass.

"God-fucking-damnit."

"—is there a spare?"

"No."

"No. No?"

"No. Fucking—"

The car door slams.

They open it again.

Dragging their equipment, onto the pavement. Out. Her knuckles were as blonde as her hair. Too many people notice. Not enough help. You're perfect. Monochrome knife under your thumb. Rubber grip like chicken skin, easy as plucking you offer, subtly, some help. Who can resist.

"I don't know, Alyson. Fucking call someone. Like, now."

The blonde was dropping her jaw for you to take the words out of her mouth.

"Do you need help?"

She looked at her band mates.

To the ugly one said the skinny one,

"Call a tow truck. Alyson—"

"What's up?" She said, catty.

"I can give you a ride if you want. Sandra—" you say, "you're on my way too—remember?"

The skinny one looked relieved.

"I know you have work..."

"How'd you get here Sandra?" you say. Casually.

While they make the decision you're indifferent.

"I took the train."

"Okay—"

The skinny one,
"Thanks a lot."
"No problem. Here, I can help you take it to my car."
You pick up the blondes drums.
"Me too." said Sandra.
She picks up the blondes drums.
"Have a good night, Rachel." said the blonde to the skinny one.

Already all together. Like ants in milk. Drudging tired to the destination, fogged cars, frostbitten spirits. The car was silent after the pieces of us jigsaw into place. You turn the key and purrrr, sputtering heat, and happiness slide under the palm of your hand. This time red leather, knobby wheels, anchors away, behind a strained stoicism a tickled laugh, happy as a clam, as cold, as calm.

"Thanks for doing this." she said.
"No problem..." you pause with a certain uncertainty.

The actor—how it all pans out. No matter the anxiety. Life's a play. An actor doesn't need to be two moves ahead. Queen's cornered. Dowry's been pawned off and your prize pig is lipsticked. Plum, not red, by the way, in this light, and her water blue eyes. Almost dead. You smile to yourself.

"Alyson," she puts her hands into the drivers seat just brushing your shoulder. Her smell—it was soap. It was subtle.

"Where are we going?" you say.
"It's by Buchser. The elementary school."

It's a 15-minute ride but you can prolong it. You drive at the speed limit, exactly, regardless of spotted, 'traffic.'

A conversation...
"It's been a while since I've seen you Sandra."
She smiles a weak smile.
"Yeah, I think we were still in school.
I don't even remember walking...
I don't remember you walking either."
You sweat. You swallow.
"Yeah I got really sick senior year. I couldn't finish any of my classes. They made me take summer school."
"Oh, I thought...I heard...you got kicked out."
"No." you say. You look into the rearview, unintentionally. Revealing weakness. Then catching yourself and smiling.
"That's funny they'd say that." you say.

The car goes silent. You turn on the stereo. You play something. It starts quiet and you raise it to the perfect volume. Enough to have to make her lean forward to talk to you. You look into the rearview. They're talking. You slow down, turning onto Alameda. Pass the mouth of an enormous city park. 40 shivering bodies congregate. Alive but slow moving the same disinterest they've been forced to live with to survive at even that level, fills you. An awareness that there are even maladaptive behaviors that can become necessary in their rigidity in certain circumstances. Can outlast the flexibility of others. Their soft lean to their soft needs. No one can bench press the weight of his existence as a contortionist. A body builder accepts his disposition—stone hard body, stiff as a board, dumb as a rock. Like it's fate.

"A right, here." into your ear. You can feel her curls brushing your shoulder. You nod.

"And then it's this apartment right here. The yellow one."

"You've parked, halfway into the driveway."

1080 Santa Clara, you remind yourself.

Somewhere by 9th.

Sandra sits quietly, waiting for cues.

She waits for cues.

"Thank you so much." says Alyson.

Pausing at the end, unsure if she remembers your name. Unsure if she wants to ask for it again. You unbuckle your seat belt and turn to her, shaking her hand, feeling her warmth cooling with your hands, two pieces of meat, one for the grasp, on over the other. Sandra looks at you like you've stepped on something. Alyson thinks little of it, though she's never seen anyone she knows shake hands like this. You don't know that, but you think it, the way her face seemed slightly less enthusiastic, which in this moments subtlety you read clearly as panicked suspicion. You tell yourself she's paranoid. I mean, you tell yourself you're paranoid.

"Chance," you say. In hopes she'll remember. You steal the ring from her finger as she quickly rushes out of the car. The door slams. Silence and the hum of your car are accents to a soft rattling from the peripheries of your windows.

Sandra's quiet. You're quiet—

attentive until Alyson has passed through the door and it's been closed for a second. You hear the quiet echo of her doors metal, fitting, like a joint, into the wood, like a socket. You imagine the air cold enough to carry the silence outside of the radius of the door click into your car, into your ears. You look eager and pointed like a dog. Then headlights pass over the back of your car. Your eyes read black and white flashes. You remembered—she's in the car.

"Where are we off to now?" you ask flatly. You notice your own tone, you can't tell if it's accidental or not.

"She lives pretty close to me."

"Oh yeah?

You gonna stalk her?"

"She's beautiful."

"You're jealous of her."

"No."

"She is. Beautiful. So—"

Your hand is on the back of the leather headrest , passenger's side.

"We're close. Where?" you say.

"Other side of the park."

You never make eye contact with her. Whether in the rearview or while checking behind you to back out, you realize, luckily, privately, that the ring is in the hand on the back of passenger's. You drop it when you realize it. Sandra doesn't notice. She's a little drunk. You can tell because—

"Remember—that night at Thrillhouse, where we both played Edward 40 Hands?"

You swallow.

"Yeah. I do actually. I was never much of a people person."

A little sad. You're embarrassed.

You swallow. You squint.

You made it out past San Fernando and step on the gas.

Your car jolts. Sandra's startled. Sleepy, drunken, singing a high note where there shouldn't be one. She leaned up. It was three minutes. You watched the city hide in the dark after the neon from a Safeway near the private university. A few streetlights after lead you out of the 'city' and into the residential crawl.

"Right, right here.

And then it's the house on the...left...right here." She pointed.

A large Victorian by an artisanal sausage shop. There was a plaza, local businesses, liquor stores, expensive salons, a real estate agency run out of a *house of all things*. A marble sphere with water running down it—you stared at it from halfway parked into her driveway. Waiting, wishing she'd hurry the fuck up and what's going on back—

"Oh my God! She must have dropped this."

Your stomach tightens. You tighten. Your eyes open a little wider. You're deciding how to turn around calmly, without interest.

"Oh," you look, "I can take that back to her it's on my way."

"No it's not..." she laughed. "You've done enough tonight. I'll bring it to her."

Sandra with such a smug smile, turning the ring around her finger. The headlights washing over the glittering white ring. Sandra looks at you, your eyes still fixed on the silver.

"Have a goodnight, Chance. It was...really nice seeing you again."

She opens and closes the door. She walks up the driveway, then darts up a lit staircase at the end of the pavement, the beginning of the house's wood.

You pull your head into the wheel at the force of a car. The car horn sounds. Staccato. She jumps back down the steps, and pauses in the same posture she started walking up. Pausing, she waves.

You put it in reverse and peel out. About 5 minutes till you're home.

▲

@abigfuckingbully

December 6th, 2013
12:14 PM

Dear Tim,
The set ended early so I didn't have to end the night early. Lucky—my timing is perfect. Things happen to me like in a film. I notice every little opportunity, so many in sequence and I wonder they could appear, so many, so sudden. Had Sandra been anywhere else I may have not taken the drummer of *Emulator* home. Alyson is her name. I knew her name but was never allowed to know it until now. This time she gave it to me: Alyson, gave me her name.

I stole her ring without her noticing but dropped it. Sandra, the cunt. She, of course, noticed it. Like some kind of rat—anything to get her closer to Alyson. Didn't believe Sandra was a lesbian until tonight. It'd been 3 years since I talked to her. The city's big enough to never see her again, and luckily, I *'don't get out much.'* She wanted to talk about high school shows.

"*Remember that night at Thrillhouse we both played Edward 40 Hands?*"

It was a Wild Boar show.

I didn't finish my 40 Sandra. We made out and you told me not to because, 'I'm lightweight,' and 'you've always had a crush on me since...'

Yeah, Senior Year. I find out you're with another one of my early ex-girlfriends. Like a lost puppy around a girl you want to fuck and a television personality when they're gone. Alyson would eat you alive.

Hahaha! I crack myself up.

Alyson lives at 1080 Santa Clara street. In a two story house. There's a reason I stopped going to these fucking shows. Something about middle class, college graduates convincing themselves their selfish decision to be an artist is really a radical political stance. Educating, poor, sorry motherfuckers. Give us some hope—we all need that. We could use a little more hope.

Sandra's so pathetic. Her state school diploma, her McWage at a desk job. All through the grapevine but I know what they're really like. A bunch of spoiled, irresponsible, repressed brats. Shoving their obsession with their own pain down the throats of a bunch of sorry motherfuckers living in their high school dunce caps. Strangled by petty grudges they've buried too deep to remember. This filthy fucking scene. All of these sorry kids playing King of The Hill. Shaking hands with us. You're still rock stars. Just small time. Just enough to satisfy your ego without looking like a snake oil salesman.

It's late—
I'm finishing this tea before work tomorrow.

▲

@abigfuckingbully

December 12th 2013

      You bring your bag with you, sitting, black leather sports bag, invisible on the black leather seats of a sports car. It's a hand me down from your in-denial dad. You're sitting in your college savings. Your dad had kids because he thought eh should have. He stopped having kids after you. You're worried—how to remain unseen.
      You start it anyway, decide it's a lot like wearing a fedora—only someone with half a brain would notice there's something clearly wrong with you. Have you ever met someone in a fedora you didn't think was an absolute piece of shit?
      You start the car.

      You can' t tell what's heating your groin. Just the denim lightly pulling up into it, the hum of the drive, buzzing like a kazoo, lights dripping across the windshield. The little fog there is makes every stoplight a dandelion. You're making your wish blowing past them.
      1080 Santa Clara St.
      There's a roundabout near the library—good place to park.
      Too close to the police station for anyone to think anything.
      You grab the bag. You notice a hole in the corner. You quietly mourn. You move on. You check while walking the block, there's a playground across the street, you take note then take inventory.

- Bag of trail mix
- Monochrome switchblade
- Binoculars
- Notebook
- Pencil
- Cellphone
- A spare black t-shirt

      Everything in place. Your anxiety fills the space, it's a little light, and you wonder why you're horrified by silence and blank spaces and free time and relaxation. 'They want me to relax...' you think to yourself. 'If they want it there's something clearly wrong with it.' Then you wonder if you've lived out all of your romantic life in that logic.

      You pull up your hood.
      You walk across the street, casually, to pass her house. You're not sure why. Highlighted by the streetlights on both sides. Fucking suburbs. You put on the sports bag like a backpack, alert you, 'stop to tie your shoes,' at her mailbox, looking, calmly in every direction. You pop open the box and pull the thickest

envelope out. You hear a door open and a man's voice calling from outside it. You don't change pace or direction, you look at the address.

MARTIN CARRIAGE

A voice approaches, and keeps getting close, you turn around, while turning you commit to the lie and your finger pushes through glue and paper—you're already face to face with a man in a fleece pullover and scarf. He looks pissed.

"Hey—" he says.

You don't respond, you continue opening the letter to read it. You look down and unfolding the sin and smiling to yourself calmly, your heart's pace a mugging at gunpoint.

"Did you see a dog go by here?

He fuckin'...slipped out of my hands and—"

"...No, no I didn't."

"Alright, thanks." You think you hear him mutter asshole.

You take advantage of your opportunity, being perceived as a law abiding local.

"Dear Martin Carriage,

We're sorry to inform you..."

You stop reading. You look in the side of the mailbox.

C A R R I A G E

in grey on black reflective stickers while jamming paper into paper wrapped in paper among other papers stuffed in paper. Sealing it, too late to have feelings about the consequences. You're confident though, you haven't met any of your neighbors. You hate them for no reason.

The winds asking questions and you hear a door open like a brush stroke. You start walking down the sidewalk, just in front of Alyson's driveway in the same act as before. It looks like Martin from your periphery. He's spinning a jacket, his back is to you, in another weakness. Of course she's the type to have a garden.

Then you dart across the street, hip the fence, which isn't easy, and smash your bottom lip into a monkey bar, crash landing into woodchips, where splintered cedar slips in just above your collarbone. You breathe in the smell, romantic aroma reminiscent of childhood and once you catch a glimpse of the stars start to relax before hypocritically choking the nostalgia and turning jade for the task at hand. Brushing yourself off. Checking your bag—there's a fucking hole in it. You knew you heard something. The bag of trail mix, 'Very Berry Blend,' fits into your hand like a football. You tear it open, unevenly.

Remembering a television show where a woman complained about men and their inability to tear toilet paper squares squarely. It hurts you knowing both that this woman exists in flesh and blood off screen, where she will drink a little extra after the shoot because of how much more indicative it is of the petri dish of her existence on this planet, female bodied, and also that that woman is a real woman, as in, the character she played is likely a neighbor's wife. You tuck a brick of pineapple slice into your mouth. Your lips gripping chimpy over the snacks.

Leaping to your highest perch, on top of the outside of the canopy for the slide. Your hand moves into the bag, still your trail mix hasn't moved. Your fingers tripping into cowhide and pull out your binoculars. You wrap them around your neck. You reluctantly drop the trail mix back into your bag, a few almonds dripping out of the hole in your duffle bag. You pull out a notebook and pen.

You spend 4 hours perched. Eating nuts, blowing hot air into your hands, distrustfully, like the story of the Satyr.

▲

December 12th 2013

Tim,

Very little going on at the Carriage household. Her window faces the street and she's in it all the time—half naked. Her body is beautiful. It's thickness. It's shape, it won't conform to the bone the way it does on other women. No matter how much of her biggest parts seem as if it had blossomed independently. Like Venus if her body, no matter how anemic, glowed with a fertile polish. She was tanned somehow. A brass back, a little torso, enormous breasts.

She didn't do anything interesting. She eats standing up and reads in a chair higher than her bed, where she places her feet on it like an ottoman. She's freckled. She ate a bowl of cereal in 5 minutes and unbuttoning and buttoning her cut offs. I'll see what's up on a weekend. She doesn't need to go to college. Dad's the office-screw-loose-stepping-out type. Typical, she was dressed for war.

▲

December 16th

  Pack the bag.
  Navy blue Dickies. Plain black Hanes Beefy-T. For shoes you've be been wearing lightweight hiking boots you 'borrowed' from your friend who also wears a size 12. You walk the same places as last night, stop at the mailbox, tempting, but continue up the driveway surprising yourself while you do it. You stop, realize you have no plan, but the Prius that was here last night is gone and you ride your own adrenaline high like you've done this drug before.
  You look in the unpaved parts of her driveway, where some salt and pepper rocks are trying to glitter by vines growing over another fence, just opposite the garden. It's lacy accent, barbed wire. You pick up a good sized rock, 'medium sized' in comparison to much larger stones next to it. The weight of a shooter.
  You aim with one eye and with the perfect pressure of a knock. It calls her to the window. She looks startled at first pushing the single hanging curtain away, crossing her arms after, conveniently unwrapping in a white t-shirt. She looks down through the two hands she had to hold up to see through her own reflection. She pauses, unsure of how to react. Clearly afraid. She slides open the window, because, you're too thin and pretty to hurt anyone. She is however still apprehensive. Her own transgression against better judgment making her twice as exposed.
  She opens the windows, lifting, like a question to God.
  She stood for a second, crossed her arms again.
  "What's up?"
  "Just pass through here on late night drives sometimes, when I'm not sure I want to go home."
  "That's really sweet but you shouldn't be here. I appreciate your help the other night but this is…weird."
  "I shouldn't be here?"
  "Look—you gave me a ride. I had to trust you, a lot."
  "You're always dressed like that, huh?"
  She looked stunned.
  She slammed her window closed and dropped both curtains. Retreating far from the entrance, you could tell by the shadows. Then, you still standing like baby bird, as if you weren't there for it, when silently, she re-emerges, in-between the two curtains. Like angels wings flapping, in-between curtains and the window with a cellphone. She lifted it like Chaplin and mimed a dial, along with her mouthing the numbers, 9-1-1. You notice another shadow behind the curtains now. One that wasn't there before. You walk back to the car with no intention of leaving. You wait for a few hours—it's the safest thing to do before returning to your perch.

@abigfuckingbully

You open the bag, find the monochrome hunting knife and tuck into your boot, the rest as it always is. Another slow hooded walk, just across the street. Of course you go unnoticed, the curtains are closed.

▲

December 16th
6:35 AM

Tim,

Last night was an absolute shit show. It's all too soon. Too much too fast. Of course she would be terrified of you. Ran into Sandra the other night, again. Also too much too soon. She was at Floyd's. The dive bar everyone's moving into. I'm not surprised. They start congregating in places locals worked hard to corral people into. Sandra hadn't bothered with the ring. I told her she should give it to me—it's the best thing to do. She laughed.

"You're the one with the crush on her, huh?

Too bad she's a dyke."

I was going to lose it.

I threw a rock into her window. I mean, at her window. Alyson's window.

Told me, I 'shouldn't be here.' which only strengthened my resolve. I spent until 4AM watching from the park slide. Around 1AM I noticed an exhausted Sandra coming out. Weird timing. She was muttering something to herself. I wonder if they talked about me. I decided not to follow her, as angry as I was. No one came out after that.

It's my fault.

I literally gave her a ring to give to Alyson. I am trying to take my failures with grace but now this is a fucking nightmare.

December 29th

Tim,

Everything holiday is settling down. Dead air for this week. I made the last 4 days a habit. The house has Sandra twice in the first two days. I made sure to 'run into her' at Floyd's again. She's gaining weight from all the drinking. Gave me a dirty look but never said anything about the window. Floyd's is the only gay bar in town, so the punx have decided to make it their spot.

The culture project seems patronizing. Ultimately arbitrary inclusion, that ends up another imperialism, are you here to immerse yourself in their lives or are you changing camps for aesthetics? I think about it, 'the scene.'

Since I was 16, sneaking into shows through the back, I dreamed of moving here. Now I'm here and I feel just as isolated as before. It's funny to me, to live in a place where exclusion wears a new costume. If you do not follow their brand of non-conformity you're branded the dominant culture. How much rhetoric have I heard preached at these fucking events, spouted off from these people, evangelical hippies in leather jackets? Glue another beer tab to the hem of it. One more year train hopping, free of responsibility as vacation. Your politics end at ideas and your right to self expression.

Your right to not bathe. Your battle against hygiene. Pitting yourself against them with microscopic lifestylism. We all need to climb up to get our point across. So pit yourself against, 'them.' Whose revolution is most righteous? And 'it's yours if you want it,' because like John Lennon said it's, 'there if you want it.' We're too busy 'asking for another television set.'

Fucking hippies. *Hippies*.

Cousin fucking rednecks in face tattoos.

The same persecuted material mindset that manufactured a more inflated sense of self. We all want a place to exist in but do you want to live where your neurosis is the new hierarchical standard? Is that your 'revolution?' Power in a different minority's hands. The straight white male put on a stake like burning man, light me up, straw man's existence. The rich Norwegians music video for Refused's 'Songs to Fan The Flames of Discontent.'

I used to believe that you want it too, a change. That dream died too—the same way I prayed that final night, to God in Sandra's basement. A few beers too early. When I had nothing—nothing but the knowledge I had nothing to keep me alive. And that's when, like a prison door close, I accepted my life sentence, a life of absolute joy if I wanted it. But I had to accept that this is the closest I would ever get to heaven. Complete acceptance of the weight of my reality. I heard my own voice, ringing tin, it's tiny, pathetic, earnestness. This is your return for believing: echos. Reverb. The silence in the same spirit as shoegaze's 'wall of sound,' and after I chose a new God. A new church. A new congregation? What's God but something new for us to hate together?

How would I learn? Replacing God for God for God for God for God?

For me—rabid, foaming at the mouth, chasing two rabbits my truth and it's convergence—with them—the world as shallow as some Venn diagram where two universes birthed into abortion where momentum eventually slingshots, red particle, blue particle, like wires to be welded. We could all be circuits. Blood electric in communion. How separate we are. How similar we are. Who you could be. How much of you you are.

@abigfuckingbully

Every day, I learn what's underneath the existential white noise: how concrete the comfort of absolute silence is. But we fill our heads with 130bpm to keep the devil away. And so your needs are never met. Fuck your god. Fuck your scene. Fuck your drugs. Fuck your chemicals. None of it is an answer.

Sandra pierced and staggering beer gutted into Floyd's tells me she gave her the goddamn ring. That night I threw stones at the door. Swallow up your pride. Choke on your needs. When will they see me? I've always had so much to offer. Still—ignored. When I'm screaming vitriol in a mic they will admire me. Until then just another fan. Until then just another follower. Pass the tithe/donation bucket and drop in your mind. I will follow you. I'll show you who I really am. I'll be whatever you want me to be. You will stop ignoring me.

▲

December 30th 2013

You pack your bag.
Extra black shirt, double check.
Monochrome knife stays tucked in your boot, pressed flat into metal, 90mph on unmonitored stretches of freeway, for it's own sake. Motor oil for blood tonight, each second of your hunger in explosive perversion. Confident you've never felt this purposed in years. Each cell in you like glass in a mosaic, the way moonlight makes you reflect like the sun makes the moon. Slowing into residential with a grin in your chest. Hollowing out a part in the night for you.
This time you're early.
From the canopy of the slide:
in two hours Alyson emerges.
A blue button up tucked into skin tight jeans, faded black.
Pacing her porch, turning, looks like she's on the phone. You can hear—kind of.
" I got it back...
well it's funny.
Pervert."
She hangs up eventually, paranoia like a snake in the grass of your ego hoping for a bite in Alyson's apple of an ass. Remember not to fuck with me—a bruise like a scar to remind her. She goes back inside. You wonder. You hop off the canopy and back up the fence. Your feet placed opposite remembering to keep the bag lifted.
Dad took you on one camping trip. During the hike he taught you how to optimally lift and carry heavy loads, including passing through water. You hiked for 6 miles just to get there. Carried a gallon jug. Convinced anemia is the main cause of being underweight for your height. Dirt shuffles under your feet as you turn to cross the street from the frame around the fattened trunk of one soft bark tree.

Down the sidewalk. Up opposite sidewalk. A slow march towards the driveway. You follow lights from inside windows, except the last before a small back patio, which you remember to look at yourself in, smiling first a sarcastic, repressed smile and then a real smile at that last smile. The thought that caused it, thinking of your dad asking, 'are you proud of yourself?'

Walk up the 'patio' which is only a foot high. Pass under an outdoor staircase, falling into a completely untamed backward, weeds as long as tall grass.

A cat meow's quietly.

You take a seat in a waterlogged chair.

Pressed by the right of the doorway.

Calmly as you had handled the rock at her window. Sitting like you lived here. Sitting like a friend who'd been waiting too long for you. Calmly in the familiarity. In the understanding. You hear her steps again, barefoot this time, on linoleum. Her weight bends the sound in and out in each step, almost as if the tile had tried to be water. Approaching the door, perfectly framed, orange-white light. Black metal accent. The screen making it darker. The creek of the door as the suction of wood like two departing lovers, her face down as she uses her fingertips to push her bob back into place.

You leap with all of your body at the sight of her breath. You feel it condensing against your hand—her tears already going. You stuff a handkerchief you kept with you into her mouth to silence her. It's as loud as the cat's meow, now.

You hold her from the back, working around her, trying to find a solid place around her soft white gut like a fish. She smells how you remember her, like soap. Tears on your hands—you want to wipe them off but get on with it.

Her hair brushing against your face, you prop her up, making sure she doesn't slip out of your grasp like a baby does, going limp. She's kicking you in the knees now. You can feel them buckling like they're being pressed into the shape of an emu's. What a strong girl. You drop her cursing. Then grab her arms. She's spitting the gag out now. She's so loud now. You drop down, her kicking. You give up trying to shut her up.

She tries getting up a few times, which has you readjusting, turning around, facing out and down the driveway into the view of the street, her face as red as a little wagon, your strength increasing with every jerk, you put a hand in your pocket, trigger the black blade, turn around again from the position of a man herding a cow, or dragging the plow, to the position you'd hold someone if you were trying to save them from drowning. Except this time you've got a knife to their throat and they're gasping for breath just from nerves. Whimpering, her screams are useless.

"If you need another sound, I'll make an extra hole—right here."

You flip the blade into your hand and tap, absolute middle of her windpipe with the rubber grip. You hear her fat flesh scraping against the driveway's concrete. She's dressed all in white now. White flesh. Red face. White arms. Red wrists. White belly. Wife beater. White shorts. Her body revealing itself, wrapper, her breasts hardly finding a place in a white tank. Her thick legs, unblemished, shaved, 'surprisingly,' you think to yourself.

You think of having it. If you wanted to you could make her do anything. The brash, prideful display. You think of how little it would take to toss the panties aside and fill her inside. Her neck wriggling in an exhausted battle against just your weight to imagine the cold and disengaged handshake as she fights a losing battle, red eyed and blazing hate. But you're not here for the pink. You're for the red. Blood red.

With your hand pulling her hair, to keep her head still, off the path now, onto the lawn, into the moonlight, the perfect place for the whole block to catch a glimpse of. You straddle her, cover her mouth again. Look up, into the garden, 'what a perfect place,' you think to yourself. Where with time food could grow, steps away from the front door. Pleasure for the parents after their child had gone all grown up. Where there was dirt, there was life. Birth the seed. Death the seed. To plant it where you stood in new ground and you remember a summer at the lake.

Your wealthier distant cousins, and their house in Indiana. Ben Rodabaugh's mother had a garden. You remember he invited you into his canoe to go, 'Turtle Hunting.' You'd never heard of it but you brought home a boxer in a metal bucket, where, in front of your house, you took a small Swiss Army Knife's blade, and sank it, with absolutely no thought, into it's belly. Through the softer, thinner part of it's shell, surprised by the ease, as if a palette of butter. Squeezing from the top, watching him, his intestines like confetti, stringing out, unraveling orange insides, splayed through a slit not as thin as the width of a dime.

Orange—brown.

Like rust, you imagine her disintegrating body metamorphosing into the veins in your basements bricklaying, like a prisoner, chained to it's walls. Flesh rotting into the negative space, sticking like dirt under fingernails. Her vacated skin, evaporating into the smell of copper and ejection of bowels, until some neighbor complains of the smell. Him drinking a beer, "Couldn't even catch a whiff of the fresh cut grass."

Your left hand, free, strangling her now. Her tits like the rest of her in a frenzied jiggle. You look for it, with a soft brush of your hand, the absolute top and center of her head. An almost lulling brush before securing the handle in your palm and driving, with the force of a pitch, a blade, the length of your middle finger, down into her head, from birds eye. You can feel how soft it is just after the bone. A littler blood welling up like an ornery ink pen, only visible by the accented glares in an otherwise black lining and then you pull the blade out from the very top of her convulsing, blonde, head. Blood spurts dramatically at first, covering the lawn, and the bottom of your fist, but conveniently missing the rest of you, as it dribbles out weakly like the regurgitated meals of an aging retiree.

You feel a chill run through you, all the way up to your thin face, feeling tears well up slowly, while the chill becomes a sting in night air. A tickle of warmth in the cold like a kiss (you can't remember the last time) on your neck. You drop the knife and cover your own mouth now. Your cheeks fatten as your face squishes up. The smell and taste of dirty pennies from the bottom of your hand. Punctuated breathing and yet no sirens. No one from a window protesting your murder of the youthful potential. A societal stand up. Comical. A subcultural icon. Her perfectly trimmed lawn, each stroke of a push mower glittering sequin in the fabric of a murder scene. With all the drama of a carpet.

You wish you had more time to cry. As if you did it to feel. The way some people go to the movies. You've got to get rid of her. You leave the body in the yard, standing up slowly, walking around the bush, back down the driveway to her patio. Firewood wrapped in a tarp. How quaint. Preservation of the middle class nucleus, down to the smallest traditions, like a functioning fireplace. Too stupid to be quiet or patient, you tear the blue tarp out, like a magician, trying to leave dinner plates in place over it and most of it claps, banging over a few piles of...whatever is in these chests around the shoe rack.

You walk. Everything in you shaking, like you'd broken a bone, like you'd sustained the head injury. Blood on your mouth, while iron filled your gums. Like you'd been sprinting for miles. You take the tarp all the way to your car, parked by the gazebo. A girl standing dead center, from afar. Her head never breaking it's line, spears end into you. She's smiling. You don't know why, you're too affected to know why. She leans one leg over her bicycle but her neck almost at attention, like an alarmed bird. You, with confidence you wish you had in different circumstances, ones that your life didn't depend on, give her a smile back. She gets all of her weight on her bike and neutral, takes a slow pedal, like a leaf falling from a tree, down the ramp of the gazebo.

You open your car door hurriedly. Your sweaty hands almost drop the car keys. You jam in the key. Pull into reverse, jam in the gas, and peel back. Looking in your rearview realizing you almost killed another one. You pull up in front of the body, roll it up into the tarp, with the care of a sleeping bag. Another life skill you still haven't quite picked up, open the trunk, and stuff her arms and legs trying to escape the tarp as you pull her up the bumper of your car. Tarps racket, plastic scraping plastic, crumpling sheet of skin.

    Trunk slams.
    Quiet steps to the driver's seat.
    Drag race to the end of the street. Catch a right.
    Take backstreets on purpose.
    Drive at a snails pace on accident.

▲

You get home from the burial grounds safe. No stops, less traffic than on the way up. Another 5hr drive back down. How you're going to manage to clean the trunk is on your mind as you pass through the back door. Your mom is washing dishes, you can smell her cooking. You're covered in dirt and blood. She gives you a full up and down and with no concern, soft, tired, smiles before asking, in her pristine morning gown, all dressed up for the rest of her day without anyone to impress,

"You hungry, Chance?"

You smile, the same, soft, tired, smile.

"I could eat."

January 1st 2014

Tim,

She didn't deserve it. I know that but I think it'd be easier if I wasn't so close to her circle. The rejection. The calm face in public but the constant private fear, at my heels like a bloodhound pit-bull mix. Whispers to a band mate in passing of that 'filthy...'

I found a good place to bury her. I raced all the way to Marin from her house, almost paralyzed. I'm surprised I wasn't stopped as a drunk on my way up. I was going exactly the speed limit on highways completely policed by traffic. As open and free as my mind wasn't. I tried not to have a panic attack while I buried her off-trail in a 2 mile hiking circuit. Far enough way to buy time for better plans, close enough 'not to be far enough,' to be suspicious. Typical enough to seem abnormal if ever discovered. Open enough to seem unmotivated. It is lazy but I buried her. Spent New Year's with a corpse. Had to stop for a shovel. Which I stole from the community college. I dropped out. He asked me to promise not to tell anyone it wasn't locked. When I finished, sunlight was starting to pour through and I ran into an old married couple in drawstring bucket hats.

@abigfuckingbully

January 2nd 2014

    We missed the New Year, a lot of us. Everyone was wondering where Alyson was, she wasn't picking up her phone. They hoped she didn't die in a drunk driving accident. They went to her house but no sign of her. Martin thought she was 'with you guys.' A lot of us met up at Floyd's because 'we had work,' like a bunch of deadbeats. Rachel, the skinny girl in Emulator showed up this night. Mostly empty with a DJ playing pop shit. I managed her open. I found out she was about 30 from someone else there. We ended up kissing in the line to the bathroom after a long conversation about the artisanal pie shop we both frequented but never at the same time. I'd thought she was a lesbian this whole time. It's hard keeping the secret from her but it's an opportunity I can't pass up. An inside look. (Hahaha!) As close to truth as I'll ever get. Understanding this city is the first step to understanding myself. My new spark with Rachel is the beginning of the darl side of the moon of my history here.

    I grew for so long with these people. Only to exist permanently an arms length away. The pillars, the ambassadors, the scene queen under my arm. In my bed. In her hair.

▲

January 15th 2014

    ABC covered it—a park ranger found her when some extreme-hiker decided he'd risk the poison ivy for a water break on a rotted out log. His daughter, almost a toddler, tripped over the log I buried it by and vomited from the smell of the mess she landed in.

"I was so scared."

He said. He was sunburnt with 5 o' Clock shadow.

His whole life he must have been living in the castle walls of a tech job that gave him the weekend off to bury me unburying her.

February 26th 2014

Funeral plans made for April 4th. 4/4/2014. As if those coincidental numbers were like destiny's stars aligning. Rachel came over last night. Hysterical. I'd never seen her this drunk before. I wouldn't ask her why. She took off all of her clothes, which were soaked in the drink she let hit the floor before bawling in the puddle of glass, her body stinging like her eyes from the shards. All the way here. Mom didn't mind as much as she would have. A pat on the back after dinner tonight.

"I'm glad you found someone like Rachel. Take care of her. You can't take her for granted."

Rachel tossed along my bed thin and in need of consolation. So unlike I'd imagined her before. Her context made her so much stronger than she really was. Because at then end of the night we selfishly want to love unselfishly. The studded armor was laid down. The radical, now screaming, that she needed my body, give it to her. (Or stand stupidly watching her cry for another 2 hours.) I pacified her, expecting her to fall asleep quietly after. Her face swollen like she'd taken a beating.

When I first brushed my hand across her cheek my stomach sank. Her quivering eyes, her bore out flesh, looking into mine for something I was looking into others for. Where bankruptcy was all there was to understand. That I, like her, had lived my life flying a black flag, promising war against them who war against us. All to build a wall.

160 decibels, a rocket taking off, 200hz, 2 tons of flesh in 16 rows, a crowd to shield her from being alone in a crowd. Turning attention into

anonymity, turning the threat into spectacle, turning the spectacle in on itself. We were all ghost, parasites looking for somebody to inhabit. We were all tired of being nobody and still, unsettled, had to haunt each other. Congregating in only the most unwanted places. We wanted to be touched. To be desired, for that part of us to finally be left alone.

In my hands was my greatest accomplishment. My masturpiece. An abstraction. A post-modernist horror. My contribution an act of unadulterated subcultural incest. Like crawling into my mother again. Seeing the absence of importance dressed so decoratively. She never finished and neither did I.

While I was bout to fall asleep, she started mindlessly digging through my night stand. Where Alyson's ring was, before burying her I made a point to take it. Seemed like a waste. She turned to me, me in hypnagogic, hallucinations of a girl eating roses, and she screamed into me,

"This is Alyson's. Why do you have this? Why wouldn't you tell me you had this? This isn't yours to keep! You're not even that close to her. Tell me—now—how you have this." I tried to explain it. She cried facing the opposite wall and apologized. Drunken.

I waited until she started gnashing her teeth to turn the light back on and write this.

▲

You put your journal in the drawer of your nightstand and sit up in bed. Turning over your shoulder sickened by the yellow like you shake, as if with a fever, your hand pivots, wrist to fingers, pinching the teeth of it's gear and twist. She's still asleep. You slip downstairs into the kitchen and grab a knife. Lifting it, blade down, below the palm, to your opposite wrist. Staring into the window. Which is dark enough to be a mirror. You press the steel to the thinnest, palest, translucent, vein-holding, porcelain and to the floor. Crying hysterically, your ribs hidden and exposed, sudden hiccupping breath like some fucked up Greyhound.

Your hand slides up a wall and grabs the pale blue receiver. You think of your hypocrisy. She had a garden. You have a landline. Years of startling neglect take shape of moans carved like Styrofoam from lungs and throat. Three numbers, two tones repeat, and stark and in night all black and white.

"This is 911, Emergency—"
"I'm so sorry." you puke up.
"Hello? Sir—
Please, calm down.
Tell me where you are."
You sob.

@abigfuckingbully

"Are you okay?"
"No."
"Are you alone?"
"No."

@abigfuckingbully

@abigfuckingbully

A NEW YORK MINUTE IS A CLICHE BECAUSE IT'S REAL

I got off work early. I was confident. I was filled with an arrogance that comes with hard work and starving. A night unlike most where in every confident step rose a perfume almost of how perfect I was and how perfect it was that I'd take it home from a train ride that felt secret and sensible more than routine. I was putting the keys in. Everything was moving with me, I'm on one side of the 'L' train platform and a girl with a black wide brimmed hat that make people look like pilgrims is on the other. She was a blonde, dressed in high waisted denim looking like a frontierswoman and we were magnetic at the eyes. We'd brush past each other with loving subtle looks, then fully expose our necks 'acting natural,' the scene: two people in love at first sight, New York City. Shy to to talk to each other. Me: thin and tall, her: blonde with waves and short like an actress. Finally we captured each other gaze unleashed two explosive spontaneously combusting and synchronized smiles at the other. I had to say it. Yelling across the platform, like an idiot: "You're beautiful!" She kicked at nothing softly in the pavement with one foot in front of the other, slightly crossed, and shouted, "Thank you! You look like you make something. Where are you coming from?" "Just got off work, from the hostel, literally like a block away." "Maybe I can visit you there sometime." She waved. Then her train ran by rattling the whole still of cement and tile and cold that's the 'L' line.

■

I was at work, 2 hours before the end of a shift when she walked in wearing the same hat. she stood right in front of the raised receptionists counter, leaning in her hands laid flat and crossed in front of her. She pat the counter flat and lifted them. "Hey, you're the girl from the train." I smiled a cocky smile, one that slides up on both sides. "Here I am. What's up with you?" A hosteller came up to the counter almost immediately with questions about extending his stay. How much it would be. If he could that. If they were going to make him change rooms or not and how he could make them stop that...

She looked nervously from aside the man. Having moved to be polite. She moved to the couch on the opposite end hidden left of staircase in front of him.

I handled it. Punching some buttons and making a few clicks. When he left she came back up to reception. She tried to ask another question when another hosteller interrupted. I punched some buttons and made some clicks for him too.

Finally she emerged from the couch in the corner and asked if she could sit with me. (Behind the desk???) I let her in and she stood behind me. Then she found a swivel chair and sat indian legged in it.

■

"So you're an actress?" "Yeah I am, also a poet. Want to hear some?" She pulled a laptop out of her bag and read me a poem. It was a really good poem. A love poem and one where love seemed real and possible even in a place was I was new to and horrified me as much as it excited me, New York City. She read with all of her being, from her gut, with her hands accenting movements that help pull her silken words and loom a masterpiece. I had to clap sarcastically to feel comfortable sincerely blushing. She bowed her head and closed her eyes and laughed, then like a shadow packed up her things. Then stood still upright uptight and told me to meet her at the bar Tutu's after my shift, she'd be there.

■

The bar was sparsely occupied. By a few locals I guess who didn't want to go farr to bee kind of depressed in front of liquor. She offered to buy my drink as we squeezed into a booth seat just after the door. Hidden. I don't drink but I got a whiskey anyways.

When we really got to talking I was in over my head. I was interacting with a whole other person, not just a New York Magic True Fantasy. I was starting to feel lost on the whole thing. I downed my whiskey once she started to get into work. I was too sober to find something to say about it. Cool that she worked on the sets of music videos but I didn't' like the music videos she showed me. The color schemes reminded me of dart boards and the music sounded like it wanted to hang out with Tame Impala. There were paint balloons popping everywhere and white people wet dramatically dancing. I finished my whiskey and found a polite nicety to shield off a potential nightmare fight as an introduction to real mind. My real mind was for people I was fucking and I wasn't fucking her tonight. We got out of the bar, iPad put away, side by side, each in one of the other's arms, through the snow to my apartment.

■

She pulled out a joint on my front steps. I hesitantly smoked it but was fine. We went in and of course there was the promise of every night that ends in seeing someone else's apartment. I sound a little ungrateful. But by then I was decided. We went inside, to my room. She peeled off her pants and laid next to me in nothing buy a T-shirt. I kept all of mine on. Like a child who wouldn't take a bath. The chemistry was a cocktail of bad antipsychotics and amphetamines and razors and candy and I wasn't going to be able to be with this woman in any other way than a soft warm body, awkwardly she snuggled in sheets close to me and kissed me. I kissed her back but it got push-comes-to-shove-close-shave, and I had to work to withhold. Pushing away. No interest. I felt sorry for her in a way but arrogant in another. We don't have to finish this tale of New York Magic, we really don't. I realized how fucked I was going to be telling this woman a shattering blow to her self esteem because of what's perceived as guaranteed as a woman at this point. She wouldn't take no for an answer physically. So When I stopped and went cold fish she looked at me, her blue eyes, a face that was beautiful before suddenly...that I as a man know I should want to fuck...but that seemed safe & domestic, I'm sorry, you're beautiful in the way lots of models are to me, an untouchable beauty, a newly common beauty, a light hearted beauty. She wasn't insulted she said but then was insulted. She said, 'okay,' when I told her I don't want to. "Don't want to?" KISS "Why not?" KISS KISS I had to hurt her to get it through to her. SO I lied an awful lie. "I think, I might, actually, like you and..." No. Fuck no. No. I can't believe I just said that. She turned away from me and switched the light off to spoon and said, 'hold me.'

■

We woke up and immediately she was rubbing against me, her hand on my cock. Kissing my neck. I decided in that early morning fog, that fog you accidentally hit snooze that the only way this actress was leaving my bed was if she was fucked. Slowly I crept up into her partly reluctantly, her snow soft body pulsing as i breathed life into her with every throat deep tongue kiss, performing. Because there's nothing more important than the performance. I did it the best I could because that's what I promised. That's what she needed. That's what I could offer. I came too soon. I was out of practice. And more whiskey than food. In New York I'd been eating Manny's Cafe's day olds. She was confused but got the picture. She leaned up with her legs as a seat against the headboard and called a taxi. She made some pleasantries while she hoisted up her underwear. Her pants. Belted them. Laced her shoes. Walked out, both of us having taken too much from the other. Honestly: stealing from the other with a polite lie of simulated fun and possible love.

@abigfuckingbully

@abigfuckingbully

WE FELL IN LOVE AT THE NO AGE SHOW

We fell in love at the NO AGE show. We were holding hands while MINER played. We made our friends jealous, I think. All the dopamine and adrenaline ran straight to my head and surging, wouldn't stop the total elation from coming. I didn't want it to ever stop. I had to headbang harder. My body was trying to find physical expression the magnitude too great for the limit of my tiny body in comparison, finding expression of such a spiritual experience. She was going to be my girlfriend because she knew what this meant to me. Winding, whirling, dizzying, droning, drowning in, a din of laughing distortion. She didn't lean in for a kiss. We both knew it at the same time. Neither of us were high or drunk. It was the purest intoxication. Just blood and lust and love at first.

@abigfuckingbully

@abigfuckingbully

I KNOW YOU STILL PRAY

A bankrupt night of liquored up infants lent her nothing on the bartender's walk home. A bartender's walk home comes with a sense of futile pride, a depressive glorious smile in the few moments of calm and unpanic with a pocketful of a rich man's change.

Which would be of good use on the turnstyle of the L she imagined hopping. It was the bittersweet mood she's in. Four women living together is about as comfortable as a canned tank of piranhas so she savored it, because of what she had to look forward to she stomached the train ride, sketchy, in that it was impermanent, never finished, and unsafe, how everything felt to her in New York City.

At home, roommates who hated her. A situation of two too alike to get along. Chores lists that hang out like clothes on laundry lines for too long. A shit that went unflushed because of one too slothful to buy a plunger in the event of this emergency. I won't tell you which. The bookish don't fuck with the ferocity of women who read and act. Actually there's the modest quiet reader and the less principled—books mean less but are read more obsessively and with more meaning than should be attributed to them by the viewpoint of the cooler modest readers mind.

She unlocks the door but she stays locked. the women on the couch scratched out a place for her to sit but passive aggressively but meaningless to them but hoping, maybe, at the same time she would be a little more 'social,' or friendly. She was always at her boyfriend's, the codependent cycle that makes all independent living situations nightmares.

"How was it?" she chimed like a bird. Somehow completely unaffected by the progress of a night. It's imminent death never a reason to let it go. "Oh, you know," she said, literally. The girl lying on the couch dressed annoyingly in nothing. Seemingly buoyant in personality because of an obviously sexual physicality. She threw her bag down by a communal desk in the living room with an enormously high ceiling. She'd shed the weight and responsibility by grabbing a glass of water to water down a drunken honesty enough. "Pretty tired actually."

She turned her back to the sink and drank slowly standing but steadily, with her only intention to finish the glass of water before she was accomplice to her own compromised character, or forced into honest silence while Dani talk longer about her fashion internship. She was always on her side as if she were being painted. Talking about how long it took to set up and what famous brand or actress she got to shoot with. Another story to tell. Acting hadn't happen for her in a while. She was feeling an undiscerning but soft hatred towards these women and towards the knowledge of how wrong it was. But she couldn't help it. She turned around to hid herself and her shoulders sank defeat and relief as she heard the 'clink' against the metal basin. She didn't say goodbye.

The room was cold but she was too and stripped down quickly, thinking to herself for a few moments of the importance of a body. In her room a tye dye flag stapled into the top of a window, a makeshift cover, curtain, or the one adjacent, a black sheet stapled in the wall over the window. Behind her: books, plays, and poetry. She closed the closet doors after placing her clothes away and looked at the night stand: a 3d rose composed entirely of green and pink beads and a cloth portrait of The Virgin Mary, in something as thick as a rug but as small as a book cover. Out of character for a woman of 24 whose love for God feigned in the blistering heat of grey New York Summers. Her heart in as much heat as animal for something like God called on her tonight though. She removed the weight of the carelessly placed rose from the virgin's portrait, then, took the position she imagined was appropriate because of film's. Knees on the ground,, elbows on the bedside and hands clasped together as erect as possible.

"Dear Father God. I know it's been a long time since we've last talked. Things are going okay most of the time. Most of the time I don't see what good it does me praying but...God it's inevitable that I come to you though please forgive me for my absence. God, please make it so that work is a little easier. That there be less pain involved in knowing exactly where a night goes. I'm feeling less than ever for people. I try to keep good face with my roommates but the longer I live here the worse it gets, can you please make it possible to move soon, even if it's with Jeffrey. God, I really hate it here. I've been alone every night I haven't been with Jeffrey and there's no motivation to move except I do want to with the oppressive silence of being alone. It's just that if there were anymore of a reason to wake up in the day...I don't know how I feel exactly but it's the difference between winning and being awarded..."

She stopped. She looked left and right hearing her own voice ring throughout the room. Then she got up, out of her stance, and rolled naked into her bed. "Amen," she whispered and passed out immediately.

A TATTOO OF FOUR GALLOPING STALLIONS UNDER HER ARMS

I was leaning in the hallway next to your doorway watching K drunk.
Her face was slowly reddening and everything she was doing was as if she were in a maddened blushing.
The way she smiled, the way she talked, the way she moved.
Was all a slow and neat blossoming little by little.
Her bright orange hair. Her bright orange freckles.
She was occupied with someone else besides I was here to see you.
It was, after all, *your* party, *you'd* arranged it, for *your* friends, and I should've understood that.
I should stop fawning over her perfectly orange hair and soft faded freckles.
You have freckles.
You have perfect hair.
Finally you stopped doing whatever the fuck you were doing, hiding in your room, and you pulled on my arm, my view was no longer in the kitchen entrance, where K was, sipping on an iced screwdriver.
There was a whole group of people at the party that we mutually knew and some we didn't know, and some you knew but I didn't but none of them were outside of your room at the time so things were private, we were alone.
"I know what I said," I said, "but I hope you changed your mind and realized it doesn't mean I don't have feelings for you. I have feelings for you right now."
"I'm not hurt. I was but I'm not now."
She took a sip of her drink.
She had light strawberry blonde hair, it was thick and cut into an a-line.
She was wearing a red-mauve silken chinese dress-quipao.
You looked perfect in it.
Your breasts were accented and you somehow had hips in it.
I was there thinking of touching you but you held my hand as I lead us out of your room and back into the party.
As soon as I was out you were interrupted, "HOW ARE YOU???" someone said with a drawl, "I feel like we haven't talked IN FOREVER."
You pulled away immediately and followed her into the enormous front porch of the building where you were once offered to live rent free if you kept pursuing your art.
I hope you still are.

I moved back to the kitchen where K still was, kind of talking to T who was already shaking my hand coldly after I introduce myself because I introduce myself immediately.
"What're you guys talking about?"
"Meditation. Chakras. Universal Consciousness."
"Oh, I love to meditate."
"Me too!" said K.
T said nothing.
Drank his drink, knocked the ice cubes against the side of the glass and said, "It's too religious for me."
She pointed a finger from out of her glass at T and said, "That's because you're a man of *science*."
She said like a kid giving raspberries.
Her voice was smoky and a little gruff.
I asked her about lucid dreaming and she said,
"I've had a few" but "I could never have them when I planned them."
Like so many occurrences in real life that struck you out of the blue like this chance meeting.
And she heard that thought and leaned in a little more.
That's when you came back and noticed us talking.
You walked right by us as you walked the the congregates at the doorway to the kitchen.
You gave me a worried look and then ducked into the fridge to pour some more of whatever the hell she was drinking, you couldn't remember what.
You were starting to worry so you grabbed me by the shoulder and pushed me to the front porch where you left me alone, without a drink, mostly sober in the night, without a lover, a night so polluted by us it couldn't do anything but blacken to watch us, the way the moon looks dead, making that fucked up face because he's so upset he doesn't have his own light.
I sat down.
A hippyish couple complimented my shoes while I watched the porch enjoy itself from down here, feeling disengaged.
Watching a party as a whole enjoy itself can be relaxing or depressing.
I was starting to feel depressed only mildly buzzed.
Eventually you came out of the house and looked down at me and said,
"We're going dancing."
Uh.
"I really don't want to dance."
"C'mon we're going dancing, it'll be fun."
It'll be fun.
"I *really* don't want to go."
"Don't be an asshole."
Then you pulled me up and got all of your friends together.
Including a pretty Mexican girl in a long dress who would get us in trouble later.
She got up and I agreed.

I got up.
We walked the six blocks to the center of downtown where at my telling machine, drawing money out I probably shouldn't, I hesitated, looked at the machine and then back at you.
You shouted at me.
You screamed,
"I sucked your cock and you can't even go dancing with me?"
"That's fair." I thought and drew $20 out.
At the club you wanted to dance but couldn't.
Your body was moving jagged to the 90's hip hop playing.
I was trying to dance with you.
Your head looked like it was hiding in your shoulders, your entire body looked like it was cringing to the music, and your lower half was falling apart.
I couldn't stay in front of you for too long without feeling embarrassed and uncomfortable as you on a dancefloor.
I was having another gin & tonic.
I was cutting a rug.
I was enjoying myself regardless until we had your Mexican friend attract an enormous bodybuilder with a sexual appetite for younger women.
He followed us around the club in a fedora.
I respected him for his bold and traditional attempt to just dance with her.
But I couldn't when I knew she didn't want to.
He continued to connect himself with our group and the Mexican girl said nothing.
Actually, she humored him.
Even though she was repelled, she moved into our group to hide, she smirked and shook her ass a little harder at the bodybuilder.
Terrible fucking idea.
I asked her, confused, "are you into this guy?"
NO she mouthed.
I was annoyed.
IT was completely unclear if she was or wasn't okay with this man to the man, who, sincerely misread a frightened attempt at keeping the night copasetic, as an invite.
Mixed signals.
I asked her if she wanted him to leave.
She said nothing.
I took control.
"Look man, you should go."
He had at-least 80lbs on me.
He really didn't like what I was doing.
He wouldn't move.
I told him again, "She's not interested man, you should go."
"Why?" he asked.
He was shrugging.

Then you flipped out on him.
He was walking away.
You beat him in the chest and start screaming,
"You fucking rapist! Get the fuck out of here!"
"Woah, calm down! He's not a rapist!"
Unfair and stupidly dangerous.
He didn't fully get the picture until I told him again.
"Sorry about her, but please, she doesn't want to dance with you."
Finally he shrugged and left.
Dissipated into the crowd.
We danced together again.
All of us.
Until the floor emptied and my clothes started to get soaked we left to your house.
At home no one was home.
Except K and T sleeping in the next room.
Their door was open.
You could hear lovey-dovey mumblings.
You walked in and stripped to nothing to change into bedtime clothes.
An I Love NY T-shirt and lace panties you preferred to pajama bottoms.
Cake was on the table in the living room.
White cake with a sweet avocado frosting you and K made.
She had an obsession with avocados.
She would fill entire notebooks with drawings of anthropomorphic avocado characters.
You pulled the saran wrap off and stuck your finger in it.
It was soft and sweet, a perfect close to a drunken night.
I sat across from you at the table in the living room.
I said, "I feel so close to you."
Then I choked on a piece of cake realizing I was lying to myself.
"Actually that's not how I feel at all."
You drunkenly stopped eating.
"Why would you say that then?" you said like you were about to cry.
"How do you feel then?" with a pointed viciousness, deserved and undeserved.
How honest can I be with you?
Maybe it's a game.
I play but mostly for survival.
She asked, her voice suddenly stable, inquisitive, "Are there any of my friends you want to sleep with?"
"Why would you ask me that?"
"I don't know. Are there?"
"You want an honest answer?"
"Yes."
There was a long silence.
Then silence was long enough.

"K."
You started crying while eating cake.
Then you fell over into an arm on the table, just barely missing the cake, "Oh, no." you said defeated in that drunken absent self-love that wants to be helped and help itself, "this happens every time." and you're almost falling over sideways with cake frosting all over both hands.
You were eating it with your hands.
"It doesn't mean I don't have feelings for you."
"You're an asshole you know that."
"I'm sorry...should I leave?"
"No."

@abigfuckingbully

@abigfuckingbully

I WAS A FUNCTION

Popular opinion is liberalism is popular opinion.
It makes me sad and then angry and then sad when I think about you and the leashes you and others have tried to tie & drag me on.
You owned three pit bulls and thought you wanted to experiment with a new social identity, which means try sex with white people, no, that's racist, I take it back, with anyone but your boyfriend,
since your racist boyfriend of 5 years was now satellite, and the choke chain he took off was the one you'd hope would fit to bind me (in)to your backyard.
You live in a shed in the back of a punk house in the south bay.
You have toured more than one nation but have no intention of leaving your hometown.
This stated for some perspective.
Unlike you, I do my best to let go of personal offenses without weaving them into a web of rationalized blanket politics for safety against personal responsibility; the creation of new inverted standard through negation, sepia tone filter from a full color photo, the child's frustration with chess and pleading for a game of Plinko, and for the milieu to reward this as talent--logic--discourse--a hollow moral superiority, a house without walls, all studs, nothing but studs, without the courage to take the responsibility of personal integrity, where one acts, speaks, defends oneself; one who believes that disinterest in closure is the same as reason to stop calling, talking about it; conflict resolution for you is on friend (your roommate) (manager) leaving the office, while I have the guts/(balls) to bring your boring Anne Sexton collection back to you in person at the counter of your work/job, the place I happened to write at for years before you started working there, does this sound petty?
Anyways--
She walked out and asked politely that I leave that Colleen feels unsafe.
'Two women came forward this year,' (coming forward makes everyone sound like a--) 'saying you were a stalker...'
Of course for the 'safety,' of said women names are kept from me, though I suspect it's a village girl whose bitter about turnout after fucking, housing, or feeding me--who just don't have it in them to say, I 'don't want to talk to you anymore,' 'I don't want to see you,' the things that cause people to stop talking to them or seeing them, like, say, you, who, in silence and absence create a sense of morality, one to be held brave--to turn all authority on into one narcissists driving single parental eye--God's eye--over policing and people pleaser--please remind me again how I am one of your dogs for having the will to bring shit up to you in person--unlike those suffering from persecution mania--whose cradle of consent culture makes incomplete stories and kangaroo courts main operative, your silence over my word.
I cussed you out--it wasn't unprovoked--anyways that's why I'm here.

To apologize to you after my trip to Portland ended and your phone calls ended.
"I think I might have feelings for you," you said.
"It's a bad idea." I said.
In bed after we fucked and you told me I was 'affectionate.'
Affectionate.
Like you were fucking cavemen.
"I think I might have feelings for you." I said.
"It's a bad idea." you said.
There it was, a fat (obese) self righteous woman in thigh tattoos and a skirt the size of a tutu to threaten arrest while an espresso machine hissed the way crickets chirp comically, the counter empty except the book, and me, now submissive, asking to justify myself, then justifying myself, it doesn't matter if you want to say sorry, she feels "threatened," so she's "threatened."
I know you've been in one relationship for five years, where, obsession with what's 'appropriate,' left blowouts repressed or navigated through with advice from zines built with tertiary sources never cited--your politics constructed, again, from what makes the most direct route to comfort and safety--where swatting flies with bazookas, magnitude is ignored, stuffing stars into music boxes, pocketing machetes...did you ever think for 9 hours from hitting your pillow one night to an unrested next morning, teeth clenched hissing at the thought of how maybe you're responsible for the outcome of our fucked relationship? Or did you adopt the logic of my ex-girlfriend, who, after my lying and cheating, holds the grudge, my transgression, over the nature, and dresses it in drag, and is convinced that I didn't try to break up with her before--that there wasn't a signal to the obvious fatigue--that long distance and love without respect doesn't make for sheltered pets instead of humans, and the stinging wrath of Fenrir, biting the hand that feeds, the Cartier adorned hand of a doctor's daughter--I'm the villain if you forget that I had my reason.
I wasn't excited when she, the mistress, turned on that B movie--and I needed ¾ of her pot brownie to share--"it looks like come doesn't it?"--the alien cesspool--or was it their gene pool?--it's on the screen though--I accepted it passively--I kissed her, passively stripped, and half heartedly fucked her as she dramatically moaned.
I must have been somewhere else.
Whatever was or wasn't really happening to her wasn't happening to me--and dying a little on the inside, like the feeling of clocking in, I passive-aggressively came prematurely, a move I didn't know I mastered until now.
Did you spend hours awake gnashing teeth and considering me your enemy, then considering, maybe, that no one acts without reason all the time, did you have faith, did you consider what part you were responsible for?
Did you stand up for me when I was right or did every rumor spread like the text you got, me naked, you cross legged on your bed, "he fetishizes women of color,"--Rick...
You're so mean scene queen.
Anything to preserve your personae.

From P.O.C. social justice warrior to slanderer and...if it was my guess...you're the fetishist.
Let's talk about how you'll fuck me and ask me to help walk your tick infested canines, affection for an animal who eats it's own shit, more respect for animals than humans, a known trait of a sociopath, but you will pull back like the sight of blood or the word cunt when I ask to hold your hand.
"Don't walk through the house. I want to keep this kind of discreet."
Kind of discreet.
Kind of discreet?
Kind of 'discreet.'
"I don't want Sasha and everyone else to know."
"Why?"
What the fuck?
Are you in highschool?
How old are you?
You're like 4 years older than me.
You've been to Europe.
You're going to hide this relationship?
I went on this walk, and then your roommate/mother figure came along, and we couldn't talk about it.
But we made the loop around the gum caked soot-strewn heated streets of San Jose, this hell hole, sometimes beautiful people will show up, but, beauty is fickle, it disappoints a lot.
It doesn't reciprocate.
It stiffens competition.
You're a good example of that.
You were beautiful.
Freckled. Tongan.
But you're a bastard.
I couldn't help thinking about it, with me, anger shuts me down, then shuts me up, then builds with every step, the weight of my thighs, joints shifting, the strength of size 12 feet.
You told me I had the perfect body.
The body of a model.
We come to the back room, we make the loop, we weave back in, like all of your neighborhoods chainlink fences, like our hands did anyways cause you know being that cold is just being that stupid in your room, I eat my anger standing, then stripping for you no matter how angry I am, I'd strip for you now, shedding again.
Didn't it bother you that I felt different.
For me it's easy to tell when someone's in a mood, when someone's mad, when someones different.
I was different and you didn't even notice.
But I can be arrogant when I'm angry and hide it inside of me well.

I forget if we fucked or not, if we had, I would write here that my body would have held the anger I couldn't express.
And that when you held me you would know most of my weight would cling to me hiding from you--you would hold something heavier and somehow more empty, like a new failed aluminum alloy.
You would have felt sad and start thinking but it's infantile to expect that kind of treatment to be taken care of, to have your mind or body read, it's narcissism to expect people, you, anyone, you, to treat me the way I treat you.
The weakness of justice projected into the world where the golden rule no longer applies.
People pleasing: treat people how they'd like to be treated not how you'd like to be treated.
Your dogs your sad fucked up dogs watched me lie to myself in a love act and sleep next to you.
Your bed has no headboard but the splintering eaten walls and something probably from Ikea that looks like a box and you're on the side by your books which I look at but wouldn't read but touch kind of anxiously and sometimes out of total boredom only to feel a bit of the spite I remind you of to be reminded is never justifiable but healthy, very much a sore loser in a way that will never be as honest and awful (annhust and hofful) as it can(t) seem trails--I get going, a good view of thought it takes too long--fingers wanted to reach/brush over and brush through them but instead--brushed through your straight black hair, jet black and turquoise dye job--to sleep and your big pretty jaw and big sleepy big eyes, brown and you are brown, and you were soft and uncomfortable, uncomfortable with/by my touch and get the impression you are always like this. All the time with him.
All I had to know was that it wasn't that I was, "so affectionate" not that's it that bad to be that offended, it does not give me the right to be expressing this because I have a right to--but it was that you were/aren't honest you suffer from touch and a lack of touch. In childhood and maybe your life now.
I was kissing your face and your eyes are closed.
It's time for us to sleep, it's not possible, it's possible we had sex, and I accepted it, and it would be the daytime when you would give me the saddest blowjob, like you didn't want to because I know you didn't want to--but I couldn't continue/get hard without it. It's later this happens.
What happens now is that I'm kissing you to sleep under the quilt and you lay facing me and I like to stick my healthy legs, one leg, over your big pretty healthy legs, like I liked that you were wearing a tank top and bicycle shorts, and you let me--my weight on you, you aren't hurting me in bed, but you ask me if you're heavy, I say no, I feel sad that I am okay with myself for feeling okay for being well/feeling safe with you.
Our legs pet and we pass out.
This was maybe the second or third night we were hanging out.
It always starts with a day after your done with work at 3 but I had a nightmare, a man with a giant axe, the tones are all red light districts, pink reds, sorbet

neons, all the film over, and he hammers his way through the wall--and then, stands over my bed, your bed, with the axe metamorphosed into a sledge hammer and he waits for me to see him at the foot of the bed and in the dream of course I wake up screaming to see him and then I wake up screaming in waking life, with all of the feelings of dying at once carried in me while I was alive, living and not dying--and all of my body felt my heart sink into it like it's possible to see poison seep through a body, if a scorpion was thirsty to be milking itself in you and you're alive to remember that it's now and you don't have to remember, it happens that way, like that.

You wake up and your arrogantly tender voice--sweet to me at the time, then filthy, now sweet to me now--and you checked to see if I was okay.

"Are you okay?"

"I'm okay."

I was okay.

You didn't pet me at all, you just woke up and asked and pass out again, which, seems like your nature now, in retrospect.

Since affection was so foreign.

We woke up the next day, you had it off, when usually you are waking at 6 to serve happy yuppies coffee, but yuppies is simplification because part of me knows that people have what they are willing to work for and I am stubborn and unwilling, like you are stubborn and unwilling, because we're both college dropouts, I think I used to be in the same camp, where I was convinced my reasons are justified, neither sloth or fear of commitment, now we are in two different camps, though neither of us is in college.

Ray Bradbury never went.

He married a rich girl though.

Like how I am now waking up in your bed enraged.

I will think of how Raven, my ex-girlfriend, someone who at this point in my anger I blame you for feeling as if I have just left the woman of my life, a future wife, for you, when I say left I mean betrayed.

I mean I'm in your room and okay because I cheated on her, not with you, but I cheated on her, and I lied to her, and I think that if you lie--and she's clueless, and you fuck her, it's rape because if she knew you were stoned and fucking another girl from work she would gag-crying and her eyes would blow out and she would scream and shatter her own ceramic art on walls and hit you--over and over again and tell you to leave--she would be saying NO in the way NO never has to be said and without being said is complete justice--she said nothing, then she said, "you can sleep on the couch."

I'm at the foot of your bed naked and uncomfortable with the way it feels to be naked around you in the day, like I should feel how you feel about yours, like you are looking at me with two stage lights and I have nothing for you tonight, but it's day and already 85 in your room---and how ugly light is when it hits cloth, but can't seem to let itself in, I felt similarly sheltered, and had a quilt raised over my breasts like a woman out of a shower trying to find pants, and socks, and shoes, and I forget who made the bed, likely me, I'm bad at it but

good at doing it--it's only right, polite and Midwestern to the core still; maybe honest to a fault on purpose, a sort of manipulation, close maybe in your life did you imagine you are this arrogant?
That there's enough of you to--
I find my socks and think of her story, her father came from war torn Lebanon to America, Middle America from Mideast to Midwest, Chicago, and he's--he's so hungry for achievement, the vision of America irrelevant to him, rocking back and forth reading medical texts for tomorrow, because he hated poverty, he had a choice, to be a cook in Lebanon or be a Doctor in America.
He was hungry, starving on forked cans of Spam thinking about a woman--about a woman whose beauty comes from an oil empire, someone he could eat cans of Spam for.
Here I am humoring art, at the edge of your bed.
He wanted a rich girl and he was willing to earn it--to work for it--starve for her.
I find my socks.
I find my pants, peel them back on, and then I stand up straight up with a shirt find myself.
Slow and leaning on each leg, shifting weight, for words, I cross and uncross my arms, your head's in your phone, at your head ¼ shaved, hair in a bun.
I'm here to stand up to you now.
"What do you mean discreet?"
Completely unaware of what you just heard, unphased, then looking up from your phone with an open mouth and then scratching your head:
"I just--everyone doesn't need to know."
"It's stupid.
Are you ashamed of me?
That idea pisses me off."
"I'm sorry...does that hurt you?"
"It's fucked up to treat me that way, like,
you just got out of your relationship but..."
"You're overreacting."
"No, you're irresponsible."
You got up and dressed--in most of the same clothes, and you hugged me.
"I'm sorry, it's not how I mean that."
Unresolved, I was walked out of the shed, your house, the room, into the house, into the kitchen, you offered me a cup of coffee but, no, fuck no, and then you asked me on the other side of the screen door, the patio littered with mason jars, what I'd be doing for the rest of the day like I didn't happen.
"Working." and left--I meant I was going to workout and make something.
I'd forgive the transgression.
I'd be responsible and tell myself that failure to accept the boundary might be, control I have no right to.
I wouldn't believe it but I'd practice it.
This was my first failure.
To accept without resentment that I had desired the fortitude to be above.

Alone.
That I let rage become a calm explanation and celibate, and tolerant and dignity you are unworthy of--I give, and it hurts, it hurts all the time.

———

The next I would see you would be at night.
I spend all day downtown and because I want to be close to you and your house at the end of a night.
Sleeping in another's bed, even without the sex made me giddy,
I finished what I was doing half-focused and pack everything up to a text from you.
The walk is how it always is.
Sad and scary like I would be mugged but I would be crying--I would do nothing but feel all of the garbage found littering the ground was piling up over my chest in my throat I would chew up garbage and mournfully spit pieces up.
Under the overpass, a mattress, bloodied with a bra and panties caked into it.
You can only imagine and I work so hard not to.
This whole city felt like a murder scene.
Senseless and bigger than me but sadder and less important.
You were starting to feel like that while I traversed the underpass, but I make it, cross the four lane teetering on the end of the thick white paint line, the left foot after the right foot, to be a big baby, a child on my way past the tarp woven chainlink fences, with the holes that look clawed out of them--flapping bits of flesh in the wind like papercuts and no band aid.
Then your enormous wooden gate past your short bus you share for tour, what a horrible idea to start a band with your boyfriend, and I think your van is stupid partly because yeah I'm sincerely jealous of you being in a band, and touring, even though your band sucks, and you kind of know that--that's what I'm starting to feel I'm here for.
As soon as I open the gate your pitbulls almost assault me.
"I'm here." I text, calmly but I'm screaming in my head, "LET ME THE FUCK IN!" and you come out dog-whispering, "C'mon, c'mon," to all three of them.
They stop growling.
They stop fearing me.
I stop fearing them, it is now clear that I am not someone to protect you from.
You're wearing bike shorts and a tank top, you bring them back towards the light coming out of the shed...your tiny cobblestone path, leading into your doorway.
It felt like that picture of Jesus they pair with tracts, the verse about God knocking on your heart or letting Jesus in.
WIth you and me glowing and being let in.
The light was gold and green just like that.
We reacquaint.
We talk about our days.

We can only do one thing around each other which is lay together and touch each other.
Your soft limbs stroke mine until we're at the hems and buttons of the others clothes falling off almost, like petals from flowers, from those tiny purple flowers in trees that they cruelly plant the squares surrounded by cement, alongside trees close enough and far enough, maybe their roots were stronger than the pavement on the surface, maybe they touch underneath there.
Holding hands, fuck, now I'm thinking about holding hands--you lay beside me, all your thickness, and I lay beside you, all strong thick limb, and we never come together but fall next to each other glowing.
It's okay that we don't talk at all during sex.
I enjoy the silence, though you seem at a loss as to what to do in that silence.
In the shed under the quilt again,
I keep kissing from the underside of your arms in a row to your wrist.
"I think I have feelings for you." You'd say.
"It's a terrible idea." I say.
About a week later, kissing your arm,
"I think I have feelings for you."
"It's a terrible idea." you say.

―――

Only ever having hung out with your friends by chance at the shows you hosted, or played,
I was surprised to have felt so close to everyone.
We passed the Museum steps you once stopped to talk to me alone in about...maybe it was family...
We ate burritos and took an obscenely long walk over a bridge to your house.
I was happy, I felt separate enough from them, but understood.
This is as well as I remember it.
Everyone dissipated, apparently for the show that was happening.
All going their separate ways before me and you alone arrived at your house.
"Are you going?"
"No."
Your car was broken down getting repairs.
You weren't going.
It was a hassle.
You weren't that interested.
You said I could stay and watch a movie with you.
You took out your laptop, but before we could make a decision, you got a text from Rick.
Rick was going to show and he could give you a ride.
You kicked me out of your house after the quick change of plans.
I remember being outside your door after packing up my stuff, and you asked me if I was alright.

Being the coward I was at the time, more passive than I could say I am now, I said, yeah, I was fine, and left. I'd get a sunburn on a bus bench texting you 10 minutes later about how I really felt.
Which was used and confused. Which was used and useless.
I would lay into you about how malleable you are as a personality and how I didn't like the idea that I was a replacement for your boyfriend. That I was stand in and on call.

Later I would wrongfully apologize to you at a jazz club named after an instrument everyone went to disregarding the jazz to eat. Even though I was spending time with someone else, I would have the bravery to approach you in your group of friends and apologize. You would take advantage of this moment by telling me "It's okay. I just don't want to be anyone's emotional punching bag." I would feel worse than I needed to, since really my only sin was trying to find the words to express... I would eat with you at your table, laugh begrudgingly at your friends jokes, slowly deflating internally. I can't remember after this, but hopefully I didn't go home with you.

———

I would be grateful in Portland for two whole weeks while I spent time with my first girlfriend ever.
We aren't exactly still in love but we are close.
We would spend as much time together alone as possible but would often run into roommates or the boyfriend, who, was rightfully threatened.
An anorexic alcoholic deluded about his role as booker at Valentine's.
He was already fairly clingy and his irresponsibility with bills, money, and Mary were all mounting.
My vacation was on saved money left over from a job I no longer had and it would be her vacation as well.
Beaches, band practice, shows, and some good food.
We would sleep in separate rooms but eventually reveal, both of us laying out on the same low mattresses, moved for a great big communal movie night, forgot what we watched, remembered passing out, she would tell me after I told her I was/she was having sex dreams.
We were fucking each other in our dreams.

Colleen would phone me late at night.
Sharing parts of yourself you may have often forgotten.
You'd say you love dating down, younger men, because they would give you something you feel you lost, they had a life that older men didn't have as those too jaded not to defile, while younger men preserved and nurtured.
Even while I was gone you would phone me like I was your new boyfriend.

I know it's naive to think Rick was out of the picture but to lead me to think that we'd stay friends.
You promised.
That stupid racist text sticking out in my mind before I'd hang up.
"He fetishizes women of color..." and nothing could be further from my mind--who cares, but then it permeates everything.
I've dated a Lebanese girl, an Indian girl, a Chinese girl, a ¼ Japanese girl, all American.
Their race was acknowledged but beyond that...
Who cares is the thought I'm having when I'm feeling what I'm saying which is "I miss you." which is too much to say but you and I both accept it.
I'd pass out and have another dream of fucking Mary.
"You think it's a good idea?" she'd ask.
"It's a terrible idea."

I come back and hear nothing from you.
I call and I call and I call.
Your phone rings and I never hear back.
When I do you're busy.
You don't answer texts either.

"YOU'RE SO FUCKED TO ME.
TO JUST GHOST LIKE THIS.
YOU AUTHORITARIAN BITCH.
I'M NOT A NAIVE PERSON,
I KNEW HE'D BE A PART OF YOUR
LIFE AGAIN. BUT YOU CAN'T
EVEN BE A FRIEND.
YOU HAVE NO FUCKING IDEA
HOW REAL YOU ARE TO ME."

That's when you spoke up.
I forget what you said.
I felt so angry I couldn't even muster tears.
I got to be like you in a few minutes, harder and harder, the soft part of me hidden deeper and deeper...
But instead I fought you more and more.
I thought if I could smoke you out of the self-righteous foxhole of your cowardly silence--your right to silences would feel stupid.
Somehow as shameful as the brow beating you were giving me through them.
How arrogant silence is.
You're winning by default.

But all you did was explain yourself over and over again.
You didn't want to get into what would make you vulnerable.
Vulnerability would have been a whole different argument.
One you'd have to see me face to face for.
Why?
You got to be the one to say, "you never get to see me again."
After another year ended, another trip to New York ended, and my apologies were wasted, is the day I'd come to your counter with your Anne Sexton book.
I'd quickly be "escorted," out on the grounds saying your apologies in person is the same thing as stalking someone. I would be a criminal and a pervert and treated as such.
Two steps from the front door, I'd pull my phone out to Facebook message you, trying to understand exactly why you weren't even going to step out to the counter.
Another argument.
Ending with me telling you,
"I hope you die in that filthy fucking doghouse you call a room."
What I didn't tell you is how much you humiliated me.
I don't mean being exiled.
I mean, how much your love humiliated me.
How much your mind boiled our entire history into it's
worst conflicts.
How the underpinnings were loose.
Love wasn't there.
I was a function.
How it could be there and then be gone.
How I would be a different person after even if I thought it was stupid.
Even if I thought I wouldn't be.
I'm only mad because I still have feelings for you.
To me, everything can be resolved.
The worst anger I've ever experienced from a person,
diminishes and means as little as it needs to.
The shit that burns off of comets.
To me everything can be resolved.
And you didn't even try.

@abigfuckingbully

@abigfuckingbully

I CAN LOVE ANYONE

I was staying with J in New York City.
She was the first and only one to offer me a space in the east coast, so of course I'd take it.
We were friends peripherally in high school, to my knowledge.
Later she would come out to me as my high school stalker, having hacked my Facebook.
She was eating a burger with me when she told me, she shared a meal w/ me at her boyfriend's work, a diner. We both laughed and not nervously, totally unphased.
I arrived at the perfect time: just near J's birthday, which she was holding at U's house.
U's house was furnished in black leather, black marble, black cabinets, all black everything.
U was a 6' black kid from Ohio living as an aspiring actor in New York.
J shared this passion w/ U, I think it's how they met.
I entered this party with uncharacteristic modesty and a characteristically but slightly less overcompensatory friendliness--this probably being a Midwestern thing but I met U and his friends first, a few dyed blonde women. J had yet to come through.
I was taken aback by U's beauty immediately.

  His big beautiful eyes and thick sculpted lips were accented by his 145lb frame and shaved head. You'd have to be a complete idiot to be unable to recognize beauty in a man but this was different than the butterflies that burn into blushing cheeks. More like fireflies were happening, I was completely sober but maybe drunk on New York. J came in and sat with us for a while, U standing as a good host, offering me and everyone else wine, there was a gentleness coming from him in modest looks that I imagine filled him with the same underlying passion it filled me with, quiet excitedly, and with the love of a woman, he filled my paper cup with a little red wine, he offered beer but I asked for, I'm always asking for what's reserved for the more selective, red wine, and even though he paused before giving me a glass, which breaks the seal and invites more than the group who'd bought it, who had contributed to this purchase. (Moocher?) But I'm always the glad happy exception to the rule. While I appreciate the dyed blonde's presences as a part of the environment, mostly forgot about them and paid attention to J & U--trying to make friends with the boyfriend, a filmmaker, handsome, curly haired, but reminiscent of a meek friend from my hometown I had severed ties with, also a filmmaker, his timidity immediately had me fishing for words and feeling watered down, I complimented his boots, "Oh thanks they're a gift from J."

  "They're perfect," I said getting up to the black marble counter, to talk to U, to flirt with U, I was halfway to being drunk since I'm so lightweight, it only

140

took two beers to cheat on my last girlfriend, wines so much harder, but U's at the counter, "You think I could have some more?"

I lifted my cup. "J tells me you're an actor." U pouring me some wine, "Yeah, well, I've been in a few things but it's not like you. J tells me you've got some work published."

My glass is filled, I look down at the counter, I find a black sharpie, used to help with some decoration, among the shining, metallic, multi colored, Happy Birthday banners, the balloons strung to the ceiling. I picked it up, clicking it open and closed in one hand.

"Yeah, I'm gonna be famous." I lift his shirt, a long tunic cut black-t, a ragged collar, holes in the neck, he takes the hems and holds them, turning his neck in gentle acceptance, to the side, his toned right breast mine to sign, and in a few lines, mine, claiming nothing but the arrogant expression itself, "Holy shit," I say. U giggling. "Let me take a picture of this, one second. Hold it. Okay, fuck yeah." He dropped his shirt.

Some time passed, I forget how it happened, but the rap playing from the t.v. was perfect, me, officially wasted, everything I see is wet now, the couch next to me is filled again as a blonde sat at the end of it, then J, tall, skinny, doe-eyed, dressed in a skin tight black dress, her curls would swing gently with every turn of her head, locks gently falling while she focused on emptying a little baggy she had of it's contents onto a small pocket mirror on the coffee table. She had set the cocaine up so perfectly that for the two minutes I watched in silence, I didn't even think to notice it was cocaine she was emptying out. That this was a drug as an ex-straight edger was one of the most vacuous, addictive, annoying, and destructive--that the stigma surrounding this drug was that, in any other situation, I would be completely averse--politely hiding total disgust for it.

This time, I was watching almost happily. "It's my birthday gift from U," then she turned to me, she was so beautiful, asking me so straight with such a sincerity, the way someone offers you another plate, while also looking empty of something, her mascara done perfectly, "Do you want some?" "Okay!" was my immediate reaction. Something about her beauty. It was a birthday. I felt safe with her even in her present absence--she snorted a line---and passed whatever the fuck she used--I didn't understand it, but I could, I used it, and I snorted a line and felt, the same, I felt exactly the same, and got up for more wine.

Everyone went outside to stand and smoke cigarettes. Everybody smokes fucking cigarettes, in a circle outside with one of the blonde's motorcycles. The blonde was U's friend, saying, "I see him as more of a character than a real person. I guess that's kind of fucked up, huh?" The blonde said, then took a drag. I'd walked into something. U looked at me, sitting next to me, stepped aside, we were both on the shallow stoop of the back door, he finished his cigarette quickly, the both of us smiling unknowingly but knowingly.

It's blurry but in the quiet of the house we came back into, U leading me to his room, sitting me down, placing our cups down, quitting the formality of awkward silence before it could happen, and looking into him, and our mouths parted and I'd taste him in a slow passion, the light in our guts growing where there was even the thought of fear with a woman, it was absent, and hands grasped up each other, him unbuttoning a shirt, print floral like petals themselves fell to the floor, he stripped me of my thermal layers, since it was intolerable in the winter cold. I stripped U down to nothing, we were both naked looking at a monochrome pile of black & denim. Me with my back on the bed, U kissing me from my neck, down my chest, down my ribs, down my stomach, until, reaching his hands over me, grabbing my cock, then taking me into his mouth, and in that instant, I was taken--by my body--rejecting everything.

      My heart palpitating, my stomach and chest concave in a desperate attempt to a sucking of air frantically, breathing like I was dying, my heart--was a crushing itself--"I can't do this."
I was getting what felt like the best blowjob I've ever gotten but was a complete panic attack simultaneously. I pushed U off of me, I roll onto the floor off my side of the bed. "I think I'm going to throw up." Panting. "Don't throw up. One second." U ran out of the bedroom, in something he threw on, there was silence for me to be convinced of the thing that everyone is so convinced of when they're about to/throwing up: that I'm going to die, I'm going to die, I'm going to die.

      He came back into the room with a pyrex bucket. Which I calmed myself in front of panting nude, while U pat my back and was mildly supportive but largely disconnected from my panic attack. He was concerned but I suspect with a harping tinge in his voice, annoyed, maybe resentment without anger, it skipped a step, being too understanding, I imagine he'd had worse experiences with other predominantly straight men experimenting with gay sex. For me it wasn't the liberal minded conquest urge disguised as openness to experience, I was following something instinctive. It should have been working.
"I don't know why. I used to be really Christian."
I looked straight up into his face.
Him now clothed in something I didn't see him put on, me on the floor wrapped around a bucket.
"Is it like...did it feel good?"
I got up having put nothing in the bucket.
I drew out my thermal underwear, merino wool long johns from the pile.
Shocked again by my body, leaned over the bucket having successfully pulled on my underwear.
But now a sudden pang from the center of my stomach, where the light used to be, now an expulsion or explosion of pins and slow throbbing poison. My torso a plank. Me apologizing with no apology while a small jet of bile drained out of me and oozed in the the outer rim bubbling ring shimmering in the edge of the bucket. U left the room again, to maybe attend the party...there's an entire party going on, people talking, about all of the beautiful useless things that are okay to talk about at a party, all of the things that make people pretty to you happen in moments modesty happens behind a red paper cup, some blushing sense in shamelessness of the vacuity that comes in propriety. I missed U. I missed J. I missed the dyed blondes.

I put on all of my clothes again thinking I'd be fine. I have amazing memory. It takes all of my obvious social offenses and allows me to present them to myself and others as if they've never happened only because of a close to psychotic confidence (w/ only a shadow of shame enough to be shameless) and invokes, even in strangers, a new love for me, a band mentality that allows people to ascribe to me like one would a member of their family but completely lacking the patronizing element of forgiveness all together.

There's so much shame in being forgiven. So much anger in being the one to forgive.

I walked back out with all of my clothes on. Buttoned to the throat, all dark denims and midnight blacks. My roses hiding underneath. I sat on the couch, perfectly set in front of the front door, where L, J's roommate would come in, along with another woman, and as a throwback played sit herself next to me, for some strange reason the entire room was empty again, except me, and L. The woman who, in the first week of arriving, I had fucked, passionately, and was starting to fall in love with but I'm not allowed to say it yet, or now either, I guess.

■

A STORY ABOUT L

I posted a Facebook status: plans on moving to New York in hellish month of December, if anyone has a place for me to stay, please, let me know.

Quickly, a comment from J an old highschool friend, or peripherally. I was surprised she even received it but my brother passed it on, always rooting for me for my success.

I had only saved $3,000 from 3 months of work but no one had to know that. I had no contact with J since a night in high school, all of us stoned would watch her crash and burn in front of one of my best friend D's house, we were all parting after getting completely fucked on pot, which is how I put it since I never really smoke, "getting really high," the conversation is like most of my memory, completely blurry, but we are/D is with us and we're all leaving but I think J, now making it painfully obvious that she wants to make it with D, the crush idiotically revealed in an amazing and brave attempt to invite herself into D's house, "maybe we could go inside and see what happens." --To see what happens? Nothing happened. We all stood there until we had-to-had-to leave. This is the last and most brutal memory I have of this woman, acquaintance, friend. Friend in a way. Friend in the biggest way because she was the only one who believed in my dream in New York.

@abigfuckingbully

Lucky it's not in my nature to be even remotely judgmental I could/I do know I've seen worse in people and watched horribles displays of affection, needs for attention, violent outbursts, tears, quiet couples fights without mediating. I love people too much to imagine they have any fucking idea they know better.

Here's J commenting: I'm in Brooklyn. If you need a couple weeks, stay with me.

Thank God for J.
Without her I would have been completely fucked and alone.
I am a child, oblivious to most of life's reality.
The exact same mind/tool that means success in my realm is the exact mind/tool that sabotages me often. New York City...to me as easy as a duffel bag. We arranged it all in PMs and text.

■

I entered the apartment with no expectation. Everything looked like shit to me on this block, disheveled. The building next door was gutted, looked as if it was puking up it's decrepit insides, bricks, copper wire, garbage, metal framing all into the caged off section for the apartments garbage. This was an afterthought.

I walked with two bags total, an enormous duffel bag I was now slinging on one shoulder and a bicyclists bag, filled to the brim with clothes and my sleeping bag, being unassuming about where I was welcome but not out of a conscious precognitive ability, like a kid at a sleepover.
I had a key, slid under a dirtied welcome mat, and inserted now on pushing into the heavy grey metal like a tomb or bank vault, opening and making eye contact with, any host nowhere to be seen, a thick woman leisurely dressed in tights and a tank--buxom and suntanned, a woman whose body spoke to me instantly of love and nurturance. It was like impact, eyes met and both of us were seized still blushing and catching our breath. She was at her laptop on her crossed legs, put her hand to her breast, "you startled me." She laughed. I smiled quietly, modestly said, "oh sorry."
"J said you were coming, I just--she's not here right now," I felt a lump in my throat.
"I'm Atticus."
   I dropped my things at the end of what would have been a coffee table but was now the frame of a coffee table with a blanket strewn over the top. I sat for a moment. I could hardly sit as close to her as I was. The lump in my throat could only be eased by looking all the way up to the ceiling and sealing my lips a little tighter, without swallowing. I was all heat but a slow warm kind, love you could tell was mutual. What would have been sexual tension was an absolute lack of--the sexual attraction was so strong, it was as if two bodies had agreed without discussing it with their brains first they were going to fuck each others

brains out. Gravity. This kind of chemistry only possible as an indication: precursor to true love. I was consumed by the feelings and our smiles knew we would try for the sake of a feigned modesty and came bubbling to their surface, with twice their strength.

I peeled off my coat and tried not to obviously survey her body which is exactly what my body wanted to do over and over again on infinite repeat. "What are you working on?"

"Well I'm working on some interviews and a photo spread I did for this magazine me and my sister work on."

"Oh yeah? What's it called?"

"We called it _____. We're the _____ sisters--so...I hear you're a writer?"

"Yeah, I'm a poet so far."

There was silence for a long time.

I got up to put my stuff away,

"J's room is the one with the door open." I carried everything in. Threw it on the floor in front of a loose full length body mirror, I surveyed the room--behind me the tye dye sheet compensating as a curtain on the window. Some original silkscreen artwork tucked behind the end of the bed I was sitting at. To my left a table cloth, a cloth prayer flag, laid out, sculpture the virgin mary, and then a rose composed entirely of beads, immaculate and sacred. A cross from the table in the corner the signature corner display of photos and kitsch. However this corner was filled with crystals, a metallic tin, some plants trapped in glass. I took the room in and sat. The door still slightly open.

How was I going to use the same room as this woman. How was I going to use the same house.

I thought I should get straight to the search for apartments and work so I took out an ipad--a choice to be productive but not rude, open enough to talking but also, still not completely dependent on conversation.

    I shyly left J's room and sat on the couch again next to L.

I sat for maybe a minute before realizing how impossible it was to be in the same room as this woman and not be touching her. I tried tucking my hands under my legs.

I rocked back and forth then silently returned to J's room until a night planned with J would turn.

■

I wore what I was always wearing in New York.

I had packed obscenely light,

Had only three out fits and would wear skin tight jeans with a long floral button up--a reddish purple covered in large print roses, three shades, three layers, and a pair of Heschung boots retailing for $800, 'purchased,' for $0.

Before meeting up with L at Baby's All Right, J and I would grab dinner at a carnival themed diner her boyfriend managed. Eating fries in an excess of ketchup I'd catch up with J who was always an actress since I could remember, and making good money as a bartender in-between.
We caught up--incredibly fucked and brief description of what I'd been doing since last I'd seen her in high school, which would be summarized by periods spent with each of my exes, the only way I can really remember it, the only way I can imagine spending it, completely consumed by the love of another person, living in between time spent without one sincere mind who knows you more, you give them more for them to know you more, "than anyone else," maybe I should have gone to college for more than a year. But then I wouldn't have met no one--that had shaped my life. That would have loved me in that unchangeable way, love really is forever, once and you've changed. But also that if I saw anyone of them again, I would still feel the same way as when I loved them--I can't hate anyone, that I have a right to--they have every right to (almost) but that's another story--I told her as she told me hers.
It seemed to me like her room.
Strong and sad and secret.
She opens up too fast like I do.
It's our nature and everyone I've ever known knew & loved, it, before they ever even met me, honestly, it's my role in their life, to be that honest and loving, where people distrust big mouths they suddenly find absolution & a foundation, I mean I burnt the bridges, but she tells me "I used to stalk you in high school. Me and S hacked your Facebook."
I should have been offended.
Aware or afraid maybe but I was unphased.
It was like hearing a dirty joke from a drunk you're lush with, but she was sober--funnier than the joke but I couldn't help but laugh with her.
Forgiveness is fucked up.
Places my needs over yours.
Who am I to be a man with the thought "who am I to judge?"
Someone else would tattoo it on their skin but all my love brands myself into the instants.
We finished our meals and stuffed ourselves into our jackets & pockets. Leaning forward together on a long crooked walk past straight lurid buildings, that I felt had a life that wanted to be crooked with us. However, J's presence was straight somehow. Regardless of our criminal postures. My brother once told me that I have a terrifying gait. I looked always as if I was determined to find someone, specifically to beat. I never took myself that way, starved skinny at 145 lbs. And 6', in New York--but probably true. I can like that about myself now.

We ended up at Baby's All Right.
I forget who was playing, a band with a play on words for a name.
That kind of music.

This is where my judgement lies, but then soon ebbs, I remember 'people,' and then like a good Bodhisattva, remember that a person isn't their thoughts, or their words, or their deeds, as much as they are. They aren't this music if they like it and they aren't this band they're friends with.

At first, no conversation.
As a welcome, L, her body warming me just by sight, buying me liquor, liquor warming me like a slow kiss, a little syrupy, she wanted to buy me something mixed, and I leaned, and she leaned, all her strong body over the bar, how shouts are like whispers.
I stood, cramped. I always loved the ramp down into the pit, was crowded by couples, clinging to the wall, shoulders hunched, leaning back, everyone a hand on their drink.
Me trying to be polite, to drink slow instead of how I usually drink, swallows.
We watched awkwardly.
Me next to L, feeling her honest desire to move in the entire time.
I am an idiot with women.
Autistic in my inability to read interest.
But this was obvious in a flattering way.
Though I resisted it strongly, it was only the bastard of modesty, how I hate it--to be on the end of propriety that turns nicety into a nice weapon, accidentally but fully, to the hilt.

J I couldn't read. She seemed to be panicked almost, her body all the time, like giving of an imperceptible shiver, it's checking the door every five seconds, it wants to be with someone else, maybe she checked her phone to see if she could hear/had heard from her boyfriend who couldn't make it.

But the set ends.
L shifts her weight in front of me from hip to hip.
Then walks me to the bar, behind the crowd, luckily not buying any drinks.
I'd never been with a southern girl before. She was from Georgia she was telling me.

We stood at the bar. She wanted to buy me another drink, I hadn't finished, and J was already asking me what we're doing next, if we want to stay or if we want to go to another bar or...being lightweight everything already seems so fast paced, she touched my arm. She had curly blonde-brown hair cut into a boy's haircut with all the locks on top and the sides cropped. It was dyed blonde. She touched my arm. She looked up at me, she looked at me as if I had a newness, the same newness New York had to me, it'd be a long time since I could see, since I could feel someone wanted me. WIth everyone else--I was so heavy to them, welcome but with a bit of tolerance. I was always the one touching their arm. Maybe how everyone else was to me. But with L, I could let her in. I could be hurt by her even, over and over again, from the start.

I was given the room to be smart in all the room she gave me to be stupid. Big male-ditz.
Existential airhead.

Her eyes were open--and alive--and giving me air--her eyes were still and strong and gave me away, I was all hers, and all she had to do now was touch my arm. I was her property. Men are glad to be property often, they wouldn't tell you that--but even if it's not in a woman's nature to be possessive, a man will settle for being a possession. J suggested, at the sound of my straw sucking wet air from my glass, _____ bar, and L finished her drink.
Then outside for a cigarette.

I never understood how anyone could wear just one jacket in winter, that she kept open, with a shirt that low cut, her presence, her dominance in every inhale, a cocky exhale, and legs to kick and stretch, displays, a demonstration...
She didn't bother buttoning it up--she bounced.
J smoked with her.
Cabs flew past the wet iced sidewalks, stopping like wreckage to pick up drunk couples.
The canopies would blow in little winds we'd eventually all, like our own pack, a band of three ragged, happy, and stupidly warm, glowing.

We made it to the next bar.
They found a seat.

I bought my own drink and staggered in after them. J was telling a story about her boyfriend, later I'd found out this is common, which would make my distraction, sitting next to L all the more crushing for J. She fell over me, L, and she was laughing, holding all of me. Everything in me wanted to return the gift but still, I shrank, men will do this, and J shrank, and slowed, and drank quieter, in a more punctuated way, she could hardly stand the sight of us. I was wasted, she was fuming, she looked sideways and kept showing her neck, while finally, I fell forward into L's breasts while she was holding me, laughing over me, I started laughing into her neck, and then kissing it, and she moved my mouth up to her lips and J watched and I could hear her saying nothing, going red, thinking, "I wouldn't stop my friend," but feeling something like a hyperlite rage, a vapor of reasonable hatred towards the tactlessness of us both. She excused herself, sliding an empty crystal shaped glass at the center of the table, we stopped, I stopped us and she said, flatly, sincerely, free of hate in her voice, "I'm going to Jesse's. You two have a goodnight."
I looked at L who got up and saw my straight face as a cue to hug her goodnight, and it was L then it was me, then it was just us. And the corner of my eye walked out J sliding, almost as if she'd lost. Conversation was useless. Just kept necking in public. We would have fucked in that bar but anecdotes about Angel Olsen were happening in the booth next to us and I was reminded that people are more real than my fantasies would have them, that I'm not to be witnessed the way I am to be dreamt, not all the time anyways. That it was wrong for some reason.

We collected ourselves and took a train, where we wrapped each other and stopped and stopped kissing, we were in a new public again. She shook in the light of the subway she never took, she always rides her bike, she hates the tubes, lost in the tubes, stumble out, onto the L, she starts shit talking a stranger but to me. I can't do it, I have to speak up, "Don't involve me in those thoughts, not here, out loud. Who the fuck cares?" Then awkward silence. She hates it. Stumble out of the L and for some reason straighten out for 10 blocks back to her place, which was temporarily our place, a binding intimacy before one could be there. Up the stairs. Through the apartment door. Shedding extra layers in the darkened apartment, on the couch. Then through her door, a bed filled most of the room. A single splintering piece of wood painted in two different pastels for a headboard. An enormous billowing comforter, a quilt underneath. We started, me sitting at the edge of her bed, her standing, me slow, her lips like a cat's, the edges of her top lip slightly above her bottom lips, her body with the strength of a lion, her hands on my cheeks, her tongue moving in waves, she pushed me down, I peeled away my clothes, slowly, piece by piece, we twisted, her below me now, our bodies too hot to even feel the winter's piercing cold against us, she fell light, and splayed, her body took mine, and deeper the bond, and the heavier our bodies, and the deeper the love, I wondered if it was going to lie to me. But it only told the truth because we both came, and fell asleep in love with the...we felt the warmth in every stroke of the other, we fell against each other, holding the other thinking of the permanence of the newness of the other. Passed out happy to be strangers who didn't want to be strangers anymore.

From that night on we'd spend every chance we could together. Though sometimes in my struggle to assert my new being in New York, I would feel suffocated by her uncharacteristically cold emotional vacancy. In times of need I would be met with a much colder woman. But days spent with the lioness, exploring the city, nights exploring each other were a saving grace.

After two weeks I'd found work and a sublet (for now) and would move out. But I was still living off of nothing, starving in winter, I'd spent most mornings meditating, partly out of routine, I'd been doing 40 minutes a day everyday for two years, and because I'd heard monks who meditated well enough could live off of 1000 calorie diets. I was always hungry and tired, walking heinous distances, but L, who worked at two different restaurants would be glad to invite me to eat a warm meal at the counter of her work, a rustic looking, western themed cafe. A horseshoe on the sign. Prepared by her hands. Instead of the usual method of one meal of eggs and rice at home or alternatively calling Manny's, a white run cafe and product of gentrification in Bed Stuy for that day's unsold pastries, donuts, scones, muffins, I would walk blocks late at night to heard and eat diabetic for the next few days.

Once practiced meditative walking, where, I decided to completely still my body until urged to move, with a totally still mind commanded to take a train to Bedford, not completely unfamiliar with the area but too unaware, where I would follow based off of my guts and legs a thread to a gross alleyway, grey and rotting to tetanus infested, but a small unlocked door would reveal, the sign above reads, "BAKERY." I went up two flights of iron stairs, found the door by warmth and scent, I arrived in a hallway filled with fluorescent light displaying racks upon racks of pastries, I stood at it's entrance, and I imagined stealing, but felt it defeated the spiritual good of the current practice, the most I could be given by nature were disposed of day olds, I trotted back out and into biting winter, where, next to an unlocked dumpster laid an enormous black trash bag, where upon feeling away the leaves of it's lips revealed...50lbs or more of pastries. I filled my pockets after eating two or three standing in front of it and walked around Bedford eating and walking like a vagabond. But I couldn't rely on this all the time. L was almost always feeding me, her big cheeks rosey behind a counter glad to see me eating. A woman who feeds you really loves you. You have to remember her sanctity from then on.

■

I CAN LOVE ANYONE .2

L entered the door, and in my drunken blur we had a conversation.
I think I told her, "I did some coke..." she was only there for a moment to come and wish J a Happy Birthday and then leave. I failed to bring up U wondering if it would upset her, if I'd done something wrong. The seat was full then it was empty. Then my stomach was crying again. I rushed to the bathroom. Sweating, convinced I was going to die, and vomited, everywhere, on myself included, everywhere but in the porcelain. Until I found it. Head down, grappling to find it. Now soiled, soaked in my own vomit, time passed, me just hanging onto the toilet going limp, my clothes soaked in vomit. The door opened politely, just a slit with J's face peeking in, looking down on me, then opened wide, there was no segue, she looked in at me, tall in her parka, "I'm leaving," she said, I looked up, and stood up, and stared at her for a moment coming in for a hug, then realizing my error, she was too clean, she stood still, no reaction, then commanded by my stomach back down on my knees like a fawn, to yak for a moment, both of us still. I turn my head to her, eyes blank and tell her, somehow without shame, "You're so handsome J."
"Okay."
She closes the door quickly to leave.

U comes in and says, "Oh my God, you have to clean this up tomorrow."
Then felt too hard on me and asked if I wanted to take a bath.
I nodded.
He helped strip my clothes away, "I'll wash these for you."
As usual taken into the arms of someone who cares so deeply.

In life I am lucky that I've been in such dangerous situations, making dangerous decisions, like that acid fast at 19, the anger that would be justified, I was always in the presence of someone who would take care. "Do you think you'd be better with a bath?" U asks."Yes," I answered, and he instructed me on how to work his tub, which way to turn the knobs, how to turn it off, I was warm and in a womb again. I calmed down slowly, all of the water surrounding me, lulling me to sleep, wading, my body slightly suspended, U came in, while I was sedated with a towel and clothes to borrow for bed. I drained the tub and dressed. But then I started panicking again. U offered me another bath. I was calm. U came in naked, me assuming that the rest of the party had left and ended. U standing tall above me while I was in the tub, I look to my right, to U, stroking his dick, asks, "Do you think we could still?" I stared and him and him stroking his cock, and said, for a minute before saying, "No."
"Sorry, I thought maybe we could."
He left back to his bed.
I was bobbing in his tub. I stared at the ceiling feeling wrecked by my recklessness, a little bit of shame and anger surfacing as I drained the tub--dried myself, put on a pair of black sweats and oversized t-shirt and walked through the living room, quiet enough now to hear my steps, and into U's bed where he laid. I laid next to him and he put an arm around me. We gently kissed before I passed out, me feeling like a complete fraud, unsure of myself and my reaction.

     Was I shocked because I had satisfied a long and deeply repressed desire or was I shocked because of what I thought I wanted, I didn't want, terror could mean anything. Maybe it was just the coke. I fell asleep in a man's arms, easy as with any woman.

     When I woke up, I suddenly felt the arm around me as foreign and I recoiled, or everything inside of me wanted to escape. Feeling unjustified in my disgust, seemingly going through with a decision I'd made last night. I would lay in bed feeling all of my resistance to him become obvious.

U would run out to the corner deli to bring me back a sandwich on a tinfoil plate, I would it eat sloppy and exhausted. He would wash and dry all my clothes, which would never fully get the smell of vomit out of them. Though part of me still held the light in my belly for him, the rest of me couldn't stay. He finished a tall can from last night in the morning, naked next to me, told me about his family in Ohio, a framed photo of his mother on a messy desk, everything towering and collapsing over itself.

In the morning I got up and cleaned the toilet as well as the rest of the apartment, covered in confetti.

"Do you sweep like a black person?" I swept. "Yeah you sweep like a black person."

With the strange winter grey creeping in through the window telling me enough time had passed, and in me everything telling me to run. He walked me to the door, and gave me a goodbye kiss which was a lie on my part.

LIBERTY ZOO

Dey don't like my name being called.
I kan tell they resent the way they're so clear when dey say it and how it so hard to watch my body struggle with the roll call.
I look left n right but my tongue waggles, like it's always out nd goes sweeping left n right.
Dey call my name before dey reach into the cage, with the electric spike, da stick, it's a stick, nd they press and it clicks and hisses, zapping, right when they unlock the cage, and I don't know why but my body, it limps and wiggles like my tongue, now it takes forever for me to understand, my body is stupid like me--they laugh, dey laugh at me.
Ow. Ouch.
The rings around my neck, dey rattle and choke me, I'm hungry.
I'm sbpossed to be eating, but they won't just feed me. Not until I do a tribck for dem.
No bell, I never know.
They just want me out da cage.
So I go--but I can't help growling.
My growls sound deeper because I can't control myself so well all the time.
I'm like the other ones, or I look like them lined up but they don't growl for some reason.
I can't help that I want to cry but when I whanna cry, I wanda kill dem. I hate them. Everyday I wake up and think that people who don't pay for things, people that think that they're good because they think they that work is good. Dey work hard on me. I sumtimes think the hardest because I'm re-tarded and easy to hate. I know I am re-tarded, Syrus told me. It's sad but I'm not sab about it. I'm happy most of the time. They tink beating me will change what I feel but I think they are unhappy. They couldn't get Brother to stop running but it either dem or him, and they thought--I mean I dunno why dey keep us. It make me wanna cry but Brother was loud and rowdy once. They shot him once, he went down, den they came close, and he took a whole eye out with his claw, now we watch them, one of dem watch us with one eye. I started purring when I heard the sound. I never laugh like a human or a monkey laugh, but I know why dey do it, they scared, but something make dem do a opposite and make that screeching noise. I make that noise with dem when I purr. Blood everywhere and I circle in the bars. The cage, they call it a cage, I don't fit in mine. I'm two times da size of da other ones, my Brothers, all of dem are healthy...blood everywhere, and everyone saw da beady eyed human, except one yee now--two of us got up and leaned into the cage walls, the bars, and growling with the humans are gone. I

was happy in a sad way, like I knew I could do better. They didn kill him tho. Dey didn't want to yet. I hear when dey get skinned and it's sad when brothers leave but dey need us. Dey use us for something. It was all in my fur, the blood was, and I purred.

But I'm awake again. All dey nothing and then da hissing. They make noises at me barking like chimps but it's hard for me to put together. I'm supposed to watch the others--they do what the other does, but I still don't know which part I'm supposed to do, it hits me before I even moved and everything clenches into that one spot, one eye open, one eye closed, we all line up and small one eyed man nails the end of my rope into the dirty ground. The center of a circle with bars again, outside think wood trees, like little flutes, with rips green leaves that tickle my ass or nose depending somethings, the light and darks are pretty and we are always safe and warm under the trees. Food is raw meat in a tin bowl, big enough to feed us all, sometimes pieces, sometimes animals in whole. No one is patient. The chains are all the same length regardless of how big we are, I choke myself eating. They don't care, everyone lines up, gets the same nail, like how I scratch at dirt in my cage at night. Today at the bowl all of my Brothers were talking.

■

"There's not enough for us here," he said while tearing apart the pinkened flesh of something he didn't even bother to identify.
"There's never enough. Certainly not this time."
"I'll take his other eye, I swear."
"They took Atlas. I could hear him, the way the hair tore separating from his skin."
"I thought they'd sent him to the circus."
"This is the circus. Welcome to the circus, Syrus."
"We shuld leave."
The brothers looked ad me.
"He's an imbecile."
"No he's not an imbecile, he's retarded."
"No he's not retarded you are if you think they're not gonna take you like they did Atlas and skin you if you so much as growl at them and you're thinking about taking out another goddamned eye."
"It was nice tho."
"They all hab to get in through the barth over therth." My tongue wouldn't go upp.
The brothers all looked at how often the stout man left the cages open to talk to other men. Often thin gapped tooth men with stubble or tall thin women who talked above him in stern tones. Who was above who was unclear.
"What do we do about the spikes, huh?"
"No probblem." I said and leapt up to my hind legs. The spike ripped out.
 I sat back down, my hind legs pushed it back in.

@abigfuckingbully

"Hey, mong's got a point."
"Forget it dude, not on your life."

■

"Are these trained tigers?" A pale Asian woman asked leaning into the cage, watching them eat, all of them somehow with their heads just lower than their shoulders.Two of them White Tigers. One obviously deformed. "What's wrong with that one?:

■

I saw dem looking at me. Brothers weren't listening to Samson.
"He's...defective."
My mouth wouldn't close, my tongue kept wagging and flipping with every bite.
"Complete mental defect."
"Interesting...can it be trained?"
I hearb the bars open and close.
Jangling, then the stick charge.
Dey kept saying my name Dumbo, but Brothers call me Samson.
"Dumbo!" Dey whistled. I growled at dem. Da woman was in the cageth now. I knew what was gonna happened. Dey wanted to see me play.
"Wanna play, Dumbo?" they laughed.
Another man came in, he hath a long rope with glass under the insides. He cracked a noise with it. Brothers moved to let me move. I wanted to kill him while I wath watching him pull up da spike. He pullth the spike up den puts a crate in the center. The man with the rope cracks it. I know what I supposedth da do but I hate it. I growled. He didn even bother w/ the whip, the other man, da one eyed man stabbed me ,deep, with the cattle prod. Everything burns and my vision blurrs and I growl again. I can't tell if he wants me to do it or not, the trick, the trick, but I know if I don't...either way. I leap on all fours on to the crate in front of my laughing brothers. "Want to play Samson? Do your trick, Samson." I leap into position, I stand on my hind legs while the one eyed man dangles da food, cut just right, he never gives it to me but I'm not sure dat's the point, da point is to be watched, for them to feel happy. It's funny that sumthingg so horrible to another living thing can be so fun for another other person, they all laugh at me. I roar right at da top of the trick--big and loud, I want to cry but I would neber chow them that--roaring keeps it away. The woman claps like a oyster and makes a high pitched happy sound over the claps, so stupid and sad, it's like a whining, it drains out like blood, all over everything, and I watch her lean over herself when I land he pulls the steak away and the one eyed man, he looks at the woman and they both imagine themselves to be enjoying me even tho I can't tell if anyone who hurts anyone this much is actually happy. But they always talking, like it very important. Okay.

"Nice, Samson, they love you."

  I walked with the chain rattling behind me to the one eyed man, who gave me da steak, and then run his hands under the metal rope, and I am perfect in his eyes taht I don't rip apart his hands is something he's oblivious too, I am too well behaved for him and I eat it, it's depressing, a down feeling, in my stomach, it's ashamed, I want to hurt him but I just eat what he give me, I hate him but myself too. I look down and try to get my mouth to move the right way while I mouth da steak he gave me. Then I watch as he pounds the nail through the loop end of my choke chain and then Syrus looks to me.

"You did it perfect, look how happy she is, she might take you away tonight."

  The woman stayed and looked at my brothers.
  "They're beautiful." She said, "how much for the healthy ones? Are they trained too?"

The man with one eye opened the cage again, rolling a tire, with a cattle prod in his hand and walked to Syrus. The tire was in the center now, wobbling. It hit the crate and stopped. A healthy White Tiger, and pulled up on his spike. The chain loosened in the back, slackened and then tightened again, just under the collar, Syrus neck tightened. He purred for a short second as a wink to the others. All healthy except for Samson. They would have whistled if they knew how but instead watched the crate was dragged through the mud again to recenter it, just outside the circle of feeding tigers. You'd think they'd be smarter than to bother an animal while it feeds but these animals were now totally compliant, beyond terrified and back under the sedative of fatigue. Fear of a captor they only vaguely understood--intuitively even the feral things will rub against their cages and be filled with sensations or visions of absolute revolt. This is nature. Some of it the most base and darkest desires, combinations of instinct which is blind but sees clearly, like bats, and intuition which screams and only asks politely to be seen.
  There was a whip brought in by a more sadistic and even less popular human. The one eyed man was more human in his vulnerability, his failures as an invincible captor actually drew him in closer as imbecilic. The man with the whip now however was all business. Nothing laughable. Just a pure sociopathic indulgence in the impersonal business of beating, feeding, taming, and maiming the appropriate animal in the appropriate manner at the appropriate time, there's nothing entertaining about his impervious weakness as unbridled authoritarian. You feel you can't kill him and that's not funny at all, it only reminds you of the desire to be free and that killing him in this case is a justified but fatal mistake, a huge waste of time and effort, and embarrassing vulnerability. For some reason, glass in the cracked whip, tucked under the throbbing and loveless bound and pound leather becomes a greater more

personal fear, the greater failures, as if you were even responsible for them in any way in your control, anyway--the idiot with one eye dragged Syrus by the collar to the crate which was part wood and part metal, hollow, and barely could hold Samson, that was the miracle. The brothers all stopped eating to watch.
"Look at him. Bout to eat some glass."
"Doubt it, they already seem proud of him."
Samson said nothing.
The man with a whip was rolling in the tire, his back idiotically, all too comfortably, placed to the animals and then held it awkwardly, pushing it while waddling next to a Tiger he was only a foot shorter than at full length. The idiots got two eyes set wide apart, kind of perfectly placed though to create a freakish stupidity to his all-too-aware mind and body.
Again, the desire for him to be stupider than he was. His forearms were enormous and with every movement revealing every muscle in his forearm. So the asshole rolls up a time chewed tractor tire, useless in a jungle, almost even instinctually to these otherwise free beasts and then plants it there. The inner rim ragged for some reason. Maybe from removal of whatever enormous machine it's supposed to be a part of. Then backs up. And Syrus knows what he's supposed to do. At the first finger pointed into the dirt, paired w/ the shouting, Syrus, like Samson, rises at his pique, roars, at his pique, and then at the crack of the qhipe, roars before leaping onto the tire and rolling at full speed back and then forward, limbs in a perfect rolling pace, his shoulders, four rolling, more like a caterpillar than a cat.
He leapt back onto the crate at the crack of a whip, then readjusted in a graceful spin, his Tiger tail tightly wrapping and curling behind him like smoke or a kites ribbon and ends in a roar but this time weakening, tapering into a resentful hiss, like a domestic cat, which ignoring having his balls, was the case. This wild thing was now an enormous domestic cat.

He was fed. They lifted a steak smiling and lobbed it flatly into dirt where Syrus sadly landed. Soft and malevolent like the tension you feel when you stare too long at a stranger, like in a bad way that becomes low-grade, pathetic. He ate it quickly in three gulps, two other Tigers tried lunging for his steak, hissing he combat both of them. The man with the whip pointed at Syrus to remind the one eyed man why he was one eyed--that he forgot to nail in the spike during a feeding, after a viewing, and how important it is to both his life and to remaining authority over the domains of these beasts, the cages. So he suddenly, red faced, falling back out of the moments he's spent blown away, every time, by the trick,like some sociopathic child, kind of smiles while putting Syrus's spike back in, like it's anything other than formality anyways, too many other oppressive links in the chain for it to matter. Eventually they both leave. The asian woman from outside the cage looked intently at both Samson and Syrus, nodded, and said, "ah." Then smiled.

■

Dey finally lefth. The day wath goob. Or it wath normal, it wath what it was everyday. Feeding. My brotherth neber listen to me. But still, I think of whath outside the cageth. Every day I wake up, cold, against the cageth. The dirt is warm. I cry at the timesth I notice the dirt. The treeth second. I get so hungry. I just let time path by pacing the outside of the cageth. It's metal reminds me of everything else outside. AllI want is to understand why every day is pained. I don't get it. Everything is hard. I get cold at night--feel good though. I like to be me more than do or be anything specific. I wonder where I come from sometimes.

■

I fell athleep quickly.

■

At the moment of birth he felt a large wet tongue on him. He was filled with a glowing warmth, of someone he understood to be his mother, thought only in dreams does he understand her function and role.

■

It was cold when I woke up. I had a vision of a girl bigger than me. She didn't have a noith or a name to her but I knew she was made for me and I was made for her becauth I was made from her. It was black like light but with nothing in the night--just darkness. But she was bigger than me, worlds bigger, and I was from her. She was licking me and I was purring, and I was from her, she was good and she was glowing. It was good. I don't know very much but I know bad and I know good.

■

The next day I was awake, I felt happy and safe with the dream. It made me beliebe there was someone made to take care of me, like, take care of me. Different than the way the people take care of me. The brotherth told me that they're called people. The knew them all even when they were in the wild. Fucking everything up, like Syrus says. They used to go into the homes of the wild animals. I only ever saw this place tho, but he said packs of tiny little humans, not the only ones he ever saw were bad humans, but he saw them in packs, getting together wit machines, they used to run like us but on weels, "driving" in, then see the wild ones like us brothers sayth and capture us. But they have these machines, they call them guns, and they pack them filled with, like, water, like, Brother calls them drugs and that's how they win...they put us in cages after they pump us full of drugs from the gunshots, and then they dragged them onto da cars and they remember just going black, black like my dream black, and nothing but the sound of their own breath, or the blood in dere ears--and den the lifght, their ears had holes in them, then plastic, in dere ears, plastic around their paws. They were bound so tight they couldn't help but bleed and scratch and cry.

    Der paws bleed while the trucks rattle and then, they would throw them out of the locked cages, like "fish," Syrus said, with one man at their head, one man at their tail, both men at their paws, yanking them but they were all tired, too "fucked upp" to do anything, and that's how they ended up here, and some of them even had parenth. A "momma" and a "papa," like in my dream. My dream makesth me think I might have a momma. I only eber remember here…Syrus lookth at me and tellth me to stop pathingg in the cage. "Hey! Stop pacingg in da cage." If I had a momma I would be more like Syrus I think. He is strong, his body moves quickly and even tho heth always annoyed--he wants to take care of uth. He is the biggeth healthiest, but heth usually…not sad but tired. He never moveth unless he has to. You can that being here, the way it ith--I mean I have seen also in my dreamth places, other places…none of us got the feelings we imagined we would have, I don't see outside the bars, but my body lights up, and starts to burn when I see it, and I want to jump out. I remember I seen mythelf killing the small things that run into the cageth…it feelth wrong, the cageth. All day nothing and then you hear before they hanged him up, they wrestled him.

    He ate becausse they feed him first and he was lazy after, he knew--a man came in and talked to the idiots, Syrus calls them the idiots, and no one took him…ith funny, the day before he wath let out of the cageth, just outside the cageth is another cages, and Tigresses live, and Syrus says they let them fuck a girl Tiger. Sounds like dying. I'm the only one who runs to da end of the cages when I hear dem, fuckking, Syrus calls it fucking, "I fucked her hard," but the sad thing is Syrus not related but Sisters of the one they took, Beowulf they call him, he was never nice to me. He used to call me retarded over and over again. Like I didn't know I'm re-tarded. But they would take him to the other cage--and he would fuck, but thing is, he has a momma here too, and so, he hath a sibster, a subling, and they don't choose, he has to, he fucks or they don't let him out. They feed him but…

    I don't understand it--but his sibster is the one they make him fuck, and he goes until he finishes once he starts, he says, it doesn't make sense to him even, he gets in there and then he screams a moan closer to a roar, then he collapses from leaning on her, and then once he catches his breath, he just hisseth ober and over again--and then they drag him back in, but he told me, I heard him crying, he told me, when we're eating, he didn't even look at me, that's how I knew--it was his sibster though, he had to make a white one like me, a white one, I'm da only other white one besidesth Syrus. Everyone wonders and then laughs, calls me retarded.

    He looked down at his meat, and he wouldn't talk, until right at the end of the meal, when one by one they took us by the collars, the chains, and dey just put us in the cages again, each one across the other, his shoulders were high, his head was low, wobbly left and right, like my tongue ith sometimes, his whole head, and his tail limp and down, turns over his shoulder at his turn and sayth, "she's my sister." Then he growled and tried biting the hand of the man and they just stuck him over and over with a metal stick with a hook over the end, and he bled in the cage, then he turned to me in his cage, my cageth next to his cage--and he roared "MONG!" at me over and over like the machines da idiots drove. He wouldn't leave me alone or shut up. Da idiots would come over and stick him to shut up--and he would and then, he would walk over to my side and roarr dat I'ma mong, over and over. "IT'S GONNA BE A....MONG! A MONG! A mong!." Then they'd stick him till he bleeds, and he'd stop and then he'd scream. Dey used an iron with a hook at the end. Talon of a bird--shaped. He went quiet. I cried, I couldn't help it. He screamed into the dirt--for me to shutup. Into his paws one next to the other over his nose.

    Later the woman, a woman, a human, she came in and talked to the idiots. After a few days--nothing happening, and the woman, a woman, a human, she came in and talked to the idiots. Aftera few days--nothing happening, and the woman, the human, dinnent eben come back. Den one day, it was obvious to him--we had all just eatden, the fed him extra, more den the resth of us, but they took out all of the spikes in da way they usthually do. I watched with all of my focus. When they got to Beowulf, he turned quickly to the hand at his thpike, and he tried biting him. The idiot didn't do anything to him. He reached again for the spikeshand den he let him loosth. But they took him by da collar after, the leash, and as he started tugging him to da door, da cage all of us wish we could see out of more--he pulled back, using all histh strengtt. All four legs, pulling back, I didn't know why, but he did, we knew dey were gonna...dey were taking him, everyting in him resisted his four legs, da shoulder rippling as he pulled himself further and further backward--dirt trailing up like from der trucks...so den dey brought out der guns, guns Syrus calls them, and dey show him right in the next. And he was crying while he fell asleep. Den dey dragged him away, not dat far away I could smell him.

    Syrus says to me, "Der gonna hang him up." He'd seen a body once--and he said they were gonna do it again. The whole night...I mean it was only a few minutes before we could smell it on the dirt and in da air. Blood everywhere, thicker than when da idiot got it in da eyes. Then we heard it, like a ripping sound, like water makes when it hits a wall, over and over, like notes held out for too long. Then, and I dunno why I knew, but I think I knew, dey started--or Syrus told me he saw him, hibs whole body was naked, no fur, just chewed up pink and rippleding skin..at night while I was trying to sleep, I heard metal scraping sumthingg dry and hard and then repeating, a cracking sound like a tree falling, it repeated for a long time and then stopped all a sudden.

    Dey sent Syrus to fuck. He didn't even fight the idiots, he just when and then as he was marched to the other cages, da girl cages, he saw it--a body, just dangling there, spinning softly on a chain, left and right a lil bit. Nothing but raw skin, the mouth hung open. It didn have none of it's teeth, it spun a little bit, without even the wind. He said he expected more blood but the only blood that

he saw was still pouring out of it's mouth, like dripping very fast, even without a heartbeat. He said he could look at that image for a long time to remember that it might be him one day. He didn't even cry. But I cried the whole time I could smell. When he told me it made it worse. I never understood why I never saw much furder den the cage. They never did anytingth with me--I dun like to think about the past so I think about my dream.
"It's a memory of your momma."
"My mama?"
"Yeah, even a fucked up cat like you got a momma."

▪

When I woke up next I woke up it was because the idiots let the woman in, the human in. She brought another human in. He was light like me and pale. He looked weak. I'm subprised he can eben hold his own body up. They pointed at me and Syrus--they wanted to do something with us, so I went to the back of my cage and started growling. Ders no spike in the cage. All my blood rushed from my chest into my retarded limbs and I hope I can fight them. I don't know if where I would go is worse or better so I better fight to live. I saw them and I know to kill them. I want to and I dun want to but it don't even matter if I want or don't want to either way, I just know it is the way. So the first thing they do is walk to me.

▪

"There's a certain appeal with that one--something classically sideshow about him. A rarity. A jewel of an individual. We'd love to take him."

▪

Dey came to da cage and opened it.
I was all the way in the back.
They came and den dey tried to grab me by the collar and so I tried to to jump up and my retarded limbs was limping, I kind of fell over myself and they had a stick but this one didn't sting like the usual one, he hit with it and I could tell right away, even though it felt like a huge smack that I was bleedingg. I roared at them, they backed up. But then I could just tell I was gonna lose, because I went for the arm the stick was in--and I saw the other idiot w/ a machine. He got on a knee and aimed it, even though I was right in front of him--and he shot it--and it hurt so bad, I roared but then...

▪

I woke up in a bouncing room. Syrus was in the same cage next to me. His feet and claws were all tied together. I saw him see me blink my eyes and he said,

"This is what it was like the first time. For your mama." I just stared. I didn't know what he meant. Everything hurt. I felt weak. I closed my eyes.

■

I had anudder dream. In the dream, I am outside a bunch of wooden tires and the tops of the trucks look like tents, but striped like me, there's a buncha idiots in dem, all doing strange things, getting dressed ornamentally. I'm at a wooden bucket, filled with water, in the middle of a dirt patch. I see a lion on one of the trucks in front of me. He is skinny and toofless, he looks away from me sad. My leash is too short so I am choking. A idiot comes in with a big bucket, and I smell food in the bucket--and the food smells so good. I can hear a splash there's so much blood. A idiot throws me, lazily, a piece of a cow, I know this even tho I cand see what I'm eating--he throws it on the ground and I eat immediately. It tastes so good.

Ebery bite fills my mouth with blood, and I feel real. I forget about my leash but forgetting reminds me of my leash and I can hardly swallow all of the too much of my food.
All of it is too much already. I feel filled with one bit but I know that I can eat more. So I eat the steak. Syrus called it a steak, he heard a idiot call it a steak--and I eat it and the blood pours outta my mouf and I love it. A idiot throws me another steak. And I eat it and it fills me. He does it again. I eat everything da idiot feeds me until I notice that my stomach is round and filled. I feel like I am about to explode. My limbs are especially re-tarded and weak. They are thin but I am fat. The lion meows like a cat. I feel I'm about to explode, and he throws me, so lazy a last steak. I can't control myselfth. I eat it but as I wanna eat, as I eating it, I start to choke, my leash is too tight, and I start choking. I leap up on my hind legs--I wake up, choking, they're yanking a metal chain, my collar...

I don't bit them like I feel I have to, I just hiss and a idiot hammers down with a stick and I start bleeding Syrus is awake and for some reason, he didn't even yell at them. We marched next to each other dragged by the collar into a giant tent. It looked striped just like in my dream but was so big...I watched a idiots lead me thru and we passed all kinds of other idiots. They were all dressed different than any humans I ever seen before. They moved like cats and other animals. They shined in the lights, they had lights on sticks. Everything was burning my eyes. They walked us through the tents. I felt sad I wasn't killing them. I knew I should kill them. But I thought about my dream. I felt weak and safe. But terrified.

Eventually we stopped, in a dirt room, almost just like the cages. Another circle. Just like my dream. I looked up and on a wagon, a cage, over the wooden wheels, a cage, and everything that fit inside them looked hung up like a bird perched--they sat us down and it wasth like we were da birds too. One idiot left while the other idiot watched us. He was quick to cut the ropes off of our feet--and then the idiot walked back and we walked, like I knew I was supposed

@abigfuckingbully

to. (Orchestrated.) Into a spot in front of da water--a perfectly round wooden bowl. Dirty and half full in the center like a moon in the sky. A idiot drove a nail down a loos end of my chain and Syrus too. Then they left without feeding us. No food. My stomach grumbling.

    I looked up around me, getting used to da new cage. Der was an empty one. Because I saw it with all da other aminals I thought, I must belong their tooth. But den I had another thought, I was angry, the thought came after in a rushing, like my dreams of chasing and killing the small critters, creatures that came in da old cages--I thought dat I don't know why, I don't belong in a cage. The cage looked at me hungry like I was and I looked back hungry on top of da cage in front of me--Syrus saying nothing--a sad ol lion, skinny. He could have fleas. He had teeth two. His lips were all fucked up. Den in a row, 4 elephants with human clothes on. Like a headdress--a girl human would wear. I seen humans wear stupid things like this before. A idiot, at least 6x smaller, looked like a bird compared to them, yelling like a chimp while swinging a hot looking stick, same as da one dey used on Syrus and Me, but longer, with a hook. He went one and one and one next each one, yelling with the stick and stabbing them near the eyes, his arm all the way extended, all da way up, they looked down at me and da one on the end, like he was throwing his words said to me--

    "Aren't you scared?" I look at Syrus and Syrus looked at me. I looked at da elephant.

    "Don't be scared!" Yelled Syrus.

    "No." I said.

    The elephants eyes watered--we blew his nose like a trumpet and fell back, raising on his two hind legsth. He wasn't sad, he was angry. He stomped forward, one foot up, one foot in the ground like a root. I could see in his black eyes that he knew how to kill, and he wantedd da kill a idiot--but a idiot had other idiots. Da Elephant looked at me ashamed. Because of his fear of the stick. But the fear of the stick was a smart fear. Yr not afraid of stick, yr afraid of getting killed. I know what killed is.

    I don't think about it so I don't say it, Syrus says it too, he says it all da time. He smileth when he sayb it. The stick made the elephant bleed. Da man yelled words that shot like a gun but stayed in the air. The blood looked like a tear--the idiot left. I felt sad but not outright...like washed away. I was humiliated at first. Not for him. I don't feel humiliated for others. Just felt what da elephant was feeling. Den I felt angry for him. Syrus looked at the elephant and said, "we know you're brave."

    The lion looked at me.

    "What's wrong with you?"

    Syrus looked at the lion and hissed.

    "I'm re-tarded." I said, my tongue stuck out, it wouldn't go back in.

    "He's a genius." and he jumped on me, his two paws forward, playing with me.

    I neber seen Syrus like this. I smiled and purred. The lion paced left and right in the back of the cage, and then showed his back. I felt hungry. I tried to moved to get tired--no one was gonna feed us, I knew that. The leash was too short. I felt like I was gonna run forever and neber stop but I had to try to. I laid down and closed my eyes.

"G'night Syrus." I said.
"G'night Dumbo."

■

In the dream--I saw myself jumping over and over again. But my re-tarded limbs failed me--a idiot cracks the whip and I do what I remember, I roar and hop on my hind legs, my tongue wagging left & right. Then stand. All four of my paws on the top of da box. Then leap off but I slam into the ground. My limbs hit dirt and all of the weight of mythelf runs up into my shoulders, and one of my legs rips off--everything vibrates. Espthecially all da tings I can see.

■

When I wake up, I was being yanked up from the ground, by my leash. I was amazed. Da idiot must really know he's safe. Dat I cannot kill him. I was too annoyed to be angry and too surprised to think about it. Syrus was yanked up next to me. Just like my dream, a idiot moved to a distanth, he had a bucket. I sthmelled da bloob. But I could smell it and I knew it wasn't as good as the dream. A idiot tossed it, a steak from da bucket, one in front of me I sthmelled it on the ground where it landed, to thee if I was real, if ith was okay to eat. It was okay. So I took a bite, from under my two paws, pressthed into da dirt, always eating dirt. I wath glad to eat but it tasted sad. I got sad…in that non-sad way I was used to. Sometimes I think Syrus is a psychotic. He wakes up and he smiles. He smells blood--he forgets where he is and just eats. He smiles and says, "glad they're feedingg us," to me.

We finish da steaks. Dat was it. A steak. Da water was too far. I woulda have some if it didn choke me but a idiot was watching so I kind of felt ashame for eben trying. I needed it doe. He immediately pulled up the spike from Syrus and walked him on into the lights and dark of the tents, I wath left by myself, looking up from the 4 depressed elephants whose eyeth seemed to nudge me back to attention to the humans. Then in the backgground a idiot came and started stabbing the elephants all in da row. He was louder than all of the other animals. Cages I couldn't see up to. The elephants covered so much. I sthlobbered on myself and den looked into a da human's eyes, and dey looked happy. I was fraid of him. Uthually I woulda wanna kill him. He should wanna get killed. Sometimes humans have faces I just by lookingg at wanta kill but he wasth different. He did his job like he didn't know he could die at all. Once, it rained in the cage, a worm--crawled up out of the dirt. It wiggled in curls and didn't move it anywhere. Once I see a worm. I didn't even want to kill it. It wath like that.

He left.

@abigfuckingbully

Then he came back from behind a cart with a box, a wooden box, and he dragged it across the dirth, lumpsth of dirt came up around the sidesth. I ggnashed my teef--and hurted my own tongue. A idiot. A people person gonna make me do a trick. He had a whip dragging in his other hand. I didn't understand it. Da whip cracked--he whipped at the front of the box. I didn't get it. I know a trick but the fuck I supbosed to do da trick? He did it again. So jumpbed up on the box, and leaned backward, putting front paws up, and roared, but I kinda yawned. Den I put all of my paws on the box. He threw a steak at me. I jumpbed down and ate the steak. I ate it fast. I felt emptier. He smacked the whip at me. Pointed sumthing and barked. Tho I did it. I went to the side of the box and started again. I waited. I looked up at him again. A idiot stared at me back. Then cracked his whip andn I did nothing. He smacked the whip again so I jumped up on the box, den I leaned back on my two paws and put my front two paws up, and then I roared, my tongue waggled, I spit on mythelf. This time my re-tarded limbs were too slow, I trip on mythelf, and stumble overt he edge of the box. But I save myself, the box wobbles.

A idiot stares at me. He didn't want to but he threw me a steak. I jumped down and ate it. I felt emptier. But my stomach hurt already. It was more than I ever been fed befthore. I thought that I sthould be happy but felt my life in the future and it made my limbsth twitch, I think I felt like the depressed elephant. It wath the first time I wanted to die. It tasted like the bars of my cage on the back of my wild tongue.

The human left. I was unguarded. But a idiot was still stabbing a elephant. I wanted to die again. Like I didn't want to go on. Because I was fed. And I was like a tree tall elephant getting stabbed. I shoulda run but that felt sthupid tho, I dunno why I stayed. But I did. Then a idiot came back with a ring. It was too skinny to run on like Syrus. It was a hoop, a metal hoop. I've seen one befthore. But I dunno where. He stood right next to me--on the other side of the box. The box wath a good idea. He lifted the hoop, I wath suppode to do something with the hoop I knew. But it wath hard to know. I did the trick I knew how to do. He cracked the whip and I jumped up on the box. Landed on all my paws. Den leaned back, stood up on my two pawsth with my two front paws up in front of myself, den fell on the box, trying to fit my whole self on it again. He cracked the whip again so I did it again, this time I roared, I think I forgot to roar. I did it again, this time I roared. He didn't feed me. He just smacked da whip at me, then wiggled a hoop at me. Oh da hoop. He want me to bite da hoop.

So I roar real loud den I jump at the hoop and bite it, put it between my teeth. A idiot doesn't let go of the hoop. Den he cracks it at me and he whips me in the side. I yip. Not becauth it hurts but because of a fear of da whip. I start over cause a idiot just keep whipping at me. I jump on da box, den lean back, I lifted my front paws and I roared den landed, alll 4 paws, den I leaped, with my jaws open onta da hoop and bit it. The idiot wouldn't let go. He whipped me and kept whipping me and whipping me. Motherfucker. Like Syrus says. So da mother fucker doesn't feed me. I start over because he hit me twice and I tink maybe he will stop if I start. I sthtart at the beginning. He cracks da whip. I jump

165

on da box. The box wigglesth but I stay on it, den, I get up on my two pawsth, with my front pawsth up and roar, and while I'm roaring, I remember when my eyes are clothed thab my dream, in my dream I jump ar. I land on the box and den I try to jump thru the hoop, I go as far as I can. But my limbs are slow and heavy, and I hit the bottom of the hoop, and the hoop flies out of a idiots hands. Hand he's pisthed. He starts smacking his whip. I hear a last crying elephant walk out. He wath trying not to watch.

The idiot smacks the whip and hits me. And I yip again. Den he runs to grab the hoop. I'm mad. I'm not even hungry but I want a stheak. I'm already fat, I know it. He brought it back. I was shtill there. I wished Syrus wasth here. He would have made sense. So it started again. And then finally I did it! I almost did it. So many times I would run on to da hoop, landing into my own clumsy limbs, I trip on to myself and my shoulder jostled before I jump and after I land. Once I landed and ate dirt. And he kept whipping. But then, after eating the dirt, my anger, it was like puke, it came up inside of me. At one point, too much time had passed they locked Syrus up next to me. Pounding the nail into the dirt somehow too deep for Syrus to escape. He was stuck. He looked at me saying nothing. His eyes moved left and right with me. But then I hopped on the box and I leaned on my two back pawth, and roared. I looked down at Syrus who was laughing so hard on his hand. "You can do it Dumbo, you can do it!" The elephants started filing in, with the same idiot stabbing them in the face. The skinny sad lion came to the front of his cage.

On the box I can see up into da cages, a monkey, a big ape, picking his nose, watching me with and without interest, undetermined. The elephant shot syrus a look when he kept screaming, "do it Dumbo! Dumbo! Dumbo!" Stho I could see it, just like my dream, my crooked body through the hoop. I roared again. Syrusth was dying. I started to laugh. He cracked da whip and I laugh so hard, I wath smiling, I leapt, and I Jumped straight thru the hoop. Straight through my whole body. I landed, when I did I tripped and at dirt--Syrus and the monkey were laughing. I felt angry now. Like I hadnt it done nothing and I wasn't gonna do nothing. I wanted to kill a idiot and Syrus too. But then da idiot threw me a steak! And I smiled big wit dirt in my teeth. And Syrus cracked up laughing. A elephant looked at it again, when he say, "Dumbo you did it, ya idiot!" I ate da steak and looked up at Syrus. "No Dumbo newymore."
"No," he said. And then he laughed.

■

I had a dream. It was the same dream--but different. In da dream, I am on da box, and I am doing my trick, I lean on my back pawth and I put my front pawth forward, and I roar, but nothing comes out. Den I land on da box and da box fallsth apart, and it disappears but I'm still der, roaring, choking on my roars. Den I jump, no hoop dis time. Just air--and I go throught, the perfect jump tho, and then I land and my shoulder pops out of it's socket, but slowly, the pain is dull and I am absence for it, no sound again, just the knowing that it snaps. The well ith in front of me. Drained fillwed with a maggots. I eat dirt, I hit the dirt and I eat it. Den, a idiot throws me a steak. But as soon as I try to eat the steak, it fills my mouth and it's rotten. I wake up, spitting out my own tongue.

■

I'm fat now. They keep training me but I work with no other tigers. Syrus always seeth the same part of my act but doesn't laugh anymore. A idiot feedth me less. I feel that feeling of the elephant less and less. Once I got mad at the idiot, he hit me over and over again. The elephant was watching and I was unashamed but I got mad. He hit me and hit me. Syrus came. He wasthn't laughing and I quit, a idiot din't feed me. And left me alone after one strong single hook, he jabbed straight into me, it came down like a hawk swooping. Da elephant looked at me, the idiot left me no food. I wanted to but I couldn't cry with all of the caged aminals looking at me. I looked at the elephant and I roared. "Dumbo! Dumbo! Dumbo!" He blew his trunk at me and I hissed. Syrus didn't even move. He stood still. I curled up against the side of the water bowl. He didn't even bother to nail my spike in. I wath ashamed. But I wouldn't say sorry. I wath too angry. The monkey in the cage kept laughing.

■

Anoder day, the idiot walked me thru the tent to a ring, there was a light on and I saw Syrus, he wath in da ring with two other tigers--doing his tricks. He did move them one. I watche him roll on the tire, then a idiot lead me to the middle of three tigers--then another idiot whipping at them, his whips were weak. He didn't have to do anything for them all to obey. Syrus did my trick, jump through a hoop but he did it after he rolled on the tire. The tire bent and got wiggly and then he jumped through, he heard another whip and ran, they all three ran together in a sea motion motion, one pack, then split at the end, separately and landing on chairs set up. I wished that I had a friend. I felt very separated from them even tho I was happy to be with them. But I wanted to run with dem. I felt unsafe but saw that they could be safe together. For some reason I liked them doing tricks. At first I was laughing, in a laughing way, but then I felt proud of them for doing their tricks. A idiot started whipping again. He looked dressed like a bird. He held a chair out and whipped and a tired looking tiger faked a roar and he followed the man with a chair backwards. Then they stopped at another chair the tiger sat on--and we sat very proudly. He didn't think like me, I could tell. He thought about thsafety and liked when he did a good job. Everytime I do a trick and succeed I feel sick, I feel like I did something wrong abgainst mythelf. Eberytime I do a trick, the trick, I feel I should be whipped again. But I know I don't deserve it. Either way.

A idiot I wath with had greeted the other idiot--they shook hands. The idiot dressed like a bird wath tall and skinny but looked powerful. They talked. The man dressed like a bird just left all da other tigers there. I looked around me. I started to notice, high, high in the air, humansth on a string doing stupid jumping tricks. Other idiots are dressed like birds all jumping, from bars to bars like monkeys. Then marched out all da elephants who were all sad and trying hard not to kill each other, or a human, or themselves. A few of them had tusks. There was a huge ball in another ring they started playing with it. I felt full of energy but I hated it. It didn't go anywhere no matter what. It just built and built and builted up. I saw everything when I wasn't hungry and I hated it all. Never felt dis way. But I felt dis way. They sthopped talking and moving hands and touching each other...then the idiot left me with the other idiot, and now I could hear humans yelling and slapping, I looked up again feeling like it didn't even matter that I did or didn't do a trick. I wanted to be with Syrus. The birdman picked up my leash, sticking histh two fingers under the collar, he dragged me into the middle of the circle--it's heated, underneath, they turned on even more light, and it burned to be under and thsee.

    The idiot whipped and everyone went back to their places. They were all quick and clean. I could imagine them in the wild, even if I couldn't remember to imagine them outside of da cage. The idiot whipped at me and pointed to the center, it wath a big stool and I thought he wanted me to do my trick on it, so I did it--except I tried to run. Syrus smiled a hidden smile at me--I ran and falling over myself jumped up the thsthool, then he whipped and Syrus and the two other Tigers ran as a pack to their stoolsth. He whipped again and the Tigers mounted, they stood tall, then da idiot grabbed a hoop--he walked to Syrus, kicking the planted tire, and then whipped again, Syrus hopped at the sound and sthtarted running, the tire bobbed and lobbed, back and forth, then da idiot picked up a metal hoop from da ground and held it in front of me. He whipped again, I leaned on my back pawth, and pulled up my front pawth and roared. Syrus looked very serious but his trick wath so stupid that I almost thought I wath having fun. I would have laughth but I wath fake roaring. He smacked the whip again and held up the hoop. I couldn't see what the other tigersth were doing. They were all watching me thought I knew. The idiot lifted the hoop--I landed back on the box and then I moved all my muscles into one spot. I made myself into a musthle and den I sprang forward but it felt like my dream. I only got halfthway thru the hoop, the feeling of my limbsth not working on the ground was the exsact sthame feeling I had just before I touched the hoop. It was my whole body but I sthalled and hit the end of the hoop face firsth. I crashed on the ground and at dirt. I looked up while peeling mysthelf off the grounb, and sthaw Syrus disabointed in me. The idiot smacked his whip at me and it stung but I didn't yip. I got up. The idiot put the hoop away. And then I was up. The idiot whipped his whip and den we all resent. But everyone was walking slow. THe pack of dem looking at me, and the Tiger that was proudest almost stopped in front of me, hissing at me, sthaid, "Do it right this time."

■

    I fell athleep.

@abigfuckingbully

I had anuder dream.
In the dream, I am outside the cage,
I'm running through a field of light
and it becomes grass.
The field is beautiful,
I am running through flowers I have never seen before, Tulips.
In the dream I know what they are.
I know I'll never see another cage again,
and I run and I run and I run.

■

I woke up and slept many days. I kept doing the trick for a idiot and Syrus too. I won. I kept doing it and doing it and doing it. I hated the other Tigersth. But they didn really talk to me stho. As the dayth went by, I noticed how many other idiots and animals were working together. I felt the lights. A idiot had started to set the hoop on fire. I overcame the fear by being with the fear. I never touched the hoop again but I always felt the fire.

One night all the animalsth got together at the ends of their cagesth.
I was nailed into the ground, sitting, watching them all.
"They're planning the big shows now," said the ape.
The elephants in a row, waddling together, looked and said,
"How do you know?"
"They do it in order now," said the lion.
Syrus looked up, lifting his face from histh two front pawsth, and looked at, one by one, every animal and at me and said, "Well I hope everyone's ready."

■

A idiot smacked his whip. All the Tigers came out in a pack and then separated, each to their stool. For some reason I felt weird. I sthaw a idiot and he came out walking backwards and waving a hand, turning in a circle. I wasth in the center, put on my stool. THe idiot cracked his whip and Syrus stood at attention. Thatsth when I startedd to notice, in a kind of darkness outside of the heat and glow of the lights, a pack of human faces. They were all smiling. A idiot kicked the tire at Syrus but I couldn't movve my look away from all da idiots to see Syrus act like a idiot. Every human face was smiling. I knew what a smile was. The thing about a idiot is the only smiles I ever saw him make were while he wasth doing something horrible. I saw a human cub eating something. Spitting up his food and laughing. My blood boiled. I have been beaten and starved and I have never wanted to kill a human more. I didn't know why. The idiot cracked his whip. I didn't move, it was like I couldn't hear him over da idiots face. He yelled something and den cracked histh whip again, it was supposed to do my trick, so, I leaned back on my two back on my two back pawsth and pulled up my front two paws fake roaringg. Den I landed on the stool again.

    A idiot picked up a hoop and turned, I realized, it was to show da whole crowd da hoop. He turned his back to me. I hated his safety. I hated his arrogant. Then he picked up a ting and stuck the flame to da hoop. And da hoop went to flame in one fast water-light motion. I felt da heat den felt sad. He held da hoop up somehow without burning. A gloves on his hand. He smacked da whip and I went compact. I wasth all ready in my body but I saw da human cub, he wath laughing and pointing. I spran but den, my re-tarded limbs, just before I got thru da air, I sa da cub and den felt it--my body got stuck in da hoop. Den I went on fire, all of me burning, all of me burning, the fur on my right side, ripping flames into me like I was being eaten alive, I was crying, now. Den I was roaring, my backside flipping around like a fish trying to kick da hoop off. Den landing with my head in da dirt: Syrus face--unmoving, looking at me. I burned and I burned, running around the circle. I didn't know how long. A idiot stood der for a whole time, he paused, didn't know what to do while I burned and burned. Den a idiot ran away. He was gone forever. I kicked off da hoop and rolled in da dirt. Burning. Den da idiot came back with water and splashed me. It burnt cold. It stopped the fire. I was panting and on one hip, trying to climb up. My flesh was open like I had once seen the fresh open of a thing, a critter I killed once, like teeth was in it. I looked at Syrus, he didn't look back. He looked straight ahead. Da humans faces changed slightly. A little bit. Den a idiot grabbed a leash and dragged me off. I heard a noise from the crowd, like a "boo-booing."

■

    "He's essentially useless."
    "Fucking retarded Tiger. Whose idea was it anyways?"

■

    One day a idiot came into the cages and I don't know why but I never saw Syrus again. I had a feeling, like when they first took Syrus, dat something bad wasth happening to me. They lifted a spike I was on and pulled me by the end of a leash. I roared and started pulling back against a idiot with my feet. I pulled. He pulled harder. A human looked over his shoulder and barked something like a chimp and den another idiot came with a gun, got on a knee, squinted a eye, aimed and shot me point blank. I yipped.
    "He's charm-tea now."

■

@abigfuckingbully

He was ripping out my tooths when I woke up. I wath on a table--I roared. I felt a tooths, my front fangs was missing and only blood all over dribbling all over outta my mouth. They were idiots. I bit the hand in my mouth and felt da bones crush really fast. Da human yipped like a chimp. Idiots had me on a table with a weak chain holdingg me down. Another idiot was leaning over me, trying to let go off da hook he wath using to crack my teeths. It grated. It sounded like a tree falling. His neck was soft and brown. I saw it flail as I spit out da broken hand. And he showed it to me again, I waited for the perfect second, broke out of da chains as I leapedd up to his throat--of course my teefs were gone, so only da dull ones were der but dey worked. I clamped into him, trying to cut into da soft flesh, spitting blood everywhere, but it wouldn't cut. So den I used my whole jaw and smashed down into the bones, I found the main bone after his throat bones smashed and I never let go. I threw his whole body from that one place, it was light like it wasth empty, all jiggling. I bit down hard and felt a snap, kept flipping him, and he started vibrating and jiggling on his own. I spit him out and he flew back onto the table I wath on before. I was panting. I waited. Den I roared. Den I roared again. Den I roared again, until the feeling of wanting to cried burned away n turned into pride--all my blood in and out of my heart for killing dem, it was starting to get cold, cold blood.

       I looked up.
       Not a idiot.
There was no cages.
I felt my whole body lighter.
I knew what was good and what was bad.
And I ran out of da tents,
tent by tent, and den alight through a curtain cracked, and brushed over me.
Da pain in my mouth was throbbing and stuckng with the wind ran thru me.
Went I got thru I saw the outside.
It was just like a dream.
I was in a field of light,
my limbs floating over the ground,
even tho it wadn't there,
I saw myself running thru the field of tulips.
And I ran and I ran and I ran.

ASH CROSS

The first time I cheated on her I'd gotten a text from my ex-girlfriend; had long dirty blonde hair, wavy and fell like rain. Thick thighs, a dominant posture, presence, and personality. The best sex I've ever and may ever have. A vice tight cunt and all of the warmth and love that made for mutual orgasms--even after the recent breakup. As sudden as the way it started with the same mutual understanding that it wasn't over, acceptable, like when I blushingly told you I was masturbating to your profile picture, and you gigglingly asked me to do it again, over the phone.
I'd gotten a text,
To come over,
And
I forget exactly what made me feel you were safe to see again, what besides confused longing, the illusion of closure like a coy look over a shoulder, promising me some relief. Closure is important to the obsessive and that's why obsessives don't ever stop loving the people they've loved, there's always the same feeling when you see them, your whole body stores every memory good and bad and you smile a smile only possible in love,

Everything blossoming and explosive.
I fell in love with my ex-girlfriend at the No Age show. We held hands while bellowing guitar washed us into frenzy, soothing us with the low throb of drums, we held hands and everything was rushing into us, the absolute high-ceaseless spatter then surge of endorphins to my head, give us both a rainbow for halos--two beautiful saints, pale, sweating, and when a song peaked, so did we--swaying and giggling, laughing ourselves to and out of fatigue, and in love.

This is exactly how I would feel when I would see her--ever again. Now I was physically/chemically bonded to her--her body spoke to me. I was spiritually bonded to her. I got the text in the stairwell of my current girlfriend's apartment, bright ona fall day, all of the cool natural light shining on my current girlfriend sitting with me, sad to hear me hearing from her.
She put a cigarette out into the perfectly white walls which matched her oversized knit sweater, the ash painting a cross.

"Why are you seeing her?"
"Just to see her."

Both a truth and absolute lie.
You got up without looking at me and started up the stairs to your apartment, "I

don't get it."
You opened the door, I saw, I heard you, but didn't see you, close it.

At Rheanna's house I had two beers, I usually never drink, but she was convincing, like a beer ad, intense conversation about, I can't remember, I was lightweight, chemically sensitive, I may as well be fucked up already, and we both calmed down and went quiet, and she layed down, you laid yourself out, and I said, "I think I'm too drunk to bike back to my apartment," both true and an absolute lie. You blushed, finished what was in your bottle and said, "You should stay here. Lay with me," it was over. I didn't even mention my girlfriend. She already knew about her and hated her. It was the honest thing to do to stop humoring honesty.
As soon as I laid with her we started stripping the other, clothes were balled up and tossed.
Her eyes looked into me with envy and spite, pounding like the hunted, certainty from the conquest. A smile of satisfaction. And heated we both came and nodded into some sad dream vivid and depressed for me, as proxy, ashamed of me the way I should have been ashamed, but unapologetic. [At this moment I remember a party at which Rheanna and Remy are at, me and Emery were throwing it. They both knew the other wanted me and would never breach the invisible barrier of being in the same room at the same time. Neither spent that much time talking to me.]
Even my dreams couldn't say sorry. Apologies are weak. If I was sorry I wouldn't have done it.
How I'm supposed to feel...

Saying sorry like a dead bouquet, like you aren't even there, looking beside yourself for a reason. Fucking arrogant.

I biked to Remy's house in the morning.
She was waiting for me in the same outfit I left her in, smoking a cigarette in the same posture on the same stair in the stairwell. I left my bike outside the cage door. She let me in then sat back down.

I looked her dead in the eyes and said "I slept with her."
Remy pushed me off of her.
Remy put her cigarette out, the ash painting a cross on the perfectly white canvas of the wall in the stairwell.

"You're a fucking idiot."
"I'm so sorry."
[It had been two weeks into seeing you, and I had promised, "I'm committed to you," I said.]
You weren't crying yet. You got up walking back up to your door. I never once saw you cry.

I saw you open the door. I heard you close it.

In a week I'd talk to you. In your grace you forgave me. A sincere lapse in judgement. Lingering confusion about how one woman's love could feel infinite and present still, how you can't see the ones you love forever ever again.

At our most in love I avoided my best friend and roommate almost in totality to be with you.
We would spend every day starved and fucking until 4pm which would be the first we'd leave the apartment, only to eat. Running only on the drugs we made inside of each other, even when we hated each other. We were blissed out and strong. Two little tanks, bouncing through San Francisco.

Once we were in a fight you told me, both naked in the shower, water running over both of us crouched near the faucet head, "I know you better than you know yourself." That cliche fucked lie. And I would hate you because it was true. You laughed and spit water in my eyes.

At my worst I would tell you I couldn't' do it anymore. Financially incapable of living in the city. Floundering emotionally. Feeling stripped of identity by my possessive best friend and roommate and my new placement and orbit in his life. My growth was stalled, choked by the expectation, the idea of who I should be for the ones I loved the most, with Emery since high school happily, and how they would hunt me down, corner me, try to drag me back to them in time to remember what I had been for them in my freedom. A vile domestication. Performer. Porn star. Love me—I satisfy the most neglected desire, regardless of how juvenile.

It's easy to look down on. Months would pass. I left the city and moved back down to the South Bay. Feelings of failure followed. My love for you was strained, exhausted by history. Exhausted by my own lack of confidence. I remember the phone conversation, "You can still visit me."
"You're an hour away. I have to get my shit together. Honestly, I just don't think I can do it anymore."
"An hour is nothing. No. You're overthinking it."
Despite my conviction I would agree with you. Allowing myself to fall out of love with you but kept promising you loyalty, myself.

There's always the question of why.
That I should have a reason.

And even for myself I'd want one.
And even by myself I wouldn't know exactly.
On my end, financially, I was unstable.
But that's so easy to fix, right?
[A memory of some shit head punky barista pulling you aside. Telling you, "You can't pay for him all the time. I used to be like this kid, lost. You have to watch out for yourself." You wouldn't stand up for me. Or for yourself. How later you would tell me 'he has a point.' And I would have to remind you of every open conversation we'd had about money. And how I only want what you want to give. It's not only animals that will take anything you offer. It goes unresolved.]
On my end I balanced no other aspect of my life with you.
You were all there was and for a long time that was good for me, for both of us, who would you have been alone? Eventually the woman you needed to be to be yourself, but while I was there, there was something invincible and permanent, and it gave you the wilderness that kept you from going soft and square in college, which you were good at, maybe you loved it more than I could tell. You were the ones w/ friends. I was the one with a best friend but even that love suddenly started to feel sick, ill fitting. There's everything about loving someone that's unspoken. What you know and see of a person is finite. But what is tacit is almost infinite and growing, waiting to be rediscovered as it grows again. As it takes a new shape breeds new light and life, bends eventually, like feeding plants. You paid for almost everything. You fed me. You never left my side. Even time spent working out was annoying to you--was a distraction from us--you were jealous. You took care of me. To be taken care of I had to put myself second eventually, even our illogical love felt illogical. Unreasonable, without purpose. You loved me so much and I didn't have myself anymore.
For a while I was glad to share my power with you, I was glad to give you my power.
But then life got ugly and I wanted it back. I wanted myself back--and this was infidelity.
And I hated it. It doesn't mean I didn't love you. It meant I couldn't the way I wanted to.
I had already changed but was trapped in some regressive hologram--acting for all of us.

It was unjustified. Evil. But I could no longer feel it, I had turned into an animal--exhaustion was the main emotion. One hot July day, I walked a block to the neighboring apartment complex for their pool. I would leap up and reach over the fence, and use my long pale arms to unlatch the gate from inside, I'd blindly strip, and then notice, as I turned to leap into the pool, a girl in a black one piece underneath the surface of the water. She would come up for air and then I would see it was Seung-ah. Her DD breasts floating perfectly at the surface of the pool. She brushed her long hair aside.

She'd walk up the shallow and stand at an immense 5' 9". A half-Black

half-Korean dream--had she been in a two piece I may have felt differently, but one piece...it's modesty was futile and romantic. "Seung-ah?" I said. I got into the shallow and took a few steps. Doing my best not to look bleedingly obvious about my infatuation, not just now but since meeting her. She was my younger brother's friend, a woman in our small town whose humor and dominant personality could take any man and make him hers in an instant. Before this we had only spent time together getting stoned on one of my brothers visits from L.A.
It was mostly her talking and my brothers friends talking and me listening. It had always been impossible for me to understand or tolerate timidity--in myself, in others--for me women had always been bulls--I always was attracted to hard women. They were more fun. They challenged you. You could learn from a hard woman. You could feel safe with a hard woman because propriety, etiquette...behavior was irrelevant. Destroyed. Put on the rack. Pulped. You could get something new. Tread new ground in yourself. You can watch all of the dormant aspects of yourself come to life as you shed useless layers and took on new strengths.

It was instantly that I knew that I was going to be with this woman tonight. Not out of bravado. Not out of arrogance. I felt safe with this woman and this woman was glad to see me, and in the defeated state I was in, defeated? It was fatigue and total acceptance of self. I shouldn't be worrying about a woman an hour away I was falling out of love with. I shouldn't think of all the reasons to continue my love with a woman who loved me but maybe had seen too much to respect me. The way people love pets. This love, with Seung-ah, was new and wild. She stood next to me and smiled without smiling. We spent some time together in the pool awkwardly catching up.

"Why haven't I seen you here before?"
"I'm just getting back from San Francisco."
Excited to be with her. I was so glad to be in the presence of a woman who was so much woman. It wasn't logic/thought. It was more natural than impulse. That this was happening was like breath. We swam for a little longer bathing in the cool water and warm sun at once. We knew everything we wanted to. We talked like friends and stood beside each other like lovers. My shorts were track shorts. I brought a pair to change into after.
She carried my wet shorts in a plastic bag she kept in her purse, along with a towel.

"What are you doing for the rest of the day?"
"Nothing, really." she said.
"Do you want to come over?"
"I need to take a shower."
"You can take a shower at my place, I can give you clothes."
"Okay."

We walked the block to my house slowly, her sandals flopping in the heat over the oppressing pavement. She stood tall without trying and got close to let me know it was okay.

We went in together.
She put her purse down and I got her some clothes and a towel, politely showed her the door to the bathroom, and, without showering myself, proceeded to change. She came out in my t-shirt, the collar cut low out of it, the sleeves cut at an angle--a sherbet orange with a faint white Siberian Tiger growling...I'm surprised I am large enough for it to oversized on her. Her shorts, my shorts, are just as short on her as they are on me. Obscene. We sat on my couch and watched cable for a long time under a blanket. Our legs and arms touching. Her bringing herself closer, leaning all of her weight on me, her legs, feet up on couch, her shoulders in mine, lopsided. Eventually got bored of T.V., we spent time looking through books, and my fridge, and my rooms, and she had something to do on her laptop. Breaking up the night w/ silence and separation, the way couples who have been together for years break up their time, to eventually in a sun kissed mass, glow under the sheets of my bed, together, throbbing, my arms over her, our legs entwined weighted with the other. Hours passed, in silence and tension. From 12am--3:30am both of us laid waiting for me to act--even with the total clarity, the mutuality assured...I was guilt wracked but also determined. I was guilt wracked and and conscious.
My conscience was silent and the need to be new to someone was so strong. I sweat next to her on her until 3:30am. I thought she was asleep.
"So." I said.
"Yeah?"
I started rubbing her back slowly.
Then touched her arm.
She turned to me and I kissed her.
We couldn't stop.
I leapt on top of her.
I bit her lip.
"Ow!"
She bit me back, my bottom lip.
I felt under her shirt, my shirt, and she stopped me as I reached to feel her enormous breasts,
"I just got them pierced--be gentle."
I forgot as soon as I heard.
"OW. Bastard--"
"Sorry."
"OW. Bastard."
"Sorry!"
And kiss was slow and guilty.
A hesitance in me and none on her part. She was certain of what she wanted.

This was intrinsic to her personality. She filled my mouth, and under the weight of the comforter, I tore away my underwear, then her underwear, soft and thin, and for a moment she stopped me, a hand, all five fingers fanned against my lower abdomen-- "Do you have a condom?"
"No."
"Don't come in me."
Then she opened up her thighs, perfectly large, and in her powerful expression took me in. I was heavy in her. She was soft and light, and we were slow at first, then I was hammering in her and neither of us made more noise than was natural--a heavy breathing staring straight at each other even in the dark, her long black hair framing her furious face--famous to me now. I pumped to come and asked, "Where should I--?" her hand around my back, holding me in while I'm holding it in--she didn't say anywhere. I pulled out after pushing out of her hands and came just below her pierced belly button, all of me in new love, guilt, grief, and relief. I got up--post coital formalities, "Do you want a towel? Some water?" She wants both. I stomp barefoot through a luckily empty house, to our fridge, where I grab a bottle of water from the fridge, and just outside the room, open a door to a row of towels and bring one in--I stand there in the dark and in the silence, and beside myself. "I have a girlfriend." She uncapped the bottle in a twist and drank, eyes lowering straight towards me, swallowed, capped the bottle again.
"Asshole. I didn't need to know that."
We got into bed, back to back.
I fell asleep an hour after her.
I woke up at near the same time.
She left immediately.
My shorts on her and shirt on her as I walked her to the door.
I never saw her again. Or those shorts. Or that shirt.
If you asked me if I felt guilt I'd tell you, "yeah," but mostly I wanted to.
I wished I could muster the emotion guilt after making such a clear decision like I usually do, sober. Always fucking sober.

I was working at a Whole Foods.
I would watch Lily bag groceries furiously, without any effort at all
I would think about her height while I'd watch all of her tacky tattoos.
She talked to men and women the same way.
She talked like a tough guy.
She was funny about everything.
Everyday I would clock in hoping Lily was in my line--making time pass faster, leaning all her skinny limbs into brown paper bags while I mindlessly scanned objects and punched the numbers on one plane, and fantasized on another, creating an impossible space for the falsity of an emotional bond to exist. The

places fantasy fill like patch jobs for sanity. I don't know how it started. She took notice of me--this is a weakness I have--to follow who notices me. (Virgo.) She would share her gummy worms w/ me while things were slow. Would ask me if I have a girlfriend. "San Francisco? Doesn't count." she says. I hated the days I would share this sentiment. Shuck carts blushing. Until one day she'd ask me in the breakroom what I do for lunch. She watched me unwrap a Whole Foods sandwich and a opening bottle of Kombucha, the depressing silence overwhelming me.
"Come to my car." she says.

I pack my shit up and follow to her raised black truck, where she asks what I listen to. She starts suggesting bands--I hate all of them. "What do you like to listen to?" She asked. The way this question is usually received like shrapnel when you start listing and the other feels similarly alien. "Braid. Jawbreaker. Bear V. Shark..." She stared at me then looked for a pack of cigarettes jammed under everything jammed under the emergency brake. She smacked out a single cigarette and took it into her teeth and lit it and took a drag and breathed out of the corner of her mouth, out the corner of the car. She finished the entire cigarette and then offered me from a glass pipe I didn't notice her packing a hit. I told her I didn't smoke weed--she laughed, got stoned and told a story about her older brother kicking her boyfriends ass for breaking her heart. I listened attentively. Our breaks were up. She sprayed perfume, like they wouldn't noticed as Whole Foods employees.

On the way in she looked to me and said, "Do you want to come with me to a party?"
"Yeah, sure." I said.
I'd never turn down a party.

At the party she kept me close. We ate gingerbread cookies in the shape of 40oz and knives. Usually I didn't drink but tonight I would, I'd even stoop to beer. I hate beer. We'd play pool with her thick curly headed friend--I would lose viciously and become infuriated with the game quickly, which would help me lose the next game quicker and keep me a sore loser. I'd break off after, spend some time w/ the host and a (sort of) mutual friend who played in a punk band that's really good--who was dating the host. They were locked at the hip. I tried not to be too focused on the woman who invited me and blow the whole night. But eventually, as a second beer progressed, I met her on the porch in a few big stolid wooden chairs. Her on the left side of the front door, me on the right, (from the inside out.) A kiss was in both of us. And we were waiting for it. It came up again, tho.
"I have a girlfriend." I said, in San Francisco.
"In San Francisco," Lily's friend said--arrogantly, and she looked at me, then

Lily, and said, "doesn't count."
"Doesn't count." Lily said back, like parrots.
"Doesn't count."
"Doesn't count."
"C'mon." said Lily.
She knew I was drunk.
I am so easily.
I am so easy.
"Don't you want to kiss me?" she said.
"Yeah..." I said.
We both looked at each other. I put my beer down on the arm of my chair and leaned forward all of the guilt loose in the margins like the way light reflects in the periphery of my sight, blurry but pretty, and I kissed her. We smiled at each other. Mine heavier. A nervous laugh to ease both of us. Just then through the heavily forested walk came a judgemental face of the friend through a mutual friend. Concerned for Lily and his girlfriend, close friends with Lily. The look was shot down from his height as he quickly ran into the party. "Maybe it was nothing." I think. Maybe it was a brotherly concern. Maybe he knew I had a girlfriend and it was the look down for guilt I should have had. I hope he never told my 'friend,' Jeremy.

At the end of the night someone would drunkenly drive us home.

At work the next shift nothing was different except we were both blushingly laughing into paper sacks about each other. We tried to keep it down but couldn't. Eventually lunch would come and she'd invite me into her truck. She'd smoke some cigarettes--no pot to smoke.

"We should hang out sometime. I'll show you this film my uncle was in, like an alien movie. I'll get you high and we'll both watch it."

"Okay," I said.

She flicked her cigarette out of the car door as she opened it and we both walked in to finish our shifts.

She texted me she was here. I opened the door and walked down the steps of my apartment and for some reason, into her car. She was wearing nothing you could wear out, jeans and a t-shirt.. But we spend a moment in her car, nervously, "what do you want to do? Do you want to go somewhere or?" I think she might want me to drink? She doesn't look ready to. She starts digging through her purse, a crinkling sound coming out,

"I thought we were gonna watch this movie?"
"Oh, yeah, yeah.
I brought this."
It smelled dank.
She peeled it open and the brittle pot brownie blossomed like a lily--and shriveled in itself. She sealed it back up without looking up for a response.
"Oh, uh, okay, cool." I said.
She was pushing me out of her car with herself and everything about her so I lead her up the up the stairs feeling like a cow to a slaughterhouse--like a cop had my arm in a lock suddenly, at the end of some psychic cattle prod. I took her into my room, where the smaller television was, my house the altar to television, and we sat for a moment. We rummaged through the hell of Netflix and found the film--a B film. It's an alien film and the film is long so she cuts straight to the scene with her uncle, which is him, dressed as an alien, in between two blonde humans, naked, all three of them in a pool, a boiling jacuzzi, of their special blend of cesspool of brooding genes.

"Doesn't it look like cum?" she says.

I'm silent. It's stupid to respond too but can't ruin the ruined moment. I look to her and kiss her. She keeps crawling towards me, all of her in my mouth. She stops. I ask for some pot brownie she was unwrapping and eating. I down half and keep kissing her we put the pot brownie on the nightstand. At this point, all dignity, and morality was modestly/politely abandoned, politically debauched. I had stripped myself of all dignity willingly...everything had a green and gold tint, it moved quickly, we were tongues, except I could feel us over my entire body with every lick, then we were wrestling, and breath deepened, and the body was glad to be with another, her cunt salivating, me pressing my thighs against hers, she stripped me and climbed--and I was so warm beneath her as she took me inside. She was moaning, and talking dirty, and I do neither.

It was melodramatic and sad to me. As if the act itself wasn't enough. This is the same feeling of abandonment I feel when someone gets fucked up and I stay straight. Being sober is the one of the loneliest feelings. There are few times I have been (it's fucked up) turned off by a body, I am usually accepting of and grateful for and turned on by any-body, but this time in my stoned freedom, unplagued by internal filters--and it was an effort to be as effortless as the act was, I found myself at the mercy of myself. Once again, passive aggressively coming too early as a cop out. She was frantically disappointed. I wanted her off of me and as far away from me as should could get on the bed. She was at the opposite end. She wanted to move out of it. She crawled closer. I rejected her early, focusing primarily on, "Can I have some more of that pot brownie?"

She was sad handing it to me, reluctantly, already pouting..."save some for me," she says. I eat most of it. I want to turn on the television, now fully depressed. Something like being completely ashamed of myself but not exactly. Not honest enough for that. If I was more passive aggressive I would have turned the television back on but I didn't. I got my underwear on and laid down.
No words for us. She eventually got as sad as I did and began putting on her clothes.
"I have work early tomorrow." She said. Her skinny legs slipping into her panties, then painting on her jeans, rolling them in reverse up her legs. There was a moment for the promise of it happening again. Our bodies pausing as she laced up her second boot on the edge of my bed, but my face was flat and disappointed. Not purposely. Not with any tinge of resentment. Just because. I got up as she stood with the remnants of a pot brownie in a wrinkled tinfoil wrapping.

I walked her to my door, opened it, the screen door after, and watched her walk down the steps and quietly inch into the driver's seat of her car. The sound of the driver's door clicking into place--even that was polite. Perfectly parked at the bottom of the steps, the door that funneled us in, funneling her out. Then the car saying goodbye awkwardly in a 3pt turn--and spinning off into the night.

If you'd asked me what drove me to do it again at the time I couldn't tell you. Maybe the distance and time away from Remy made me feel distant. Made us feel impossible. It wasn't the strong sexual desire or temptation that everyone imagines it is. It's a kind of stubborn quitting. A giving up of dignity. Self-destruct. Feelings of self-fulfilling cowardice as prophecy. The feeling that if I'm quitting I wasn't good enough at all. A desire for a loss of control. Fatigued to the point of wanting it so badly to end. I used to think I would feel awful at that time, but I felt guiltless, and depressed. All my infidelity like the poisoned apple rolling from my hands.

In San Francisco, in bed with my girlfriend Remy, after having finished fucking. She was in a bathrobe sitting next to me, clipping her nails before a bath.
I get a phone call suddenly from Lily from work and she asks if I can cover a shift.
I put the phone on speaker unthinkingly.
Remy can hear it in our voices.
She leaves the room and turns on the hot water, which can be heard through the entirety of the house. "I am notorious for not taking shifts," rings out in my mind, my ex-best friend Emery used to tell me. I am reminded of the whole of my time in the city. The whole time I am in the city and I am unaware of my time was collapsed sinking on itself like the pus in the cracks of broken limb.
The water cuts off, the sound of someone sucking in air. She came back in and

sat next to me a full head of curls wet and dangling. Cross legged next to me without looking at me asks,
"Did you sleep with Lily?"
I look at her and lie.
"Did you sleep with Lily, you can tell me."
I hesitate. I look up from the phone and lie.
"No." with it wavering at the end.
Trying to bury itself.
"Don't lie to me."
"I slept with Lily."
She moved to sit right in front of me.
I tried to begin explaining myself.
How would she have even known?
The friend of a mutual friend. Bastard.
Nothing like a snitch to play friend for a sin. Fucker.
Her voice was strong and unshaking.
I tried to explain myself and it was wrong and stupid too.
Tears and anger filled her eyes and she still wouldn't let go.
Total control.
Shaking, looking down on me.
Cross legged.
The conversation ended before it started.
"You can sleep on the couch."
I packed all of my things into a bag while she watched me like an animal.
No anger to unleash on me--to bond us together--to justify us--to rationalize the anger.
Complete suspension. Removal. Disintegration. The act of composure the true testament to love too dignified to be bastardized in a last ditch effort to say it happened, it has worth.
The moon in the guest room was huge and staring into the bay windows.
I fell asleep surrounded by the sounds of wood creaking. Contracting. Expanding. It was as sad and silent as the room looked. I couldn't get myself to cry.

I woke up the next day and left down the narrow doorway. The steps deep and low, the curtains light grasping for sun. I took the N train the wrong way on purpose to the beach--to see if Ashton was home, but a block in knew, I didn't want to feel better and I didn't want to see the beach.
I got off at 35th Ave. in Ocean Beach, I stopped dead in my tracks, looked up, dropped my bag, and ah, yeah, started crying. Felt something like a short surplus of remorse, for a whole year of love and hate then apathy, burning the bridge I was standing on. Fucking idiot.

@abigfuckingbully

I WAS A FUNCTION 2

Molly calls me at 3am.
Molly doesn't want anyone to know but me what this call is for and that she was ever there.
She wants discretion, not to have to take full responsibility, the safety of anonymity I provide but sometimes with strings attached.
The main problem is my mental illness is only half of my bad reputation.
Suffering from untreated acute Schizophrenia I let everyone I'd ever know exactly how I feel and no one in my village was innocent.
Everyone was completely torn apart by me.
I left no one alive.
Outside of my village, every artist I knew of and added on Facebook was accusing me falsely of rape. Or I was convinced. I was hearing voices I was convinced were from God.
They told me so.
Some people in my village accused me sincerely of stalking them.
I wouldn't know, cause I'd never hear it from them.
I burnt every bridge and am a social exile.
Molly knows me from way back, 11 years since I've moved to California and throughout our fucked and tumultuous relationship, believes only some of the rumors and trusts me as a very loving, forgiving, man, as brutally honest, selfish, and sometimes problematic as I can be.
Molly doesn't give a fuck either way.
She's here selfishly to be serviced, sexually, and I am willing for multiple reasons.
I am, as pathetic as it is to say, lonely.
Slowly through the isolation I have become progressively accustomed to the almost irreversible nightmare of desexualization.
I believe it's important to be there for people who need it even if I am selfish: reaping temporary benefits like sexual satisfaction and the comfort of company.

The saddest part about Molly is no one listens to her.
She is sincerely half-insane but the other half is intellect worth engaging.
Most people, especially men, are ignoring her.
I will be brief about some of the influences, like a physically abusive father with a strong incest urge, a dead mother since she was 8, and the curse of being her dead ringer.

This together made for a home nightmare.
That's for her to tell you about.
However she's always with men who ignore her in some way.
I am always her valuable, trusty, pressure valve.
An ear to chew off when the standard social milieu turns against her and her unconventional ideas. All artists have unconventional ideas.
The sad part is that there was always on my end the hope of being a committed partner.
It's a wash.
It's 3 am and I'm lonely too.
People aren't listening to me.
Maybe I just feel that way, it's a Virgo thing.
Naked, I'm answering.
It's small talk for a minute before I cut it short, we both know what this phone calls for.
In about 30 minutes she calls, I think I may have fallen asleep in that time.
Wake up-stumble to the door in pink boxers I quickly slip on-open the door.
She's dressed-it's an all saints striped, thick sailor T with a cut down the breasts, tied together with a string, white & blue striped.
It's a crop top.
Tight jeans.
Some high heeled boots in a light brown.
She always dressed like she was out Saturday night.
But it's Saturday night.
A conversation on the couch in the living room about my recent weight gain.
"You look different. It doesn't look bad."
She smiles.
She reminds me of Sigourney Weaver with her long curls and white skin.
"Let's go to my room." I say.
I have this license from the last few times she's been here.
And we move to my bed.

No frame.
Just a mattress on the floor and a few comforters.
She falls over onto the mattress, onto her stomach.
Like a kid.
I roll onto mine, next to her, like a kid.
She starts talking.

"They don't listen to me, none of them. Mitch's boyfriend is cheating on him, like, he goes on Grindr and hooks up with fucking random dudes. All the time. You know he's like 30, right? But he's finally found all of these messages on his phone--and Mitch--he acted out. He's cutting Jason out. He told him he never wants to see him again but for some reason, it's fucking insane to me, everyone's mad at Mitch for kicking him out. I'm like, how the fuck? I'm behind Mitch all the way. They said I was insensitive got mad at me."

"Well as someone whose cheated before I'd never see the issue as that clear cut off the bat but, yeah, sounds like he's unreasonable."

"You think I'm wrong?"

"No you're right. You're absolutely right." I said sincerely.

I turned to my side and like last time I'd seen her, where she let me feel every inch of her through all of her clothes without asking, I patted her ass.
She turned and took her head out of her phone and laughed.
Then I pulled her close to me.
Things felt different than last time.
There was no spontaneity.
Just a sad understanding of how necessary the mutual use was.
The rationalization of its being beneficial, then a kiss.
And then her laugh.
And then her boots coming off-she places them neatly by the end of the bed as if everything deserves a place.
And the sound of the knocking wood heels on purpose.
And I felt her again, my hands groping her breasts through her shirt sadly.
Pathetic in its heated honesty.
Sometimes when I look at them, my turn ons are so open and revealing they display little flickers of suffering.
This why I have a quick immunity to pornography.
Why something more novel becomes necessary, like Hentai.
I felt her from the outside and could feel nothing inside.
First through the clothes expecting more excitement than I received from the sensation.
Then under and it always been this way with her the love act opening me up as much as I was opening her up.
There's this idea that women are more vulnerable in the act.
Which is true in a way.
There's also this idea that those who open up are stupid. Less vulnerable in their vulnerability.
That the initiative is somehow for the brute.
That in every act of love as one pushes forward he is somehow numb, and taking, giving as a woman passively receives instead of granted the same agency,

mind, need for safety, humanity.
With every attempt to reach her, I was emptier.
I stripped her and felt stripped.
A hand under a bra now self conscious.
Self-conscious not self-possessed.
Watch as I take advantage of myself through the act of attempted self expression of love through sex.
I actually started taking off her clothes after one final grasp over them--looking for something, first her shirt, she said nothing.
The kisses were soft and tired.
Shy but asexual.
Pathetic and requesting.
Wanting and not wanting, all of the appearances of a desire for power, whimpering, parental, pathetic.
Then, I took off your jeans and skinny pale legs went stiff in anticipation.
That they would be touched like everything else, and loved and wondered about.

Finally, you were naked, and I put myself above you.
You asked for the lights to be out and I was ashamed of my body.
But it was okay, maybe it was better this way.
A simulated anonymity.
The love I will always have but push down for you, to be with you, I have push down for myself, to stomach you.
A kiss on your belly button that I thumb.
It tickles you, you hate it, but you laugh.
I kiss you.
Then you take both of you hands and put them around my face like I'm a good dog, and you say, " You can't expect anything from me, from this okay?" You kiss me. "Promise me you won't get angry."
I lie to myself, I won't get angry I lie to myself.
I nod seriously and lie to you, and say,
"O.K."
Then I peel away your translucent cotton panties, the ones with the soft embroidered roses, and stop my hand at your bra.
And squeeze. And feel happy and warm. Then mourn.
Selling myself out.
Then I lift you to take away your bra.
And then I kiss you once before stripping myself.
And you look down yourself as I move between you-and you look to me, over my shoulder and ask up to the dark, "Do you have a condom," and I answer no, "aren't you always, how do you not have a condom?" The assumption, common.
Offensive and flattering--like how Remy once tells me, "I love that you could kill

a man."
"When's the last time you were tested?" you ask.
"A long time ago. No I don't have a condom."
You and I are both there when we're thinking, "well you must trust me,"
"He must trust me,"
"She must trust me."
Last person I slept w/ was you.
I'm not sure you could say the same about me.

I can't expect anything from you.
Means I can't feel anything from you.
A fuck stripped of it's affections.
What is a fuck stripped of its affections?
What is my purpose?
Like love without a human on the other end.
A metaphor for itself, it happens once and then again.
It happens as I watch it.
Unrequited love a collection of all my resentments.
To be invited without a right to be.
To take without taking.
Now you're under me and I can feel myself filling you and how gone you really are.
How little I matter.
I am a different kind of gratification.
Who is this? I am over and in and sharing breath with?
How can I be inside of a person and outside of myself.
Make a decision, you fuck.
But I don't tell you, I hide it from you, that I'm here to want to enjoy it and I can't and I'm semi-erect, mostly going soft, and you don't notice, you keep telling me how big my average sized to small sized cock is and oh yeah, yes, yes, like a script, fuck me, fuck me and it's without a condom endangering both of our entire lives, like last time, but I am controlled, I am amazing at holding myself back, of pushing it down, of keeping it all in.
I watch your enormous breasts shift and jiggle in rhythm.
I am hardly moved.
I long for your love more as your body presents itself perfectly, as if love could be reached in the promise that lust dangles before me like a trained animal.
You are the perfect shape to another man.
Who are these sociopaths who can separate love from sex?
Here I am (trying.) (I'm fucking one.) (I am one.) I can be one.
We both arrive at boredom quickly, me deeper than you, you ask to switch positions.
You turn around, your legs slightly parted, somehow the sides faces bulging at the calves, most of them touching the mattress, you look like you can stand.

I am still pumping like a good man and you start moaning and I am still soft mostly,
It's taking me forever.
I watch your curls bouncing and your body bobbing, and I try to find pleasure in your soft white ass, small and pale.
I grope it.
I look at the dimple in your back and decide I want to come here.
This thought is very real but still fails.
You can't tell and I can't tell you.
I half love you. I half love you and I half love you, half hard still.
Continuing following through while following through with the hips.
We switch positions again, you're above me now
Quieter now,
And I hold you still,
And pump,
And pump,
And braced to satisfy myself,
As if there was more to give,
And as the heat wells in the base of my cock, all of me rising and lowering, a throbbing sea rolling through me watching our breath and you pant, and I pull out, I pull you off of me, and you make a noise like a sad sigh or a stuttering before a question, and I grab my dick and pull up on it and everything stills, even air, as I clench my teeth to come silently, all over you.
You and I both stop.
And your lip is curled like it's still happening for a moment.
And your curls bobbed with your breath, draping over me, then, you rolled next to me and asked, "Did you come in me?"
"No. No way."
We sit still breathing.
Yours is dramatic like it needs to be good.
And while I hate the brutality of silences this is the only time I hold it over someone, sex.

We sit for a moment.
Together.
We can feel close to the other without the responsibility of love
Which is supposed to be easier.
It drives me insane.
You start getting dressed in the dark quickly and the suns coming up.
We lay for a bit talking until blue hour.
No need for the light,
We talk for a few hours.
"You can't write about this."
"Okay, can I Tweet about it? JUST CAME."

I type it in and 'TWEET SENT.'
You laugh. I laugh.
I'm never proud of passive aggression--but as someone typically as direct as me my cowardice shows itself in awful ways.
We start talking again.
"I can't believe they got mad at me."
"Yeah that's fucked up.
They make me feel glad I've been exiled.
Do you still see Colleen?" I asked curiously.

My exile: during my acute Schizophrenia, suffering from paranoid delusions and auditory hallucinations I eventually, in the haze and disconnection from reality, began to believe were from God--there was a night I cussed out every last person I had ever met, known, or heard of, spending a solid 4 hours writing and sending vitriol online to every person I had known and met in my village. Accusing artists publicly of rape or accusing them in my paranoia of accusing me of rape.
No one responded.

My exile: events two to three years ago, a blow out. I've known Colleen for 7 or 8 years peripherally. Sometimes closer than that.
We'd met while I was in college.
I remember walking into her house, the family of punk kids and friends and the roommates together on the floor, along w/ Rick all putting together an events calendar for the local underground. Music, protest, politics, get togethers, anything.
Seeing Colleen for the first time was stunning--I had to act hard away her beauty.
A face perfectly set, a big, soft but square jaw, high round cheek bones, big brown eyes, long hair in a bun, black, freckles over her perfect tan, in the perfect place, the cheeks, the nose.
She looked up and smiled.
A smile I can't remember seeing ever again as if something between then and now had taken a part of her only she was unaware of.
I would spend time w/ her in the margins of shows she either put on or played.
The boyfriend would also spend time but we were never close.
I remember him insulting me passive aggressively for being who I am essentially.
Expressing an interest at one point in modeling.
A dated ad for a hair salon with a skinny white dude with frosted tips and spiked haircut,
He stopped me on 5th street for a photo, pointed and said, "hey, it's you."
I posed not exactly understanding how racist it was at the time.
I'm half latino and those people still get my fucking race wrong.

But I was never one of them.
No matter how many shows I went to, no matter how many political events I attended, the more books I read, the less I could believe in the cult minded mass of punx who, may always be more involved in the community, but to me just as likely to lynch someone as an unread redneck.
We shared a lot of views and none of the spirit.
I saw the most potential in Colleen as a person and artist. She read.
We would have conversations inbetween sets.
I was always glad to be around Colleen.
We'd both felt close to each other during our time and both possibly, totally, attracted to each other but couldn't act on it.
I thought her band sucked.
I thought the whole fucking scene sucked.
It was as if the entire social scene was a bad boyfriend and the love we had for each other would remain stunted, unborn, still born.
As long as her legendary boyfriend, who slays at drums, and is a really great writer now, was in the picture we'd limit it.
We played music together, starting and ending a very promising post punk band w/ my brother Hippy Jonny and my writing partner at the time Z.
I loved Colleen at that point.
She had a released a poetry zine I read once at her house in her room.
She was modest about it but I believed in it--so me, Colleen, and Z, did a reading with Jesalyn Wakefield in San Francisco.
Colleen fucked up majorly by offering us a ride but operating on punk-time.
We were an hour late to our own show.
Half of our audience left and Jesalyn (amIhuman press) was pissed, almost left herself.
Even so, the reading was good.
One of my favorite memories.
Then,
Molly,
Who I was w/ right now.
Having all these memories thru.
Stopped working at the coffee shop we (me and my close friends, none of whom I have now, part from anger, part from clarity, part from my Schizophrenia) all frequented and soon Colleen started working there. There was love and comfort in the consistency of Colleen.
All my fetishes are emotional.
Watching women work is one of them.
She was always there.
If not at a show, if not on tour, working, serving yuppies without thought or pretense and I could write in the comfort of her presence, sometimes distracting her with my friends, what was going on.
Years pass.
I move to S.F.

A year passes.
I come back.
I don't know who I heard it from but a secondary source, a reliable source, maybe Molly even, that the impossible happened.
Colleen had broken up with her long time boyfriend.

For a long time Colleen had been writing songs solo, on guitar.
When she usually played bass.
Her shitty band broke up, even w/ Legend on the drums, they sucked.
Her solo act was strong, I'd encourage it.
She'd played in a lot of bands, maybe I was a stubborn individualist but I thought what she was doing was more promising. But now she was alone too.
How to describe it? The love I had for Colleen for so long, I pushed down the way I push down my love for Molly.
I once got into a fight with a girlfriend at the time (before Colleen and I could be together)
"If there was someone else you wanted to fuck, or be with, who would it be?"
She was disgusted and surprised when I answered who I could love now, Colleen.
In my mind the physical expression of love I stored for Colleen throughout my life had built and expanded. Things blossoming. Inside jokes. Bees pollinating. A real, unpained smile.
The weight of her body against mine in her bed.
To get to say, without waiver in my voice, every little feeling I have for her.
I would fight for her again and again and again.

I found out she was free of the Legend and texted her as soon as possible.
"I want to see you."
"Come over after work sometime."
It was natural and immediate.
It was like it had always been mutual.
Like the nights I remember most, sitting there in her living room, her and the boyfriend watching an old movie, both eating.
"Are you anorexic? I never see you eat." They ask, sincerely.
"Oh no, just ate, I'm not hungry."
We watched the shitty, dated, film intently.
Then, they both retired to bed together.
A moment of intimacy shared in a look she gave me while she asked if I needed anymore blankets before I slept.
I would spend the night and have one of my first jealous thoughts of him and her.

A sincere, wholehearted wish, to be him.
To sleep alongside Colleen.
Jealousy is such a pathetic emotion.
One I've worked my entire life to police and weed out.
It weakens you.
The actions resulting from jealousy are never justified.
Maybe I would passive aggressively take a photo as a racist joke and return the hurt.
Never. I hate jealousy. No one deserves it.
As in is worthy of it or deserves it's reception.
But that night on her floor all of the time we weren't spending would fill me near to heated tears.
I'd write a poem about it which would be published in the year we had both been separated and I would bring it to her, the collection it was in, along w/ a few other poems about her.
There was a mutual combustion on the night we finally met again, like two kids who had waited so long to play with each other.
Love was at the root of everything, I felt cared for the way she held me and listened.
We fucked the first night.
It fell apart just as quickly.
In two months I realized that I had become a human doormat.
A stand in on call rebound fuckboy.
The love I had built up fell apart.
It ended with me cussing Colleen out.
The only expression I had, a primal expression to defend myself.
When you find yourself replaceable, by a phonecall, kicked into the street when the ex boyfriend came back, literally, you find that reason is a failure.
The expression of anything other than unmitigated anger is a square peg in a round hole.

All these memories through Molly.
I looked up at her.
She said,
"Yeah I still see Colleen. She goes by a different name now.
Prefers to be called them."
I nodded.
"They have a new partner now."
I nodded.
I thought about Molly,
Hanging out with a group of people I fundamentally am unwelcome by, wouldn't get along with, but still somehow missed Colleen. I imagined her sitting at a bar

I was banned from, sitting at rain eaten, splintering wooden tables, under the canopies, pretty and pounds lighter.
The love I couldn't have from Molly was the love I couldn't have from Colleen. Was a selfish clinging to misunderstanding.
Maybe I should feel more resentment.
"You know what happened, right?"
"I kind of heard."
"I'm not a naive person you know.
I really loved Colleen though.
I could see her ex coming back, but she said she had feelings for me. She said we were going to stay friends and then he came back and she ghosted. I cussed her out, then she painted me as this stalking abuser to people.
It's bullshit.
But you can't convince me to hate her. I miss her.
I still love her. Or care for her."
"You still love her?
You can't think about people who hate you. There's plenty of people who will love you."
"But they're not Colleen." I curled into my blankets, then got on my knees on the bed, then fell on my face into a pillow.
"You can do better than Colleen.
She sees herself as a pillar of the community. She's sensitive. She wants things to be a certain way so she insulates herself w/ all of these politics, like a bubble."
"She humiliated me.
She made me feel so small.
I wanted to show her I could make her feel as small."
She stared.
"I didn't realize it until I said it.
Actually, thinking about Colleen makes me want to cry."
"Why?"
"You can't convince me to hate someone I've loved, no matter how they feel about me.
My love is...unconditional."
She burst out laughing, falling over herself.
Started dressing in the morning light.
Eventually grabbing her boots and putting them on.
Then left to grab her purse in the living room.
The bedroom door now open.
A hand on it's side, cracked.
She slanted to one hip.
"Do you want to get coffee?" I asked.
"Coffee? Not really, I should sleep."
"I'm past the point of no return."
She squat on her haunches, looking powerful in the height of her heeled boots.
"You expect too much from people, you know, if you expect too much from

people, people will always let you down, you know. That's the reason we've always fought. You want more than I'm willing to give. People suck."
Then she stood back up and leaned in the doorway again.
I was infuriated.
It was the dumbest fucking thing I'd ever heard.
It was the vacuous condescension of a parting sermon from an airheaded nihilist.
How it's possible to be the brilliant artist she was and a total idiot.
I forgot I was talking to a valley girl.
Literally, from the valley.
A complete ditz.
The blood rose and all air was still.
She started closing the door and asked, "are you letting me out or--?"
I said nothing.
I'm no moralist but I have my principals.
My threshold.
I turned my face down in my blankets and imagined I was shedding tears my body never let me.
You're the only one at fault.
When you are comfortable thinking she has good use.
Using yourself.
Letting yourself be used.
I couldn't sleep and went unbathed tho I didn't wash the scent of her cunt from my mouth or hands.
The scent on my breath made everything in the morning beautiful and gave it a determination and I felt loved being alone.

PRESSURE WASH THE WORLD

"Some jock asshole? What does that even--mean, dude? Because he invests?"

"You know what I mean."

"No, fool, what DO YOU MEAN? Because he invests in his body?
You get what you put in, man--if that dude could look into your life as an artist he would laugh his ass off--art is so fucking lazy, people parasitizing a foul political climate to climb into a mountain of social currency. There's men building houses. Doctors. Firemen. Construction workers. I'm not here to say they're more important than you okay? That's not what I'm getting at. You're important. Art's important, like...do you think that guys life is less important than yours cause he's--and I mean you don't know what this dude even does, like--because he's not producing--and he could easily be an artist, but like...do you think this guy suffers less? Like less than you? Everyone suffers."

"Some young conservative guy..."

"We're all athletes. We could learn from those attitudes, that perseverance, the almost masochistic willingness to face pain. You wake up every morning, faced with the weight of existence--the required monotony to excel, and you lift: over and over, everyday, the heavier the burden the stronger the animal. All your emotional, mental shit. And you do it because you know you have to. And everyday you get a little stronger, and a little faster--a little torture and then the growth."

"It's vanity."

"It's not.
It's not fucking vanity."

"Relax, dude, why are you so offended?"

"I'm not. I'm not offended, I don't get offended--you're being an asshole. I take you, I mean, I consider you an open minded guy, but I'm starting to think, like, don't let all this punk shit get to your head."

"What do you mean?"

"C'mon dude.
This shit is some herd minded manipulative shit! Think about punks man. They just created a new social standard, through negation. They inverted the criteria--they can't compete in dominant culture, they can't cope with the culture, so they deviate. These people are just rejecting what they feel rejected by. These people aren't oppressed dude. These idiots need to go to college. Like, yeah, talents succeeding, the artists are the most progressive here, and let's be real, they are insanely intolerant people--they want some utopian world of equality, fucking, cultural marxists, you blame society? You're a fucking college dropout, you are in a first world country, you chose this path dude. When you choose not go to college and you choose minimum wage work, I mean they pay you to go to college so...it's like a model. You're making art. There's even a certain freedom that comes with your poverty. You choose fucking bohemia and to risk it all for your art. If you want to guzzle beer, get a face tattoo, and commit your life to following loud music you're not even NOT a fucking deadhead, man."

"So you think class is a choice, it's just as easy as a choice. You think this is fair? This is just?"

"Not exactly, like, of course there's inequality, it's not even an injustice. I'm disgusted by the profit motive but I'm not about to believe money's a completely abstract concept, when it has material effects. I don't fight gravity, except at the gym dude. Like, but in other ways too. These people are attempting a tyrannical utopia. They seek purity, no sexism, no racism, no homophobia, no transmisogyny, no this, no that, whatever the fuck, iron out all the kinks, create a new order, doesn't this,

it's so disgusting to me, the idea we're just going to bleach the world into it's perfect little hateless place, the imposition of a new morality, a carrot on a stick behavioral procedure, it's reductive, it's annihilation of free will. The liberty these people are seeking isn't even not stomped out like an organic-cigarette in it's seeking to enforce new 'high minded,' behaviors. These people aren't introspective. These people aren't more open minded. They don't look INSIDE their hearts for truth or what's right, by boiling everything down to systems they actually STOP SEEING things in a human way, they become fucking machines, systems essentially. I don't SUBSCRIBE, fool. It's an integrity that comes from inside, not a drop down menu of beliefs. You're a baby, you're in denial. You want equality? No one's equal. I mean, yeah in a certain sense, and intrinsically, but not in real-time, on the ground...it's not real.

Society will always exist. And for most of us, I mean this isn't a prehistorical Indian society, man. This is civilization. And let's be real, how much of what we know of these primitive societies is real? Like these peaceful, ecologically stable, anarchic societies--I mean all of that 'noble savage' shit--like, get a fucking grip dude! Indians were murdering and enslaving each other. They got white people to help them! Society exists and it's going to in part, be evil and inequal. And it's always going to want to police people, and war has always been here. I'm going to do what I want fool. It's my job to make the right choices. To be adaptive."

"Society's sick, it's maladaptive. I mean we shit in potable water."

"Yeah, dude. For sure. Society is sick and it has it's problems. Including turning living trees into dead words. Books. Art. A fucking record is plastic. What the fuck are we doing? We have to fight for liberty always. We have to transition to farming. But are you realistically going to do that? So then stop couching your own inability or refusal or whatever as some bullshit politic..."

"What about war?"

"What about it, fool? Was he wearing a USMC T-shirt or some shit?"

"You know how much violence is rationalized by our society? It's our job to end war--it's the duty of our generation."

"Look, dude, war is COMPLETELY FUCKED, but on a certain level, no matter how much it disgusts you, the life you're willing to live, it only exists BECAUSE OF WAR. Your critique is sad because it's out of touch with your life's dependency on it. You got a car, right? You tour, you need oil. Jimmy the Jarhead from Wherever the Fuck Idaho, who you think is a brainless sell out, shot at least 100 brown kids in the head so you could fucking drive 500 miles cross country and play shitty music nd eat a vegan dinner in what was a black neighborhood ten years ago."

"Okay..."

"Look, dude, war is wrong, okay? But don't deny you live off of it."

"So war, and rape, and racism, we're just going to accept it? What about sexism...what about feminism dude. You just some fu-cking DARWINIST?"

"Like I said, equality is intrinsic, oppression is extrinsic. You have to fight it okay. But if you think utopia doesn't require brutality towards people in order to enforce...how much self-denial is required to create the society these people want? And feminism will never stop rape dude. People don't respect women's bodily autonomy aren't "entitled," they aren't taught wrong. They weren't "socialized," to abuse or rape women. They know what they're doing, fool. It wasn't porn, or violent video games, or a rap song, okay? They're evil. They're not entitled. Entitlement causes small accidents, oops I ate too much of this popcorn we're sharing. Asking for too much from a girlfriend, it's not "oops I raped someone." It's greed. I want what I want when I want it. A kind of sociopathology."

"Yeah, let's see how women feel about that theory."

"Look, dude, I'm not one of these fake pretty-boy-poet-boot-licking-male feminists, man. I've met them. They're fake. I believe in empowering women. I believe in their intrinsic equality. Men who act concerned about women, the ones who say they care the worst aren't even not THE WORST."

"The fuck are you to say that?"

"I just saw on Twitter the other day, and I mean, who can be sure this shit is true, it's fucking Twitter. I mean, I just read an article that cites a female lawyer: 40% of rape accusations are false. She's sick of defending false rape accusations. But this asshole: long hair in a single braid, bearded, cardigan on, mr. mountain man softy heartthrob, Father John Misty looking motherfucker, calling the girl whose calling him out for rape a "cunt" in text--guys known in the SJW scene,"

"Social Justice Warrior..."

"Okay..."

"Guess what his t-shirt says."

"..."

"No--guess, fool."

"..."

"I'll save you the time, because it's impossible to fucking imagine,
In BIG BLOCK LETTERS, white on his black t-shirt, it says,
'THIS IS WHAT A FEMINIST LOOKS LIKE."

"Jesus..."

"These are the people who are making decisions about what's moral in our society?"

"Jesus..." he said. He kept his arms close in, limp, soft, and weak. Crossed one arm over his stomach and propped the other up, lifting a 40oz like a baby bottle to his lips, puckered nd sucked, his lips pulled off and the bottle made a "POP" sound.

"Dude, these are the same kinds of fuck-ing people who are deciding who gets published, whose rewarded. I was fucking censored by Dostoyevsky Wannabe. They loved my manuscript, they were into my poetry, then I make the mistake of following them on Twitter and they followed me back--a month later, after they sent me cover art, w/ my own fucking photography on it, this photo of Akila," I showed him the photo, bringing it up on my cellphone. "They send me an email: we're pulling your book, we've seen the content on your Twitter and we're concerned about some of your attitudes towards women...we know you might feel censored...but..."

"What were you Twee-ting DUDE?"

I showed him my phone.

"HOW I FEEL ABOUT TALKING TO WOMEN W/ HEADPHONES IN: ONCE FUCKED A GIRL I YELLED AT FROM ACROSS THE OPPOSITE SIDE OF THE TRAIN TRACKS
POSSESSIVE MALE FRIENDS ARE MY FAVORITE 2 PISS OFF WITH BORDERLINE SEXIST BEHAVIOR."

"What do you even expect? They can't represent that."

"They don't have to because they don't. "The opinions expressed are that of the filmmakers," or whatever...they put out the book, I control my Twitter, I should be able to say whatever the FUCK I want. If people think I'm a misogynist because I produce 'problematic' art or Tweets they're fucking dumb, man--like, people aren't their thoughts, it's just an extension of who you are, and yeah you need to be responsible to an extent but there's something to be said for authenticity. What about sublimation? The same idiots who want to put a cap on masculinity making arguments against violent video games, surprise surprise suppression doesn't work, the neurosis shows up in some perversion somewhere else...another fucking perverted zombie game. How many evil people are considered good because they say the right things to the right people at the right time? I'm open about my shit, I don't hate women. I don't violate their space--I mean I have if a conflict isn't resolved--I mean yeah I guess I'm problematic but not in a dishonest way, not in a malicious way."

"Sounds sketchy to me man, I think we need more responsibility in..."

"It's bullshit dude. It's a bullshit fucking argument. If all I did was murder and rape women in my art and it had artistic merit then it should have a place in the art world. We need less responsibility. Less laws. Less pressure! We keep pressing people to "progress," and it's blowing up in our fucking faces..."

You ever hear of that book 'Suicide?' You know the story on that?"

"Nah."

"Okay, it's a 'fictional,' book, but really it's this account of a guy's friend's decision to commit suicide. The whole story and how he got into it, why he did it. In real life, the guys friend blows his brains out, and the author documents the whole thing. The book was so fucking depressing, had so much impact, that the author himself committs FU-CKING SUI-CIDE! And that shits famous? That shit is praised as a masterwork. That's disgusting to me! But do you think it should be censored? A book that drove it's own author to suicide should be published and circulated by my poetry should be censored, not because of what I write, but because of what I fucking TWEET? That's disgusting to me--shit should have a warning sticker and an age minimum--you should show I.D. to read that shit--but I sure as fuck would never say it should be censored even though it's impact on society is probably worse than any "sexist," Tweet, it's a real fucking account of life too, okay? That Tweet is a true fucking story and a funny fucking joke.

You ever read the book Necrophiliac?"

"No."

"Well, it's a STAFF PICK at Green Apple Books. Guess what it's about? It's about...A FU-CKING NECROPHILIAC! Also doesn't have an explicit content warning or minimum age to purchase or read--that's disgusting right? I mean Jesus Christ--am I the only one who's confused? How the fuck am I being censored? That shit's a masterwork too but I open up about being problematic and...I mean I think Mellissa Broder's Twitter presence is disgusting dude. It's truly toxic but because fetishizing yr own sadness isn't one of our more obvious political ills she's not censored. She's doing fucking great! And she deserves it dude because it doesn't matter if I like it or not, it doesn't matter how I feel, you can't fuck with her as a writer! She's an amazing fuckinng writer, dude. There's like 500 women smashing the like button on her self-destructive prostitution of her own degeneracy. He perverted suicidal worldview."

"So, again, you just think--"

"Dude--no--don't say it again, okay? Do you know what the theory on serial killers is?"

"No, who cares? Don't kill people."

"Curbed creative impulse.
Look dude you may be satisfied with the moral structure nd everything, but I

have to face my evil. You ever get around a bunch of happy people, or like, you go to these shows nd you see these people all getting along and spouting off a bunch of the same fucking political--like--whatever--like, I see them sometimes nd on some primal level,
maybe I just have a Napoleon Complex, a conquest urge: I want to fight all of the men...it's like that in every social scene. I want to fuck all of your women and fight all of the men. It's inside me dude. Perfection doesn't exist, nd morals aren't real if they're just a cover, just make up for your evil..."

"..."

"Sometimes I wonder if I like anyone."

He took a sip of his 40oz in the same whimpering stance.

"Dude just didn't want to be a worm-person anymore. Decided to be athletic...you want to catch this set?" I asked and nodded towards the cellar door. The noise of an unplayed guitar wavering thru the amp.

"Yeah, sure."

We walked thru the grass of the yard and opened the beaten, rotting cellar door--the last ones into the basement. The ceiling was draped with protective trash bags. The ceiling beams were broken. It smelled, classically, like B.O. The light was a low orange. We stared at the backs of heads...I met eyes with a man in an overpriced slick back haircut from a trendier barbershop and a North Face style jacket with PERMANENT RUIN written on the back--nd the asshole mugged me. I immediately barked uncontrollably at him like a literal dog and all he did was turn back to what he could see of the band not playing, then playing, the sounds of a sawmill, 8 songs in less than 2 minute intervals--a scrawny white transsexual was gripping the mic in a shredded homemade tank top--screaming--MY HAND CAUGHT IN THE GEARS. CHEW AWAY MY WRISTS TO SAVE MY LIFE. THROW IT AWAY WITH MY LIMBS--over the bellow of some noisecore.

Next to the scrawny transsexual was a fat, beautiful, freckled Tongan woman, sawing out thunder on her bass, humming God. I saw her and decided then that I need to know this woman. She was sweating profusely through a crop top t-shirt with a switchblade xeroxed. Her freckles accented how her skin glowed, I looked back at Stephen, in a disaffected mood, likely depressed by our argument, deflating, who was now pouring the remains of his 40oz into the heel of the asshole I barked at. He was oblivious and headbanging. Stephen caught me catching him and laughed.

"That's so passive aggressive, dude." I said.

@abigfuckingbully

"Whatever."

@abigfuckingbully

UNWELCOME EVERYWHERE (The New Amerikan Brutalist)

"See Oscar,
I don't need what you have.
I'm going to create it myself, with or without the help of others.
Validation. Social Networks.
Love. Acceptance. Friendship.
I've gone for years without them already.
And I'm starting to change my attitude.
      I used to believe that being who you are the way you want to as boldly as you can was the most exciting, intoxicating, empowering thing. But what's weird is that the more I became myself, the fewer people I had in my life. I've never been bad with people, you know? It's easy for me to talk to people, to reach out, to make friends, but then I started to come into myself and somehow everyone disappeared. When I became who I really was and wanted to be, no one wanted me anymore. Feelings have changed. You think for all of your self determination and creativity, passion and love--your strength that something would be returned but even that's a need, a repulsive need. If you want to succeed in society everything has to appear effortless. I started to realize that people weren't interested in people. People don't love people. People love what a person is or has or does or exercises. Yeah, everyone likes a "good personality," but a good personality isn't even a determining factor. Shitty people succeed all the time. Great artists are some of the most horrible people you've ever/never met. And nothing changes for them. In my head, you come to know a center of an otherwise nebulous self and become powerful but it's a myth. You don't matter. I don't matter. For whatever reason I was ignored, neglected, rejected, abused, exiled, so I started to think differently. I was naive. Passion doesn't matter. Passion's a crutch. Boldness alone doesn't work. Power is the only thing that matters in the modern world. A thought arrived to me: if people don't love you for who you are, be someone else. If you can't join them beat them. I don't know what I did wrong but indie lit's rejected me, man. Neglected me like I said. I guess a psychotic break is essentially unforgivable. Nobody cares. Otherwise people would have treated me differently. Oscar, you have friends. And a book. And publishing credits. And a beautiful large breasted wife. A brilliant artist."
I place my hand on his shoulder.
      "A wife who's a better artist than you--who if you weren't fucking, see if you weren't fucking a brilliant artist you wouldn't even be on my radar. You're a great writer and everything. I mean I think you're shit is really safe. It's just so...clean nd safe nd composed...boring."
I take my hand off his shoulder.
I'm looking him directly in the face, but how the neutrality in my face is terrifying.
Shifts sometimes into a sincere smile.

"I'm sorry to do this to you, you know. You've never done anything to me. I mean I know I told everyone on the internet I wanted to fight you. See, to me, you're a just a poster child. A symbol for all of the people I've reached out to only to have them spit in my hand. It's senseless my hatred for you. Maybe it's jealousy. It's just a choice really. You've never hurt me. You probably didn't know I existed until Sarah told you I wanted to beat the shit out of you. Maybe I'm just a violent person. I'm unhinged. I know why Dylan killed those people. I know why Columbine happened. I understand like no one else."
Oscar looks into my eyes. I'm smiling cocky. He's smiling cocky. I'm full of shit to him.
"It's okay.
I sympathize with school shooters." I say "I am Dylan. But I'm different than him. I'm stronger than him. Dylan was weak. He snapped. Life is suffering. Life is about enduring--so instead of taking my anger out on everyone, I store up all the little abuses. And smile in the face of the big ones. A woman I love fucks another man. It's simple: why let it hurt you? I'm called a faggot all the time in my hometown. Street harassment is a regular thing for me. Once a drunk felt so comfortable he farted in my face imitating me while I was stretching my legs in the street. I should have acted out but I don't know how far I'd go. You know there isn't single woman I've fucked out of the 21 women I've fucked in the 8 years of being sexually active that's respected me. Not one of them. It's okay tho. It's all just fuel for the fire."
Lucy looks up from a glass--alert. Alarmed.

"I'm not really a jealous guy by nature. Abuse doesn't really bother me either. I read this article recently, let me know if I'm boring you Oscar--about social ostracism. That when someone's iced out of a social group or cut off or ignored, that the psychological effects are actually more effective and traumatic than suffering direct abuse. Including violence. I guess that's why I am the way I am. Social ostracism is a form of abuse that drives home the message, you're just not even worth the fucking energy. You're no one. But I'm good at this game. The international artist Michele Bisaillon once gave me the compliment, "You can survive off of nothing." A survival mechanism I've mastered my whole life. She's another woman who would fuck me but refused to be seen w/ me in public. A lot of women are ashamed of me I guess. It's wild to be as ugly as me and pull a girl's number. I've got that going for me. My boldness. You get rejected enough and you become numb to it. Things get a little easier because you actually find more power in the expectation of rejection--that's an alpha trait. You're a beta male Oscar. You're an inferior artist to your wife. In both content and status. I look at you people and start to wonder what I'm doing wrong. See I started talking to Bunny. It went terribly. I'll spare you all of the details...couldn't have been more beta. It hurts me so bad to know I've failed so hard with the only woman in America I care to know. When you love someone that much and you find yourself destroying so much potential...so I started reading The Redpill, decided to take a page out of their book and start a harem. Fuck it, why not right? D.I.Y. EVERYthing. Life's too short to wait for what will 'come your way.'

I'm a tiger not a blobfish. I don't…I mean don't blame women for their rejection of me. They're responding to something primal. I was weak. I've been reading a lot of books on P.U.A. and the attitude laid out is simple: if you don't get a girl it's not 'cause she's a bitch, it's because you don't deserve her. That's everything in life. I'm terrible with women now. It's nobody else's fault. Learn to turn them on or fucking fade. Adapt or die. Everything is seduction. No one cares until you make them. So if I'm lonely or rejected…see this is kind of a roundabout idea but it'll make sense in a minute…you look nice Lucy. You look great."

    I smile at Lucy. I smile at his wife. She's dressed in a tight floral dress. I smile on her as if she were my own wife. And she's outwardly disgusted by me--but she can actually start to see that I'm a very honest person. Who wishes he could be a part of the group of artists that most inspired him growing up. She's seeing me again as Josh waving to me in the Spreecast. Hahahaha…What I wouldn't have done to have been next to Lucy at that reading watching her open a tallboy. What I wouldn't have done. I would have stabbed kids for ticket money…

    We're outside of a trendy bar somewhere in Brooklyn. A real "banger" starts playing but I replace the sound with Nirvana's Milk It in my mind. Looks more and more like San Francisco everytime I visit. "What was I getting at? Oh, right. Identity doesn't matter…most of what it means to be a person that's loved is to be someone in the society--you're only as important and real as other people believe you are. So it's incredible. Watch how the resilient respond to abuse. Those who cross you aren't even not creating their own best competitors. There's this Chinese lady. They interviewed her on the radio--she was imprisoned in an internment camp as a kid. They put a gun to her temple. She's like 8 or something. They tell her to lift up her skirt and take a shit in front of them. So she lifts up her skirt and takes a shit in front of them--and they don't remove the gun from her temple. They say, 'eat it.' And with a gun pressed into her temple she eats it. She's a billionaire now. I have a lot in common with this woman. All that matters now is that I succeed. I will be the person I want to be in the society. You're speaking to an incredible person. An important person to the culture. I will be valued by society. I will have a harem. I'll have the fandom and social proof. I mean think about Pollack. I hate what he makes. It's fucking trash to me. But he did what he needed to. He convinced us it was art." I laugh. "And so it is."

    "See…I'm not certain most of independent literature isn't just marketing…it doesn't seem to want to breed success, you know. It's like, I read this interview, I think it was with Mary Miller, one of my literary idols at the time. I know better now than to have an idol, especially a woman, it's dangerous. We focus so much on the victimization of women in the culture. Think about how they're raped nd stalked nd then there's this compensation that happens--this sort of angelic quality that women take on as victims and martyrs. We're all our own martyr, right?" I laugh. "Clearly I've got a persecution complex. But women are somehow viewed as more pure. Less interested in sex. This morality is attributed to them as if by nature the "fairer" gender. Anyways.

It's Mary Miller I think and she posts this really annoying Facebook comment that at the time I thought was really, "real." and some sort of solid advice to writers, "Getting published doesn't change anything." People who are published--you privileged fucks--telling us unpublished to enjoy our/accept our being essentially unheard and nonexistent in an art scene. It's the worst advice I've ever heard."

"Better advice is to be determined. Assume that if your work is being rejected it's because you suck. Be content in your discontent. But want more. 'If you're not pissed you're losing you're cool with being mediocre.' A poem doesn't exist until it's read by someone else. The difference between success and failure is achieving the goal you've set out to do. The difference between a glorified hobbyist nd an artist is that he's acknowledged as the artist he believes himself to be. The difference between being a writer and not being one is that you were fucking published. Sorry...I've lost my train of thought. See Oscar, I said I wanted to beat your ass online and I know it's wrong but what you don't know about me is I'm not just a cybertuff. The problem I'm having right now is that, I am up for the fight, I mean, I'm a nihilist. It just doesn't mean anything anymore to live. Although something about by suicidal tendencies has this deep undercurrent of determination laced in it."

"My issue isn't fear--because for some reason, besides losing all feeling, except for hatred and a desire for vengeance--I've lost all of my fear of the things I should fear. Like violence. What I'm afraid of is the consequences. In order to succeed and finally prove people in your scene wrong about my value in society I have to stay free. We're in the middle of the street in Brooklyn. It'd be wildly cinematic--the perfect place, in this parklet with your beautiful wife watching the merciless absurdity of uncontrolled release...here by this parklet--"

I point my entire hand to the parklet. Someone rides a track bike by the front of it. A girl twists her hair seated at the benches. Cars honk. "My issue is to become the person I've set out to become I have to stay out of prison. See I've been institutionalized before for suicidal behavior. Twice. God had me driving a knife into my chest at the sink...because even God hates me. He hates how I've been living. I have to change. The psych ward is a horrible place. I can only imagine prison. I mean. I can't even imagine prison. I can't afford to have your friends here call the cops and have some pigs drag me off to the clink. I just got here to New York. I'm alone and one phone call would go wasted like a prayer. But if you want to fight--I'd love to. I'm just looking for an excuse to take out my senseless misdirected aggression--pent up from years of resentment towards your social scene, and break your small Parisian frame into the concrete. I'll agree to a fight if you want but there's conditions. We choose a private location, indoors. No one films or takes evidence of the event. Sarah and Lucy both have to be there. Any men you bring are totally unallowed to step in. And we flip a coin at the beginning of the match to decide whose playlist we use for the fight. Before the fight I record a legally binding contract that I'm responsible for nothing--and you accept full responsibility for yourself: time, date, name."

Oscar looks at me--
"Okay."
"Give me Lucy's phone."
Lucy looks at Oscar.
Oscar looks at Lucy and silently asks for the phone with a gesture of an empty palm bobbing up. Sarah walks up from inside the bar and steps up behind Lucy. Sarah's in a white Nike Run Joggers cap, which I'd seen her wearing in a dream I recently had of her, a crossback tank top in grey and black highwaisted jeans. I couldn't see her feet. Her hair's in dual braids sticking out of the cap. She looks at me--surprised by my size now. My shaved head. My height again. She sinks under a glass and her eyes furrow. With seething anger at just the sight of me. Oscar hands me the telephone. I pound out my number and call my own phone. "Just so you know it's real." I lift my phone from out of my pocket, simultaneously ringing, and place it back onto my butt pocket. I put a hand patronizingly on Oscars shoulder and look him in the eyes--
"Have a goodnight, fool."
Look up to Lucy and Sarah and start running off without turning around, and then spin into a swift soft run. My black rain jacket fills with air.

■

I get a text from an unlabelled number with a time, date, and address--I'm so excited by the lingering sensation of the vibration. I smile--holding it in, perverted to be this joyous alone in my rat's nest apartment in Bedstuy. But I can't hold it back. I start rocking back and forth laughing out loud--through the hollow of my house. My nude body, subpar by my own standards, nude, revealed to no one. The uproar shakes me, I fall off the bed kicking my legs. A woman downstairs pounds a broom into my floor/her ceiling and I laugh even harder.
"Be there."
I text.
The light of the phone illuminating arms pounds heavier than the year before. I've always been proud of my arms--but not always for what they make.

■

I entered Sarah's apartment.
All the walls were white and the lights were bright.
All the furniture was modern.
There was a banner on the wall, letters strung across like a birthday welcome.
"BLEED HIM."
I think that one's for Oscar.
There was a piece of embroidery on the wall I knew was Lucy's, a cover of Christine's World. That crippled girl in the field.

@abigfuckingbully

The house was full of bodies that I passed thru--unnoticed, unknown, as I'd always been by these people. The room was packed wall to wall. Beers were in everybody's hands. Like tickets had been sold. And I felt when I closed my eyes, a light in my right fist. I could see it. Everyone was beautiful. I walked deeper into the, found near the couches Oscar--standing, drinking a beer. I shook his hand and finally people noticed who I was. The room pushed themselves into the order of a ring: all the bodies to the wall and a floor for the both of us. Lucy and Sarah sat on the couch beautifully placed--like actresses in a film. I smiled--not a vengeful smile--a sincere smile just happy to finally be meeting them. We didn't the rooms silence for agreements: I spoke into the phone clearly and handed it to Oscar who spoke his testimony and I hung up.

"Ay, shut the fuck up! Fights on!" Someone said as we entered the ring.

Oscar handed his phone to Lucy.

I handed my phone to Lucy.

I peeled my shirt off immediately, I know I'm scrawny, but I'm still proud of the small mass I've built. I was proud to inhabit my flesh, myself, my armor. Sculpted arms, a stronger chest. The hint of ribs I'd shown Bunny in so many photos. I felt like an American. I felt violent and happy. I saw the eyes of all the writers that I love and who hated me now. Elizabeth was in the room. And I smiled at her knowingly. Her face was hiding all of her anger in pure neutrality. The disguise--it's all writing is. It's all anyone is.

"You're a great writer." she once emailed. "You'll be published a lot, etc. etc."

"Send me a poem anytime!" she once emailed.

It flashed thru my head.

Tonight I was all of the men I was jealous of her loving in her books.

But I was different than them.

I want to be the one to wash your blonde hair.

New Amerkian Brutalist.

Bunny said it best, I just don't translate well to paper.

I'm better than anything I've ever written.

"We'd get along in person." Bunny messages, once.

A purple ribbon appearing in my cellphone with the sweetest words, satellite to these people. "It was so funny to me," she messages, "you talking to me and Sarah like we're in-kids." She's an outsider too. It's why I love her.

Bunny would hate having given me those words now.

My blood was rising and with it--with Oscar in presence...

■

At my worst, after all Bunny had given me, I ceremoniously burnt her book in the kitchen of my mother's house. The same room I promised I'd make her my wife. Hahahah...

A fucking loser.

A psychotic.
A stalker.
An "abuser."
A "failed" artist.
All I had was what I felt for Bunny and when it went unreturned it mutated, took the form of boundless hatred, I couldn't help looking at the kitchen table--a portrait painted on the book so widely recognized.
"It must feel good to have a book published.
A book is a powerful sculpture."
What a beautiful thought Bunny.
That's the sweetest thing I've ever heard.
Her book...it was true for her.
The portrait: her long, shining brown hair draped over her rail thin ballerina's body, in a simple wooden chair. Green velvet dress, plumb purple stockings...
But she would never look at me.
'The symbol of the face always turns away.'
Infuriated I finally grabbed the paper back and turned on my camera--I stripped down to my underwear and started filming. My body wouldn't be new to her. I lifted the book into view of the camera--and held it, then turned it, and demonstrated the strength of my arms, hips and ribs in view, and with my other hand, lifted a grey lighter up to the corner of the book and sparked the flame, while the book burned I read a review:

    BUNNY IS HARD NOT TO LOVE
    BECAUSE OF HOW HARD SHE LOVES
    THE BEAUTY IN HER POETRY COMES FROM A MIXTURE OF MALE AGGRESSION
    AND FEMALE SENTIMENTALITY
    PASTELS & FLOWERS
    COLUMBINE
    SO MUCH OF THIS WORK IS REMINISCENT OF VERA PAVLOVA
    IN IT'S DENSITY ND SPEED
    IN IT'S BREVITY
    IT'S GRAVITY INESCAPABLE AS A BLACK HOLE
    SOMEHOW CAPTURING A LANDSCAPE UNDISPUTABLY AMERICAN
    THIS WOMAN DESERVES AWARDS FOR HER WRITTEN WORK ALONE
    IF YOU'RE NOT IN LOVE WITH BUNNY BY THE END OF THIS BOOK
    OR IF YOU HAVEN'T FOUND A SISTER IN BUNNY
    THERE'S SOMETHING SERIOUSLY WRONG WITH YOU
    YOU'RE A FUCKED UP HUMAN
    I LOVE YOU BUNNY

I calmly collect the ashes and put them in an envelope addressed to you.
I still have your address.
I display the final product for the camera, obscuring the envelopes details for privacy.
The feeling was overwhelming.
I felt the camera rolling and left the camera rolling.
I picked up Sarah's book and demonstrated my arm, then lifted the grey lighter, Bunny's favorite color, right? to the book.
A book that I believed at one point had 'saved my life.'
Had filled me with the desire to live when I would have otherwise taken my life.
Hahahaha…
The book burned so peacefully, cleanly and economic, like my rage.
The pages folded, blossoming quietly with a crackle into a black rose, which I shake into dust, onto my floor. Out of view of the camera.
I continue filming.
I find Elizabeth's book.
My mentor. My bane.
Hahahah
And I dig thru my books, all stocked in a pile, in the corner of my entirely empty bedroom. Next to the single size mattress. And a dream journal.
I pulled it out of the wreckage, a monument of my own failures, books of artist I loved who hated me now. And with all of my heart I returned the gift of rejection.
I lifted the book to the camera.

∎

I'm shocked out of the memory. It's Elizabeth. She throws a half empty tall boy at me, full force, no sympathy. Spatter catches. Her blonde hair shakes over her face as it moves forward with her body's screaming, "Piece of shit!"
And I'm so blessed to hear her beautiful voice which sounds out like music.
The audience loves it.
I sustain the blow without resistance nd turn my face back to Oscar.
I say nothing.
I accept the abuse.
Two way torture.

∎

Again, I remember:
I lift the book to the camera.
I lift the lighter to the book.

I'm surprised the fire alarm hasn't gone off.
I let my thumb slide down the lighter.
I celebrate the book and watch it burn.
I watch it burn.
I'm Hitler collecting Bibles.
(Sorry Scott.)
I'm building better people one book burning at a time.
Fuck you Elizabeth.
"Fuck you tho
 I love you tho"
Ashes collect on my kitchen floor. A pile of love. My hand japs into the stop button.
Fills the frame before going black.
One day I'll fuck an artist.
Hahahah
I'm a genius.
I'm Dali.
All I gotta do is sign the canvas.
I press 'Send' on an email of the video addressed to every indie lit writer I've ever exchanged words with online.
Everyone knows.
Who I am.
Watches the film entitled *Sour Grapes 0*.
Who I'm not.
If people don't love you for who you are: be a different person.
If you won't accept me as a friend, accept me as a villain.
You only know of me know because I'm someone you can feel free to hate.
Sorry about my Twitter.
I'm a racist. Blah blah blah
I'm a Transphobe.
I'm a hypocrite.
I'm a misogynist.
Fuck you Dostoyevsky Wannabe.
I guess I should know better than to have any opinions.
I guess I should know better and keep my mouth shut.
It was a true story, you know
It's not a testament to who I am, it's just how I feel.
I was so good for so long.
Once I did bad, that I heard ever.
Twice I did good, that I heard never.
I deserve it.
I'm a psychotic.
Sorry Elizabeth, for all the shit I said when I lost my mind.
My total lack of boundaries nd professionalism.

I used to have a lot to say.
Now I don't know who I am.
I must have hurt a lot of people.
Fuck you, Alex for not defending me.
Fuck you, Joseph, for virtue uber alles.
How tyrants think of people just as objects/obstacles.
I'm pariah now.
I'm going to act like it.
Non platform me.
Censor me.
Label me.
Tell me how I see things.
My brother says my last piece in Fluland reads like the Isla Vista Shooter.
'Entitled white serial killer shit.'
But the only compliments I got were from a woman.
The hot Virginian girl from work.
With a shaved head nd a bull ring.
Thanks Cheyenne.
'I loved it! It's a story you can really put yourself into. It's really good.' she says.
Ben loved it.
Thank you Ben.
Joey loved it.
Thank you Joey.
Why was it that the only people disappointed with my censorship from Dostoyevsky Wannabe were women?
Thanks Izzy.
Thanks Alicia.
Thanks Brigid.

∎

The issue I'm obviously having is the failure to believe in myself. To believe I have a purpose and influence on my own. Nihilism is lazy, an aversion to being held to standard.
In a dream Kimiya, the pretty, petite, freckled, light skinned persian girl, the one who dresses like an anthropologist, she looked better before the rhinoplasty...someone who I loved but who I only ever shit talked in poems, is in my room, sitting across from me on the floor. Her legs to her side. She grabs a case of .9 pencil lead and opens the top. She holds me down and pries my jaws open, stuffs the case in, I choke to death on the breaking pieces. Rarely are dreams this merciful nd direct. You will eat your words. Here I was to eat them.

∎

On a trip back form Santa Cruz, Jennifer, visiting me from New York City, the woman who had given me a start to my life in the east in her apartment while I settled myself the first time I moved, a woman I had complimented, prized, and insulted in writing…a light skinned Arabic woman with long, curly, black hair, big sad eyes, here she was driving a red car wearing a pair of stonewashed Versace jeans tight around her beautiful ass. I noticed when she was pumping the gas. Tho I think I'd first noticed on her birthday in New York City, when it was wrapped in blue velour. Smiling, doing a line of coke, she'd done her mascara perfectly.
"I liked that you wrote that. I liked that line." she said at dinner.

On the way out of the diner, she pulled a pipe out of her pocket, a one-hitter, sat herself loosely in the front seat, car doors open, one leg off the side, foot on the pavement like a cowgirl, and took two hits. She passed me the pipe, having packed it for me. Everyone knows I don't do a lot of drugs so they do sweet things like give me baths when I'm puking drunk or pack the bowl for me, I'm always visiting. I accept: take a single hit which is more than enough for me to spill my guts. The night drive gets darker. Jennifer drives aggressively. I'm paranoid. "I can't believe I survived this road stoned. Weed and driving is a terrible combination…" Highway 17 is a nightmare, it's a constant turn, winding. The car goes silent for a while. Jennifer broaches a topic that I feel may be a polite and indirect way of suggesting I correct some behavior. I'm too stoned to remember *anything* but also, I have a terrible memory. Bunny noticed.
"Am I an asshole?" I ask her, my hand stretched over the hot air pumping out of the A.C.

"No." She says sadly, stiffly, looking straight forward at the road. The way your face gets tight when you don't want to cry in front of someone,

"But you're too blunt. You're too honest. Like, you've always been abrasive, but…you told me you wanted to take pictures of girls you were sleeping with naked and post them on Instagram. You told me you were starting a harem. I don't like that. But you've always been like that." She didn't look at me. "I'm just used to it now." Her jaw clenched.

I would never say sorry.

I'm so tired of saying sorry.

But something in me…for 2 years solid after being given the red letter in my punk scene because of accusations of me stalking and 'abusing,' a girl: I've written so much about this at this point. Hey Christine, I still love you but I hate you. Don't fuck someone who's had a crush on you for 8 years, tell them you have feelings for them, leave them for your ex-boyfriend, cut of all ties of 8 years of friendship and be surprised I literally wished death upon you.

"I HOPE YOU DIE IN THAT FILTHY FUCKING DOGSHED YOU CALL A ROOM. YOU AND YR THREE SHIT-EATING PITBULLS, BITCH." Oh, you don't want to talk about it? Surprising. Well bitch, I do. I'm at your job, with the book you loaned me, because I got words. They might have to drag me out by the collar like they did when I brought Jess flowers to her job…The real issue people have w/ me is access to sex. Pull the lynchpin in a tight knit social scene and everyone knows who you're fucking and everyone has something to say. "He fetishizes women of color!" Hahahah, I'm a fucking person of color, I'm just light skinned. Everyone looks at you differently and expects you to act a certain way. Even the people you're with. "You're so affectionate." she says after we finish coming. Oh no, I'm weak to her. When I finally got angry...it's like the only time I've ever been real to these people...people cannot believe who I am when I'm openly angry. I'm not violent. You thought you'd have a white boy as a pet forever but now you're terrified. You start a fight you finish it. Under the guise I'm a threat, under the banner of honoring consent, people shut me out without any interest in resolving the conflict. Nobody gets mad off the bat. People get mad when people don't fucking listen to them. Okay, I'm a stalker. I'll get better with stricter policing. Alert the community! Hahahah Nobody knows what you've done wrong, I'm clearly insane.

Then there was the psychotic break: verbally abused writers who barely knew me. Asked to be Sarah's whore. Burnt every bridge. Cussed out the entire literary and punk scenes I was even marginally a part of. Accused strangers of rape. Sorry wasn't good enough. *Sorry, I lost my fucking mind.* A catalog of failures with women I had to finally confront were a result of just "being myself." Yourself isn't good enough. Yourself isn't good enough for respect. For 2 solid years I cultivated an individual who served absolutely no one else. Who was unapologetically blunt. Who said everything I had to say when I wanted to say it. Who didn't wait for someone to take the time to notice me to talk to them. Every woman I wanted I approached. Every magazine I wanted to be a part of I submitted to. But maybe I've always been like that. I was someone more concentrated now. Harder. More aggressive. More powerful. The problem was in the process of putting an old self down like a sick pathetic dog, I had functionally suppressed everything in me that allowed me to feel. While I tried to forgive myself and move on I hated everyone in my past. I was @abigfuckingbully. I was a Lil Tank. All kindness is weakness. And emotions are in the way. Emotions were my hustle. I had plans on converting myself into currency. I still do.

I looked at Jennifer who had lifted a hand to her temple, hanging there now. I was suddenly...feeling something. "I'm a little hurt." I said, cringing, crumpling into my own body so uncomfortable with how pathetic it felt to feel anything at all. Especially, "hurt." I both couldn't resist and hated myself for acknowledging and expressing the emotion. It had it's own momentum. It was independent of me. "You're hurt?" she said, neutrally. And I thought of our history. How for whatever reason we had spent our youth together but I had never spent any time actually *talking* to Jennifer until I had moved to New York. I had always isolated her/alienated her, rejected her. We spent every moment together for summers at a time and we made little to no contact. Just staring across Misty's room hoping a conversation wouldn't happen. Invisible as we filed in from 24 mile city bike rides, rack the back in silence on Misty's wall. She wasn't real to me.

Jennifer wouldn't like me mentioning it here again, it's already been written, but she once hacked my Facebook. Was my stalker. "I resent that you describe me as your stalker it's a very self-aggrandizing description." she said. She never said if she had romantic feelings, so I shouldn't assume anything. For whatever reason she had held a place in her heart for me and of all people wanted to visit me while at home in Santa Clara seeing her mother. I was in her car now. Something clicked.

"Did I hurt you?" I asked sincerely confused. She knew what I meant.

"Yeah, you were always mean to me." She put her hand back on the wheel. "I knew just by the way you were to never approach you. Everything about you told me that. No matter how much time we spent together." She was suddenly becoming especially beautiful to me. I never listened to this woman before. I wasn't going to say sorry. No matter how horrible I felt. But what was happening now was that I was understanding my role in this woman's life. I felt sick. They just kept coming all of the 'feelings.' :))

"That's so fucked up." I said into the car, loudly, alarmed by my obliviousness. By my abuses.

"Here's the thing,"

"Why was that?" she said.

"See, it wasn't that I thought poorly of you. It was just, the way people talked about you, it was like you were unimportant. They never talked shit, it was just as if you didn't exist. I can't believe I was that impressionable, I didn't even make my own decision about you."

Her eyes were watering.

Her face was still straight.

"You're a valuable person to me!

You're an important person to me!"

I yelled at her.

I wanted to touch her so I touched her. It was part desire and part impulse. A function of wanting to care for this woman. Her legs were warm. Her back was small. Her hair was under my hands.

"Stop. You're pulling my hair." she says making a face and fidgets out of my hands, wiggling her shoulders.

"What did I do?"

"Listen." she said, pulling into my driveway. "I don't want to talk about it."

" I really need you to tell me."

"I have too much to say about it." she paused. "See, it's disgusting to me because these conversations don't serve me. It's a lot of emotional labor for me to get you to understand how you've been treating me." She shifted something from the front to the backseat. "Look, I have to pee. Can I use your bathroom?"

I said yes.

I didn't tell her how disgusting it was.

Our plumbing doesn't work.

She's a film editor in Versace jeans...in our shithole apartment.

I stood patiently in my house, introduced Jennifer to my mother, and my mother's rapist.

She smiled and asked me to come outside with her.

"So we're okay?" she asks.

I don't know why.

I was infuriated.

How was it that I turned from neutrality.

Feelings of superiority to this person into full affection for them.

I was horrified by myself.

"See I was interacting with this concept I had of you.

It's so sad.

We just delete people because of an *idea* of who they are.

She was red in the face.

She could cry but she's smart enough not to.

"Why are you like this?"

"I think..." I ate it. For a solid minute. She was patient.

My face contorted. I couldn't tell if I was being honest or manipulative when I said,

"It's because I like you."

I like you. Hahahah

You fucking animal.

"Don't say that." she said.

What I couldn't say,

I thought you were ugly

but I wanted to fuck you

so I kept you away from me.

(Success. I'd become who I'd wanted to become. Someone who navigated their emotions so 'well' they ceased to exist. Complete unawareness. Like water thru water. Don't think that because I've got a big mouth I'm not repressed. An interview with a BMXer comes to mind.

"How do you deal with fear?"

"I'm completely numb to it. Either I do the trick or snap my neck, that's it.

I do have these night terrors tho...)

Anger rose, like heroin through a vein.

I lifted my finger and pointed to her.

My posture clear and terrifying.

"You're not being fucking straight with me." I growled.

(Projection)

"You're being really scary right now.

I'm not mad at you.

I told you everything I could, okay?

Can we hug?

"Okay." I said. I put my finger down out of her face.

We embraced for a weird weak hug.
Both of our bodies felt as if they were slipping away from each other.
I wanted her in my bed now.
I wanted to watch her peel off a pair of stonewashed Versace jeans.
I wanted to take a picture of her doing it and post it for the public.
I wanted her curls to fall over me.
I walked back in from the balcony, and stripped away slowly.
Collected myself.
Slipped under the single blanket on a single size mattress in the floor of "my" room.
How pathetic.
Never tell them how you feel.
It's my bed. I'll sleep in it.
I leaned up, spat in my hand and masturbated to the same image of her above me, her face focused down on me. Present but distracted by pleasure. Watching her curls drift nd bob. Versace jeans by the bed. And came.

∎

At the club (cafe, Hemingway called them clubs I think)
I frequent as to work a woman whose name I forget was acting strange towards me.
She didn't smile as she usually did. She was curt. She neutralized facial expressions, jammed them before they happened and avoided me. She's a barista there. A writer. I had gotten her phone number but never called. I wonder if she was feeling upset. I ordered a coffee at 8pm regardless of how poor sleeping patterns exacerbate my Schizophrenia and sat in front of the mirror where I like to write. I know everyone in the village which is why I'm alone in the mirror.
People don't think it's weird anymore. I feel bad. Apple's here who's number I also got but who I've never called. She's too young and I'm too heavy, I honestly don't think she could hang, and if you're not my age or within four years of it I don't want to fuck you. And I'm not calling women who don't make art or who I'm not fucking for "personal reasons." Sorry I pulled the number Apple.
The plain girl whose name I forgot looked upset still. She moved from the counter to the bar seats in the back where employees took their breaks. I saw her white legs sticking out of pink shorts. It's unlike me to care enough to gauge why one of many village girls are upset with me when so many village girls are upset with me. Everyone's got a reason, I don't blame them. But remembering Jennifer--I got up from the mirror and the small wooden bar I was at and moved to stand by the wooden bar she sat at.
"Let me sit with you." I said. Standing with a bag on.
"Okay." she said.

I sat down next to her. I was feeling close to her immediately. That I had commanded a seat and not asked for one and was now close enough to smell her turned me on and I wondered if I was sending or receiving the same interest and excitement. Apple came to the back with us leaning on the banister and slid over to me a huge Pellegrino which I took into my hands like an ape, unwound and started to drink from handling by the neck like it was hard liquor. "It makes me want one the way you drink that." The plain girl said and smiled. Her voice was tired but energetic still. The way time can slow if you move fast enough. She looked pretty to me right now. Apple was there, freckled nd doll faced. Focusing this much on the plain girl was a direct offense to Apple but I moved forward without hesitance or consideration. Apple watched politely but with anger. With my hands over the green glass bottle I looked at the plain girl and said, "You look upset."

"No, I'm just tired." She smiled. "How are you? How's writing?" she asked.

Looking down the cafe if she needed to help anyone.

"It's great." I said. "I'm writing a story about beating the shit out of another indie lit writer."

She nodded. "Why?"

"It's a long story."

"I'm listening."

Detailed the psychotic break.

Detailed repeated censorship of my work.

Problems with Elizabeth my mentor.

Who I made feel like my momma.

Accusations of harassment, racism, transphobia, sexism, etc.

"He's sort of a poster child of a scene, all of these people I really loved."

She was bored.

Got up and helped a customer.

I felt stupid.

I compensated with good posture.

Took out the story and started writing again.

Sucked on the bottle.

Forgot about my coffee.

Watched Apple bend over in black sunbleached cutoffs to clean things and cook things.

A man in front of a computer is fucking ridiculous to me, dude.

A man in front of a notebook is worse.

What am I doing here?

Are any writers even sane people?

Who could enjoy hours in front of paper and absent of women?

There's a person writing and then there's a person outside of me watching me write.

All of my own thoughts.

I've already had them.
I didn't enjoy composing it.
Most of it's just real life with the names changed.
I'm a journalist not an artist.
Only the insane could enjoy the act especially when so rarely rewarded.
So weakly rewarded.
It's social science, dude.
Punished or ignored: dissolves.
Criticized: dissolves.
Praised: begins again.
I'm a masochist.
This is what I learned from lifting.
I'm a part of a hyper competitive society and all I want to do is win.
I like it when it's read.
I like the product.
I like being heard.
Bunny's seeing 4 men right now, "juggling men" she says. Men say spinning plates.
4 men that'd beat the shit out of each other for their shot.
They fight for her at museum exhibitions.
Something to be aware of.
Stop telling me arts not a competition.
Stop telling me love's not a contest.
Stop lying to me, okay?
James Guida wrote this aphorism:
There is after all a criminal element to solitude. It too would like to snuff out the witnesses.
Another I can't find from *Marbles* about how if we were to watch footage of our own lives for a week we'd likely kill ourselves.
Agreed.
"Tie my noose tight."
Kick the footstool and smile blue in the knot.
The plain girl came back with her pretty voice and looked at me commandingly.
"Can I ask you a question?"
I look at her smiling, cocky.
"Yeah, sure."
"Do you think the reason people are afraid of you is because you don't know what you're capable of?"
"What do you mean?
 Am I an intimidating person?"
"Everyone's afraid of you."
I smiled.
"It's because," she said, "you don't know your own limits."

I was confused.
"I don't understand what you mean?
Are you saying I'm unpredictable?"
That's an alpha trait, I thought.
Am I being punished?
"Well you just told me you cussed out an entire art scene--like, you can only have so much sympathy for a person, you know?"
"I don't need sympathy."
"That's not what I'm getting at."
She stared. She was being gentle with me which had me feeling attracted to her.
And that was making me angry.
She looked flustered.
Her thick lips pursed.
She looked away, cocked a hip and stared at me again.
I tried to do everything in my power to hide everything I was feeling.
That none of it would show on my face.
I used to be able to smile a real smile.
But it'd been so long since I'd loved someone enough to smile a kind of smile that starts to mark your face that I had a total neutrality.
Everyday I was taking a mugshot.
I took a sip of Pellegrino to hide myself while asserting myself.
"You read Catcher in The Rye? You know Reznikov? Or whatever...He doesn't know he's doing something wrong until he's gone too far. He doesn't know he's done something bad until it's too late. He's crossed the line. People are scared of you because you don't know what you're capable of."
Apple looked around us nervously, bending over to clean things. A broom fell. She picked up a bag of trash and huddled over, passed in front of us acting like she couldn't hear. Ignoring how close we were becoming so quickly.
The plain girl turned for a minute, didn't do anything. I liked her pink shorts. She turned back and sat at the bar. I looked at her. Honesty even if cruel or a misread is a sign of respect. I had learned early that people committed to you would witness you and if they witness you, they think of you. There's a potential respect there. Can never tell who's looking down on you all the time. I'm a terrible judge of character. I'll be hard on art but I won't be hard on people. Forever forgiving. I wanted the plain girl. I'm sorry if you're reading this right now. I'm sorry I called you the plain girl. You're beautiful. Apple's staring disengaged. She also seemed upset, but was it with me? Her eyes looked wet. She had questions she wasn't asking. I probably hurt her all the time like everyone else.
I took a swig from the glass bottle and I looked the plain girl in the face, feeling her warmth from here. "What are you doing after work?" I asked. She got up and walked to the other side of the bar. Looked into a cellphone to change the song playing.

"I'm..." she did everything she could to be distracted, put the cellphone down, her eyes looking down, big and honey colored. Her face was soft with rounded features. "Going home, cooking a meal for me and my partner, watching some..."

Half Right by Elliott Smith plays.

I think of Bunny.

I want to cry.

All the texts I sent Bunny about walking downtown with a knot in my throat. It had gotten to the point where I was so lovesick that in order to "relieve the knot" I would excuse myself from work or public, and find a bathroom--then lean into myself, falling over and scream as loud and as long as legally possible. I've been arrested for screaming before. This was the only way to treat the "knot" and it would return in ten minutes much worse. My heart/chest would become tight and I would only be able to take shallow breaths. My face would contort. I'd never be able to cry. Maybe they would have been fake tears. *All my tears are real except in front of you.* And she didn't deserve them. *"You're really irresponsible guilting me like this!"* she texts back. Missing the fucking point.

I look at the plain girl. I'm stung with rejection.

"You have a boyfriend?"

"Yeah, well, we don't just fuck and walk each other to school, we pay for shit together, we live together, do life stuff together, so he's my partner not my boyfriend."

I felt stuffed.

I stuck myself into a notebook.

Then pushed it aside obviously agitated then looked her in the face and said,

"I'm mad you have a boyfriend."

"I know." she says matter of factly.

Turns around and shows me her ass, making herself busy. She starts putting up all of the chairs. Surrounded by so much wood, like prison bars. She puts on a boys camo jacket in the back door/cellar hidden in front of me, then politely tells me,

"Atticus, you hear that? We're closing at 9, we didn't make enough money to stay open tonight."

I nod.

She stays close fixing more chairs, just off to my right shoulder.

"Can I ask you a question?" I ask.

"Sure." she walked over and stood tall looking to the side at me.

"Why'd you give me your phone number if you had a boyfriend?"

"Oh." She sort of hung there in her camo jacket huge sleeves hanging over her skinny hands. It's like every girl who gives me the time is some skinny white girl. "Well we have a lot of good conversations and you seem interesting. I'm sorry. Is that a black and white thing for you, like it has to be sexual or romantic? I understand."

We were both silent.

I was almost ashamed.

It was like the left side of my body "unlocked" and fell into the rest of me like water.

No matter how tight my body wanted to get--I wouldn't let it.

"Sorry if you felt lead on." she said.

"No. It's not like that."

I packed my shit up and walked out of the club.

Rejection constantly.

You can't even bother feeling burnt.

Everything in you goes black.

My face broke and I finally cracked mask.

It was twisted into rage.

I walked like I always walk but bigger.

Jacob says, "You walk like you're going to beat someone's ass, it's scary."

I know.

I know.

Oh, shit.

Her name's Layne.

■

Crying about Bunny: she blocked me on every social media outlet.

I asked too many questions she didn't answer them. So I got mad and asked her more questions. In a DM Jacob says,

"You push her too hard.

You're constantly testing her.

You keep pushing all of her buttons"

"Yeah, I'm just like that.

Pissing off a girl isn't the worst thing you can do though.

Get under a girl's skin and you're doing something right.

She's mad right now but I think she'll come back."

"You're deluded."

"Yeah, probably.

I mean, I think she might like me. Hahahah"

"I think you're the horniest guy I know."

"Absolutely.

It's not like that tho.

I think I'm in love with her."

"Really?"

"Yeah."

"I guess you've pissed off a lot of women in your life."

I laugh.

■

She just doesn't believe me when I say it.
But I've only ever had nightmares about her so...

■

I release a two part video one hour each on YouTube titled Sour Grapes 1 & 2. I'm terrible at being mean, I'm just not that intelligent, creative, or critical enough but I do my best on reinforcing people's worst beliefs about me. *Racist, Transphobe, Misogynist.* You want to see a Transphobe? You want to see a Misogynist? Hahahah Someone accuses me of being an "unsafe male," by saying "I'm scared to live in the same town as this guy." People report feeling harassed by messages in a thread Joseph started about my being a Transphobe nd that it's vital "we" don't support a magazine run by the likes of one. It's another instance where, sorry, I guess I've got a big dumb mouth, but I'm really not this horrible person you're making me out to be. As if my opinions on your gender even fucking matter...so I start in:

"Hey C, let me tell you as both a man and a stalker myself, since I'm so well connected in the scene: you're rape proof. Even the most self-abasing stalker has more self-respect than to follow you--down a dark alley way. He's got better shit to do. I've got better shit to do."

and

"I've seen enough Protect Trans animated gifs to want to kill a trans person. I no longer want to protect you...I don't feel safe..."

In Sour Grapes 1 I choose some targets in the scene at random and some out of a need for vengeance. I mean, you've already basically kicked me out of your scene, I figure, for myself, I may as well get a word in before finding another venue. I have no idea how many people I'm pissing off. How this will effect me since we know when you piss off the wrong person you're pissing off a lot of other "friends in high places," that will likely have the same instinct to extinguish you/leave you to continually isolate. I do a lot of dumb shit when I'm mad.
I announce in the video that I'm writing black female pen name that's doing better than when I submit as myself. The truth is I write under several pen names to avoid people I'm writing about finding the specific pieces I abuse them in. Hahhaha I skewer Alex publicly for her newfound feminist vigor in her Twitter feed after disowning me as a "broet," and disowning her participation in my magazine, which wasn't an issue till I cussed out Joseph and botched her privately discussing the issue with me. "I don't like what he said to me." she said initially. But again, I get so angry sometimes...I just can't let shit go, no matter how much it preserves my power.

The magazine's unimportant, tho. What's important is that people are privately accepting of me but quick to disown me in public. "Alex, you're not a feminist okay? You fucked a guy you told me you think might be abusive, then you called him out for abusive behavior, then you override your judgement and invite him to do the reading. I'm doing the reading too but you don't offer me a place to spend the night until you're too scared of the guy and ask me to be muscle in defense of you in case he 'does anything.'" Hedonist in private. Moralist in public. "Bitch must think I'm a tool." Elizabeth never forgave me for the psychotic break and all my 'unprofessionalism.' Or something else I'm unaware of. Won't get into the rest of the video. Except that at the end, I attack the only girl in America I want to know. Pathetic, I know. Dangerous, I know.

"YOU DON'T SEEM LIKE THE TYPE TO HAVE VAGINA DENTATA OFF THE BAT--BUT AFTER A CLOSER LOOK, SHOULDA PICKED THAT UP."

"I REALLY REGRET BEING SO EAGER TO FLY OUT ND JOIN WHATEVER FUCKED UP HAREM OF LOSERS WHO WANT TO FUCK YOU."

"THERE'S THIS DEEP SEEDED BETA MALE IN ME...WANTS TO...EAT YOUR PUSSY ND--GIVE YOU FLOWERS...IT'S SO PATHETIC."

"YOU KNOW YOU'RE THIRSTY WHEN YOU LOOK LIKE ME ND YOU'RE TRYING TO FUCK SOMEONE WHO LOOKS LIKE BUNNY."

"I TOLD YOU YOU HAVE A PRETTY VOICE BUT YOU KNOW IT'S GONNA PICK UP FUCKED UP GUYS LIKE ME, SINCE IT'S ALL PITCH SHIFTED--AND MASCULINE."

"YOU'RE A MEAN DRUNK--THAT'S FOR SURE."

It's sour grapes.
I wanted to take back my power.
I had subbed myself with every compliment I had given Bunny.
Compliments are currency.
I'd robbed myself.
I'd made her head so big.
Like a child,
I decided to take it all back.
People say, "you can't take it back."
I disagree.
All the good I ever gave can just as easily become a dig.
I know there's smarter people than me, who would have so much more to say.
If I'd even end up on their radar hahahah

@abigfuckingbully

All the nights I spent cross legged on my hardwood floor listening to your readings like a favorite album.
I know one of your most popular poems by heart.
I have a night terror of you:
I'm a preacher offer you a light in the form a jade stone, carved into a rose, from a future-primitive/organatronic console, a glowing jade green: a map of the tunnel system we're in. I want to show you the way out. I'm sincerely happy to offer what I've found--and you hobble forward, in muted purple, long hair, and a muted purple headband, maybe it's a ribbon in your beautiful silvery hair. You take what's in my hands, snatch it and race away, becoming a light. I'm hurt. I'm supposed to come with you. "Where are you going?" I ask with all of my heart, shouting you down. I chase you but the closer I get   you turn on me, and you're hissing, you open your mouth wide, slightly unhinged as if a snake, revealing a mouthful of knife-long fangs, bloodied, as if rust. No sound comes out out. Your eyes/pupils are filled with a skull each, and parallel to your howl, they howl silently. Tho I am horrified--I'm numb. I disappear.

I author an image macro that's accepted in @nulithouse: a white pillow centered in a black background with white type, *IN ALL OF MY DREAMS YOU ARE GOOD TO ME*. It's a lie.
You've never been good to me (in a dream). Maybe it only seems like you're good to me. Maybe you're just bored and like the attention. Maybe you're just "being nice."

In another nightmare you appear to me. Again in a muted purple dress. Sitting at the edge of my bed, the view from above obscuring your face. Your hand is a fist in your lap holding what I understand to be an invisible knife. You're grinning.

Michael has a dream you rape him a day after I show him a photo.

I attribute too much good to your face.
Halo effect.
Fuck you.

I send the video to every indie lit writer I've ever emailed with…It recieves 21 views. Significantly more than I expected.

I record a video of new unpublished works: essentially cellphone notes. Fuck it, I mean, Darcie's doing it. One of the poems is titled a racial slur, on purpose, just to piss people off/disappoint them, which I won't repeat here. 17 views, a thumbs down on YouTube. Significantly more than I expected. I'm such a valued artist.
       Hahahah

I snap out of it: the apartments filled to the brim. Darcie's hissing at me, *"KEEP MY FUCKING NAME--OUT OF YOUR MOUTH!"* Most people have cans but she's drinking out of glass. I have this respect for her for that. Wrapped around the bottle, I notice, neatly done purple gel nails. I always notice gel nails. She's wearing a skin-tight black cotton dress. Her bull ring pulls up she keeps screaming at me, which stresses me out--I feel stupid for having been mean online. She was really nice to me on Twitter, should have left it at that. I like her bowl cut because I like girls who do boyish things. She won't stop hissing at me but I find the attention to be a form of affection at this point. I'm always impressed by this level extraversion. Thicker girls usually like me but I don't think Darcie likes me. Her body makes me feel really safe. She's beautiful. I'd love to be with her. I'd love to be held by her. Enveloped in the warmth and nurturance of her large breasts. (Alex once said, *"She's popular on Twitter and has big tits, it's whatever. Of course she's getting published."*) I don't smile or respond. My blood's rising. I try to harness it all for the fight.

■

Sour Grapes 2 is a video in which I apologize without apologizing. In this video I praise everyone I've ever had a chance to read, meet, email, DM, be published by. The sad thing is, is I thought I did my best throughout talking to these people to demonstrate how deeply I loved and respected them as both artists nd people. Even as someone who's been critiqued, censored, ignored/destroyed by the group he wishes the most to belong to, I know that there's so much good in showing people the good they're doing. I understand now it's unrealistic to believe in friendship as an artist presenting themselves in a scene. I want to learn from you. I want to be in your light. I believe in you. I believe I have something to offer. I believe I have a place in your world and that if you'd spend time in mine, you'd see how much fun it could be. I keep going back to this memory of a portrait I drew Lucy, it was terrible but it was an offering. I know why it's a problem to be this way. I ask for a lot I guess. It's my job to bring people into my world, it's pathetic to want to join someone else's.

There's this Jungian idea of the Shadow. All of the aspects of yourself that are evil, destructive, anti-social...you'll become aware of theses aspects around age 30. All of a sudden you start having these terrible nightmares...If you're a psychological success you integrate these aspects into yourself while still being aware of their danger. Me being the impatient and curious cat to be killed thought he might risk potential self-sabatoge by "meeting" my Shadow thru meditation.

Meditate:
You're on a boat and you crash thru green seas in your small white two man canoe, as a passenger. Rowing is a man, a hooded figure whose face is hidden.

You crash upon the shore and find yourself on the sands of an island. He silently leads you down the sands into a jungle, a stone pathway leading to a camp fire. The hooded figure leading you sits down on a log of large beachwood and pulls away his hood to reveal the face of a jackal. His black hands point behind you, where you're confronted by another hooded figure. As you approach, your vision becomes clearer: what do you see?

I put out my hand to the figure: a hooded anthropomorphic tapeworm. A parasite with a stark human face. It's eyes colorless, hollow, and without pupils in the face. A constant state of fear. However it was smiling now., I recieved his hand, with disgust and then acceptance. I was here to meet myself.

His first words to me are, "You *need* to know me. You *need* to be my friend."
The vision ceased. I was clear again.
You all need to be my friend.
I'll make you.
Hahahha
Sour Grapes 2 details my love for Lucy and Sarah and for their words.
Suicidal and schizophrenic, Sarah's words saved me from trying to drive a knife thru my chest at the sink. At least that night.
I cried tears of relief and joy.
Thank you for being here, Sarah.
I thanked Elizabeth for her mentorship, for her kind words and support.
"You're a good writer. You'll probably be published a lot etc. etc."
"I want to be Ian .
I want to wash your hair.
I'm jealous of every man in your books."
I applaud Scott for his groundbreaking work, it's healing qualities.
He's another author who has time to write back.
As much love as I can give--and final statements on my political alignments.
It gets 41 views.
Twice as many views as Sour Grapes 1.
Evidence that you can potentially catch more flies with honey.
Or maybe no one's actually seen what I look like when I talk.
Everyone's curious again.

■

    Bunny just doesn't have the time.
    I don't blame her for her rejection of me.
    My interest isn't what matters. No matter how strong, deep, or sincere.
    Truly intelligent people known how to create curiosity in someone else for who they are.
    To whet an appetite in a man/woman.

I wish I understood that in the beginning.
Bunny has several alpha traits.
You can tell she's stubborn. Independent. Speaks softly, carries big stick.
Is hyper industrious. A ballerina: an artist, an athlete. Plays basketball lately: invests in her body. High impulse control. Makes herself scarce socially. I'm learning how to be a man from women who know how to be men better than me. I have my own skill set. But since we're not talking much and Bunny's on my mind 24/7, a form of burning idolatry, the way monks have that kind of time to think of God, partly on accident as a result of exposure to her art, poetry, beauty, and other clear expressions of power,...(Bunny, why the fuck aren't you an actress?) It's at the point where I'm so strung out on her that when I get messages from her, and either that avi of her with Gazlene's pendants shows up, or that avi of her purple ribbon on Tumblr, I laugh: giggling like a little kid in public. *"Sometimes I do this impression of you. Sometimes I giggle at just the thought of you."* Or I scream out of uncontainable energy, the words, *"Fuck yeah!"*
Which I sustain for at least a solid 20 seconds.
Once I received a message from Bunny who I asked the question, "Do you think you ever really know the people you love?"
She responds back in 24 hours an abnormally long waiting period to me, but at this point I've waited something like 5 days for a message back. I should have better shit to do but I'm kind of in an aesthetic period at this point.
"I think this is where 'you always hurt the ones you love,' comes from..." her text starts.
I'm in my underwear 30lbs overweight, I make a fist, (*hahahhahh!*) fall on my knees and scream into my empty apartment at 9am: *"FUCK YES!"* Sustaining it for a solid 20 seconds, then repeating, "Fuck yes. Fuck yes. Fuck yes..." to myself as I prepare a 600 calorie breakfast of 3 eggs w/ cheese and 2 pieces of peanut butter toast, I don't stop repeating "Fuck yes." to myself until I receive the next DM. Bunny's just not that interested tho. I scare her a little. *"I'm scared of ur big mouth."* She doesn't greatly appreciate my output here. My curiosity seems a perverse obsession to her. Sincerity is stripped from it. The more I speak the more I'm robbed. My ethos is misunderstood. I misunderstand her interest. *"How do you feel about me?"* I ask.
"I'm not in love with you, sorry." Missing the point again. *"No. No. No. What the fuck? Not what I was asking."*
In one text conversation she compares me to another one of the many dudes in her DMs, a(nother) mentally ill Englishman who wants to shoot the shit about her art--
"It feels like an interview." she says.
"Two things I don't talk about," she says, "My art nd my dad." She hardly ever asks questions. Bad sign. I should be infuriated as the topics broached but everytime I hit the wall with Bunny, I find myself thinking about her size/height. With her 5' 10" I feel compelled to resolve all misunderstandings

between us. Her size is accented by her super long hair, it commands a respect from me. Even online, I just imagine her standing here and I can't give up on it--I've never met this woman in person but I just imagine her with her head slightly turned and a hip cocked, telling me this stupid shit with a straight face in all sincerity, oblivious to how passive aggressive it is. Everyone I know is telling me to stop fucking with her. She doesn't appreciate you. She doesn't care. You're not real to her. She's a stuck up, rich, anorexic, white bitch. I hated it. I wouldn't listen. But they were probably right. I wasn't holding her or myself to standard. I was making so many excuses for her/"us" Hahahah

Here's some criteria:
- Asks questions
- Respects my art

("...and I don't hate everything you write." she texts.)
- Texts within 24 hours

"If you're not interested in him, why do you respond to him?"
"He likes to vent to me."

A passive aggressive dig/hint. My rules for texting Bunny were that I never text when I'm bored, depressed, or lonely. If I'm happy and thinking of her is the only time I can text. It's totally wasted on this woman. I must come off as some kind of hermit/pussy beggar. Tell a girl you don't know you're in love with her though, and you think about her all day and you've essentially handed her your balls so she can hacky sack with them. Smash them between two bricks or something. You're not a man. You're not an artist anymore. You're a cuck. You're a child. You're a psychotic. You're a loser. I knew things were going to be hard with Bunny.

Just look at her face.

She destroys men.

But if a woman doesn't intimidate you/scare you, why are you even approaching them?

No risk/no reward.

"I crave what I don't understand."

Tweets Alex Severino.

I'm attracted to what might destroy me.

4 Lokos. Hahahah

The beauty of wild animals.

But what I'm getting at here, is after being blocked by her on every social media outlet--I reached out again after creating a new Tumblr, specifically with the intent of talking to her again. I'm aware under other circumstances, this qualifies as stalking and harassment. Hahahah

A sincere apology for pushing so hard. I waited patiently after communicating myself. Days later she responds. The number 24 appears in a bubble next to the smiling speech bubble/messages icon.

"I wasn't mad." she said. "I just wanted you to shutup."

Success!

I knew I needed to give her space but I still wanted her attention. She lies and says, "no one's messaging me," Which...if you're a beautiful 5' 10" elite artist and popular American poet in New York City, there's no fucking way, there's *no fuckin' way*, that there aren't like, 50 dudes--potentially wealthier, hotter, more well known as artists, bigger, yoked, dudes in your DMs. Competition is stiff here, so I have to be aware of what it takes to be an individual--to make an impact. Hahahah

Bunny hates poetry so I notice. She rewards nothing composed. Luckily, I've been a terrible poet lately because I've been spending time writing these lengthy 'relationship stories,':
(enjoy.)
       I post some music.
       Also ignored.
       But, I started writing these relationship fantasies.
       I'm now keeping a catalog of thoughts and fantasies on my Tumblr for Bunny.

RELATIONSHIP FANTASY

It's a phone call and I need help shopping somewhere trendy, I say, like Topman or something,
"Bunny, I don't know anything about money, or like, how to dress..." 'cause I'm your date to The Whitney.

She responds to the entry by smashing the heart and responds with sincere laughter: "hahahahah." We'll get into a fight later because I misinterpret it as passive aggressive. I feel bad for it. I guess I calibrate incorrectly and expect even some of my best intuitive/impulses to backfire. I expect rejection and am surprised by success. I can't even believe it worked. Hahaha

RELATIONSHIP FANTASY 4

Bought the ticket.
Lost the weight.
Gained the muscle.
Grew my hair out for 6 months.
Bought new skin tight jeans that I highwater over just fat enough calves.
Scrawny dudes who highwater...I dont get it...
Another floral print shirt from some popular/trendier brand/store, again prolly Topman cause, fuck dude, fashion is lost on me.
Buy a new hoody, one that actually fits you hangs tight around the middle, just below or above the crotch. Buy Summer Jacket. Am I wearing pants or shorts to this thing? Can you wear shorts too a gallery, New York is like a hole when

its this hot...okay yeah pants duh... Gonna need new boots cause I would never wear black with brown.
I trimmed my nails nd toes.
Trimmed nosehair, just in case.
Have been clean shaven.
Now that I'm really her date, moisturizing my body with light amount of Coconut Oil.
Chapstick all the time.
Brush 2 times everyday instead of how little I usually do.
(grooosssss...)
Cant come to New York empty handed and Im a terrible gift giver, what the fuck could I ever buy Bunny?
Flowers and wine are a must not cause I think its a gift just because thats what yr supposed to do...the thing about wine is it could be really tacky under a certain price...jewelry seems good,
I mean I'd buy her Cartier if I could...
Buy Argon oil, should be conditioning everyday. Need to buy a new bag. An excuse to get a haircut finally,
Ive grown it long enough to get a pushback but is that going to make me look like a typical New York guy at this point? Maybe a trendy bowl cut. Fuck it Im big enough to get my headshaved and look alright maybe.
Call Bunny about it, what does she want with her at the exhibit.
Seems kind of like a beta males question.
Bother Bunny about it.
Don't bother Bunny about it.

"I like Relationship Fantasy 4," she says.

DETERMINATION (RELATIONSHIP FANTASY 12)

Alone in my kitchen
overwhelmed by my realities
determined I slam a fist into a palm and scream to the darkened empty room
"Bunny
Rogers
is
my
Wife!"

■

"Can I tell you what I thought about all day today?" I message.
18 hours later:
":)"
Bunny is my wife. Hahahah

Omg, I'm gonna smack you." She texts.

∎

I care about you.
I can tell you're different.
You have a spirit.
I respect that you're so much yourself
even when it hurts you to be.

    She messages.
A few fights later,

        (*"I don't like being known. I tend to keep people an arm's length away."*
        "Bunny--I would cherish the opportunity to be an arm's length away.")

and we're still talking. I was going to write friends but...friend is a strong word.

        "I admire your persistence. It's how I've made a lot of my friends. Just by them being here."

        "Am I your friend?" I ask. *"Friend is a strong word. It would be an honor to be called your friend...I have to meet you Bunny."*

        "If you're ever in New York, I can agree to coffee with you."

An insult more than an invite.
Too non committal to be affection.
I'll be in New York in a few years.
But I can't waste time/money on a visit if I don't know yr gonna be there/free.
If you want to see me, commit to four days.
Khalil Gibran: *Do not love half lovers. Do not entertain half friends.*

∎

I write a relationship fantasy after being rejected.

RELATIONSHIP FANTASY 15

At the Whitney:

"That's the exact wrong thing to say.
Is that a joke or am I the joke?"
"..."
"Dude. Get a grip. Is that a joke or am I the joke?"
"It's just a joke."
"Give me your fuckin' house keys."
"No."
"Dude. This isn't a game. I'm leaving. You can have whatever other guy who's gonna torture you not giving a fuck here tonight. I'm fuckin'gg gone."
People are starting to notice. The arm gestures get bigger. I stick my arm out wide nd lazy like a bird. Hardwood floors...the rooms so empty...except for ppl. I shake when I'm mad but not 'cause I'm scared because its not what's outside of me I gotta keep away/out, its what's in me I'm afraid of letting out.
"Don't be a fucking idiot. I didn't mean anything by it, relax."
"Give me yr keys."
"I'm not comfortable doing that.
I'm not doing that."
"Okay..." I take out my cellphone. "It's like 9. I'm going to a fucking HOSTEL. I'm gonna sleep in this fucking silk shirt and I'm gonna sleep with my fucking boots on and hope my shit doesn't get stolen."
"Okay."
"You really let me down, you know that. You really FUCKED THIS UP FOR ME. I know it's arrogant. But these fucking men don't love you! They're wasting your fuckin' time! I flew out for this shit. I want to be here with you for this. But this isn't self respecting."
"I'm sorry. It's really not a big deal you're overreacting. Yr embarrassing me. Yr embarrassing yourself."
I squint like Im watching an animal dying. Like girls who notice you but want to look casual. Like when you want to notice a landscape but its your face and I'm pissed.
I do this thing, my dad used to do it, je would sort of take his fingers and wipe the sides of his jaw in one handstroke nervously. I look back into my phone.
"You should just stay."
"Are you asking me to stay?"
"No. I'm not gonna ask you for anything."
"Lift up yr skirt."
"–the fuck?"
"If you want me to stay–lift up yr skirt–in the middle of your show nd show me your ass."
"Fucking psycho."
"No–fuck YOU. I'm not a psycho. I'm punishing you. If you really want me to stay, you'll lift your skirt up–in the middle of your fucki-ngG show nd you'll show me your ass."
"Wow."
"It's not about sex, okay? It's about commitment."

@abigfuckingbully

"You can leave."
"Alright." I turn around nd then remember: "I DON'T KNOW IF YOU'RE GONNA RESPOND TOMORROW BUT I HAVE UR ADDRESS WRITTEN DOWN ND I'm gonna COME to PICK UP MY SH-IT AND IF YR NOT THERE M GONNA PITCH A BRICK THRU THE WINDOW OR SOMETHING TO GRAB MY BAGS ND LEAVE. OKAY?"

In addition to the fantasy, I post Carly Rae Jepsen's "Call Me Maybe."
I know this is high risk but I thought it might a seductive quality in it's drama.
It's my taste for drama.
I also have to demonstrate that I won't be nice all the time.
I get ugly easily.
Things with me get so ugly.
Things get so ugly with me.

"I hate this new Whitney Fantasy.
It grosses me out.
Call Me Maybe is cute." she messages.

■

"Call me right now or I'm never tallkkingg to you agin." She messages.
She sends her Skype handle.
She's *"obviously been drinking."*
It's 11pm Pacific.
Two thoughts at once:
I've vividly imagined receiving the first phone call from Bunny and I was fully aware even in my own fantasy that she would be drunk. She's just like that. I know I should say, "Thank you...but..." and tell her I can't call unless she's straight. The other part of me is so happy to hear from her. Carly Rae Jepsen had gotten to her. It was too funny not to phone. We both knew:

"We'd get along in person, I think, we just don't translate on the internet." She says.
Bunny's always so sweet on accident.
Every other message is accidentally funny.
Every other message is a poem it's so thoughtful.
All day, everyday, I've wanted to hear her beautiful voice again.
Never be this eager.
Siren's song.
I call immediately.
She answers--drunk, wine glass spilling, she carries it around her--waving it, drinking from it--floundering. Dribbles down her chin. When she answers I start cheering,
"Fuck yeah!

@abigfuckingbully

Fuck yeah!
It's Bunny Fuckin' _____
We've got the International Artist on the line.
Fuck yeah!"
She smiles.
I don't know if my enthusiasm matters.
I'm quickly disappointed.
"Why aren't you wearing any clothes? You're totally masturbating to this." She cracks herself up. You're the hardest person to sexualize ever. I'm too in love with you. I want your heart not your cunt. There must be something wrong with me.
I'm infuriated.
How all of my affections being boiled down to perversion and obsession.
I just don't wear clothes when I'm alone.
I keep smiling.
I push down how I really feel.
I should be grateful to hear from her.
I push down how I really feel,
which is like an ashtray.
We'd make a great couple.
I fill your wine glass.
You put your cigarettes out in my wrist.
"You went dancing?" I asked.
"Yes. Yes I love dancing, until these guys came up...*hey baby, you've got a great ass,*" In the voice of a man.
"That sucks.
Are you a good dancer?"
She sits back in her swivel chair cross legged and erects herself--stares into space, lowering her head and says matter of factly,
"Yes. It's very sexy."
I smile.
I don't doubt Bunny on a dancefloor is sexy.
"Are you a good dancer?" She asks.
"I'm alright. I like to.
I have to get drunk, tho.
Where are you?"
"I'm in a hotel."
It just devolves.
I forget what happened.
"I'm not scared of you, you know." she says. "People are scared of you, I'm not scared of you."
I'm a choice amnesiac.
It's how I survive as myself.
I have a terrible memory.
Maybe it was acid.

Maybe it's my Schizophrenia.
But why remember all the ways that people hurt you?
She smart and funny.
"You're white, huh? But you don't like to talk about it unless you have to, like every white person."
I laugh. It's funny but depressing. I think I might hate this woman. She's exactly like Michele. She's exactly like Akila. She's like an ex-girlfriend I'm submitting myself to again. She's a hard girl. She swears she's not. *"I'm careful, not cold. You keep acting like I'm the big bad cold bitch..."* I forget it all on purpose but I can't.
"Are you disappointed yet?
 That I'm just a boring northeastern white girl?"
"No. I like that you're white."
She moves outside to smoke a cigarette.
I just keep smiling.
I just keep faking it.
How degrading.
I could be anyone.
I could be no one.
You are who associate with.
I am no one.
I say the wrong thing.
She's barking at me down a lit cigarette.
"You fuckin' cocksucker! Cocksucker!" She laughs.
Cocksucker. Cocksucker. 'Hahahah'
She just keeps laughing and calling me a fucking cocksucker.
I politely endure to the end of the phone call until Bunny excuses herself to a bath.
I hang up.
I hate who I am.

■

> "The point of the phonecall was to show you I was nice.
> I was mean?
> I'm just a cunt I guess."
> She messages me the next day.
> I'm just used to this kind of arrogance.
> I grit my teeth not to cry.
> Not a tear for her.
> Bitch doesn't deserve it.
> I'm at the gym.
> Pitch my phone into my bag and lift 80lbs over my shoulders.
> If I accept it, I deserve it.
> And I tear myself apart.

@abigfuckingbully

∎

"I dont' think I can talk to you anymore." I message.
"You've said that shit before, dude.
You wishy-washy cocksucker.
I'm sick of taking care of you pathetic baby men.
You all think you're so beautiful and talented.
Lie to me about how you're gonna marry me!
Stop looking for yourself in me, in your projections of me.
I'm not like you.
I'm separate from you.
You've hurt me too, you know?
It's not like you've never disrespected me before.
I know you're an asshole.
You say all this weird, perverted shit to me.
You hurt me all the time, I just accept it.
See, the first sliver of humanity and you feel out of control.
I have agency and suddenly you want to run.
You blow this fucking phone call into something entirely different.
I'm careful, not cold.
You're fucking arrogant.
Leave me alone, okay?
If you want attention or something.
If you've got something to prove.
Look at yourself first."

I wasn't unmoved--but I was controlling my emotions.
It's my fault she didn't want me.
I failed.
"If you don't get a girl, you don't deserve her."
You want an apology but, you don't deserve it.
"We always get what we deserve."
I choose to accept it as data.
Information.
An opportunity for self improvement.
I'll remember you forever Bunny.
I can never make this mistake with someone I love this much ever again.
I will become needless.
I will become invincible.
I will secure the love of the next woman I value this much.
If I can ever love again.
Hahahahha...

@abigfuckingbully

▪

The crowds getting louder. The sound rising like a chorus. Greek colosseum. Everyone wants to see my blood. I can't silence them but we have to start the fight. I'm impossibly high, shaking and terrified. A bug to be crushed. An offering.

"Before I paint the walls with you Oscar." I point to the walls. "I want to say...this isn't your fault." I look to Lucy. "I want to show Lucy and Sarah who I really am. These women are here to witness me as a whole. And though they may fight their deepest reactions, their most primal responses, to watching me beat your scrawny ass, with intellectual resistance about my character, something almost heroic will come thru. They're going to lose respect for you Oscar. There's something beautiful about senseless violence. It's a lesson in logic as a failure. It's the necessary reminder to the moralist that no matter how much you feel in control through your values, there are some things that are just greater than you. Somethings don't have any reason whatsoever. You're being chosen for the very reason you are innocent. The reason any martyr matters. I want these women to witness my character thru my shadow. The underside of my darkness is all of my virtue. Though they are repulsed right now, after I bury you, these women will be having wet dreams of me, repeat in slow motion--in the faint impressions left in sleep."

Lucy makes a sour face, it contorts and turns sideways into hate.

"Shut the fuck, up!" Sarah shouts.

"Lucy," I turn to her. Lucy's freckles are obvious here unlike my freckles. A face like an English Doctor. Strong facial structure like any woman worth noticing. Cheeks that make it look like she's always smiling. Large breasted with good posture in a floral dress. A dignity and authority to her. The biggest blue eyes I've ever seen with a sadness and awareness to them commanding you to stay there. She's seen enough. She understands enough. She's seen too much. Just don't hurt her. "I've always loved your art. I think you're an incredible person. I wish we could have met some other way sooner." I laugh "As friends maybe. I'm sorry to do this to your husband. I hate him. I'm so jealous of him. Thank you for being here."

I look to Sarah. Sarah has a face like a giant teddy bear. Long cheeks that start high with a small near the end. Her eyes are very dark nd heavy but look cocky and happy. The dip above her lips, the bow, the philtrum, is deep. Thick silky hair drapes down. Big eyes look up. Stoic and forward. A powerful figure. It's a white t-shirt and jean shorts for the fight.

"Sarah, your words have saved my life. Your poems mean the world to me. I'm glad to have shaken your hand already, to have spotted you on the subway, to have waved to you thru a screen, with a smile, to hear your voice. Thank you for words. Thanks for being here. Say hi to Bunny for me."

I centered myself in the circle and standing tall,
"OSCAR

OSCAR
OSCAR
OSCAR,"
The crowd started chanting. It was going to be an especially ugly fight considering how hated I am and how loved Oscar is. How determined I am to win. My predisposition to violence. My absolute loss of sense of self. A determined suicidality. I stood in my flesh like armor. That I was willing to lose gave me an advantage. When I break oscar how hated will I be by this mob? I peel off my shirt and toss it to the couch. I reach deep into my jeans pocket for a quarter and show it to Oscar. I flip it, in the air off my thumb. "Tails," Oscar shouts for the call. I catch it in a palm and slap my palm on the back of my opposite wrist.
"Heads." I display it to him. I smile. I look to Lucy, who I've trusted with my phone. I point to her. She drops Oscar's phone and presses play.

[BLUSH by TITLE FIGHT plays]

Last year, I tried to learn
What makes me so insecure.
What better way to pass the time?
I lost myself in my mind.

I just want to hear the words you speak.
When I'm not around, what do you think?
Think I'm hopeless, I think I think too much.
Bruised and broken covered up in blush.

Tell me what's wrong
With forcing myself to write it down.
Never made a sound
I never second guess I'm right the first time.

I'm the fly on my wall but I'm too blind to see.
I'm the view from your room, come look straight through me.

Oscar puts his fists up and prepares for me, walking in a circle already. I follow him. Raise my fists and turn to my side to minimize my size. But it's already over. I lean into myself, movement from the hips as I cock an arm, clench my fist, and launch it with a thumb untucked, as if a whip and push through to Oscar's face where I immediately feel the impact of his pretty little nose, which turns to mush under my knuckles. I feel all the bones go to putty. Looks like I broke his nose. *"Augh."* He shouts. Blood shoots out of his head like a squeezed Orange. It's dripping everywhere. I stood there with my fist clenched, shirtless, my jeans high waisted, belted two loops too tight. My hand looks like the one cut, draining down his face, his blood on my chest. Spatters on my lips. I am already taste my victory. He folds in half and grabs what's left of his nose, breathing through his mouth moving in between gasps. *"Ah. Ah. Ah. Ah. Phubck."* He's sobbing. I can't help but laugh. He's shocked still. The crowd gasps. Then boo's. Then screams.

    I bend over and put two hands on my knees lift my head up to look at Oscar in the face, who can't stop moaning. Then I hobble forward smiling and put my hand on his shoulder without changing my position and ask, lovingly into his ear, "You alright, guy?" I fall over myself laughing. The dude just keeps spilling blood in front of him. I sucker punch him in the jaw for fun and he falls to the floor, toppling sideways, like a child. The audience is enraged. The audience is pitching full beer cans at me, that rattle, roll, and bubble up their contents into the floor in front of me. It's like running through a broken fire hydrant. My arms are so white. So exposed. I'm so made of myself.

    Lucy runs to the center of the circle and falls over Oscar's body, crying. Her floral dress ruffled and sticking up different directions at the skirt. Her big white legs crossed, some sort of keds. You can hear her crying, it's really sad. It makes me feel like I hurt somebody. She feels so deeply for her man, I'm almost moved. If I die here, no one would care. If your mother's the only one who loves you, you're a failure, we all know that. Don't bother coming to the funeral. No one else is. No one's gonna cry when I'm gone. See, I thought art was the perfect place for me. If the greatest human drives are sex and the need to be important, I thought I'd kill two birds with one stone. I felt I belonged to these people.

    When I imagined my success, I imagine eating at their tables. Spending some time in their pretty apartments. Sharing a dirty joke alongside them at the bar. A quiet moment in the car with them, *"have you heard this song?"* The volume knob slowly turns. *"No?"* It's always something new with you. The crowd is so loud everything is mute like a silent film. They're gonna call the cops so I take one last look around the room. Mira's face is in the crowd. Ana's face is in the crowd. Both of them in the exact same posture. Shoulders weak and bent, hands draping loosely. Juliet alongside Elizabeth. The same burnt out expression. Does sadness wear away our faces or is it a result of heavy drug use? A million other faces without names. All of them I recognize from photos, smiling with more popular and successful writers. Writers I also wish I could have met. If just to have a friend. I just was never cool enough. I guess I just wasn't a good enough artist to be anything at all to these people. *"Pleasure to meet you,"* I think. I take note and then without hesitance dart towards the door, but am met with resistance. All of the bodies in the room won't release. A wall of them.

    Hands jut out, palms on my chest. Hands across my biceps and that's when I'm kicked in the guts by a fat, bearded, redhead, with a big animal face, hooded in black, with holes eaten at the elbows. Tattoos up his neck. I fucking hate tattoos. I can't tell what it is. Just faded blues and red like everyone else's. His girlfriend seems to enjoy it. It's like an activity for their Tinder date. This is

what a Tinder user looks like to me. I drop to the ground and am grabbed by another stranger, dragged closer to a mob:
Elizabeth
Sarah
Spencer
Scott
Juliet
Darcie
Ana
Mira
Chelsea
and from the crowd suddenly emerges Bunny. All 5' 10" of her. Hair pushed back in a muted purple ribbon, revealing giant silver hoops in her ears. I was always a fucking sucker for hoops. She smoking a cigarette inside. She has an entire bottle of wine ($100+) which she palms at the neck. She leans over, hair drapes over me and touches me while she gets a look. Darcie moves forward. I can see up her skirt. I laugh. I love everything about women. I hate that I love women so much. The way they dress. Watching them get dressed. Their idiosyncrasies. Their hairstyles. The way a skirt flies up. The way they fix themselves. Comb their own hair back. The jokes they make. Their friends. Their voices. The way they drink. The sounds of them cussing. Their posture. The way a girl gets quiet. The littlest things kill me. It's a mans boot I feel drive into my ribs. They shatter and are pushed deep into my core, the skin gnarled and loose like a broken drum head.

    Spencer starts in on my face, hammering down with one fist, his post-office blue 5 panel cap falls of his head in the first motion, then across my chest, under my opposite armpit, his whole body moving into it, a lightweight sunflower yellow nylon summer jacket fills high with air as it inflates like a parachute. His fist makes perfect contact with my right eye. At first, just blackening to swollen. But as the motion is repeated the bones around my eye socket dilapidate, weaken, and then break. Elizabeth watches patiently smiling. Her perfect lips closed flat. Her blonde hair adding to my love and hatred for her. Arrogant friend. Humble enemy. Sarah rushes to my body, laid out flat, like a martyr, like a patient, and spits into my face, gets a few kicks in: her style is to raise her enormous asian calves above me, my pelvis/hips, and then to push all of her weight into the kick like she's starting a motor bike. Darcie immediately imitates this style but isn't satisfied breaking me in at the hips with Sarah. It's too crowded anyways. She does it in a perfect run: Darcie likes to dig/thrust her heel in when she kicks me. *"Fuckin' pig!"* She squeals, laughing. Enjoying it now. I smile.

    He heels drive into my sternum. I don't know if I'm just scrawny or suffer from some muscular deformity but the middle of my chest is the weakest part of me and is fully exposed. Megan looks down from the crowd and pours a little beer in my face. I once told her about a dream I had with her and Elizabeth in it. But then conversation turned to nightmares where I overshared about being anally raped by a demon. A recurring one for me. Needless to say, the back nd forth ended quickly after. I also have a deformed breastbone, which curves deep into my chest, exaggerating an already alarming fragility. Darcie's big legs break me immediately. I can see her big underarms while she jumps into each motion. The bones are now twisted and carving into my heart like thick splinters. I can't breath and I start blacking out for seconds at a time. I lose my vision. But then regain it as Spencer's relentless onslaught appears a red face then an eclipse. The fist is blurred in between as if I'm being beating with nothing. So repetitive I start to leak blood out of my single shattered eye, it's popped out of the socket. Burst blood vessels raising my now red eye to the surface of an indeterminate mound of flesh. It's locked between two misplaced bones and is rattling in violent spasms--my vision is now distorted by it's random and lightyear speeds. I want Spencer to end the horror of this twitching but for some reason he stops. Body inflating as he pants and drags himself up. The smell friendly face of a ferret. I don't know him but I hate him. I don't know him. I hate him. I fucking hate this guy.

  All of a sudden I hear Lucy crying again. It's really pretty. I don't think anyone's ever cried over me. Definitely not over my body. Darcie's skirt flies up: sternum, chest, throat--Gabby peeks over a shoulder, her light brown skin glows. Her big cheeks. She looks very serious. You can tell she feels sorry for me for some reason. I once saw her for a moment in a pair of two tone sunglasses on an M line detour due to construction on the subways in New York dead winter. We both looked as if we would approach each other, the light bulb went off, but we didn't. I felt I'd honored enough people who thought I was invisible to have the sense to ignore at least one back. (Fuck you Mitch.) My windpipe shatters and her boot falls to the back of my throat. I can't hear the sound of it snapping over the crowd but I can feel the vibration of everything breaking piece by piece. My crumpling like slush. I can't breathe.

  Blood pours out of my mouth like vomit. I keep coughing, which causes wine red plasma to launch out of my mouth like the stream of a pressure washer. Darcies boots drip. I black out again. Then wake up to Bunny's long sad face, the face of some exotic Russian woman, the face of some famous American actress, the face of a beautiful broken woman, grey eyes large and sullen too tired of you to be afraid, the most enormous cheeks, "apples for cheeks," I said, the muted purple ribbon in her hair dividing her bangs from the rest, wiggling, as she falls over me--spits a mouthful of wine onto my head, which is a scalding pain from the top of my throat to the bottom of my spine. The cigarette she's hardly smoked is in between the thumb and finger of her free hand and she puts a cigarette out into the fleshiest part of my left pectoral. "Cocksucker!" she growls. In her low smoky voice. The one I'm so eager to hear. Her long thin fingers hold the burning cigarette down. *If she has an internet presence, she must have hands.* The muscle and skin around the cherry and cling to the weapon and her hair brushed over my body, it was like we could have kissed. This is the closest I've ever been to Bunny. The cigarette is bent and blackened.

Somehow the cigarette stands perfectly erect in my flesh like a monument. Like she made it a part of me.

The burn calls just as much attention to my awareness as the popped eye, still spasming. But there is so much release. Alex Severino tweets: *ALL PAIN IS RELEASE AND THERE IS SO MUCH RELEASE TO BE HAD.* The smell of the cigarette, the wine, the spit, the sweat and breath and heat of the crowd wake me up. I start to cry finally. It's been so long since I could really cry. It's been so long since I've been touched this much. First tears of relief. Then tears of joy. I black out again. There's this theory on punk kids: loud/heavy and erratic music drives cortisol levels to an unnatural high. Has an almost addictive effect. Cortisol, the stress hormone can become a staple for some people. When you're a kid and you get upset or stressed out--your cortisol levels rise. If a parent doesn't take the time to console you, to touch you and relieve you of your pains, you don't just become familiar with rising cortisol, you start to become addicted to it & averse to the touch necessary to heal you. Touch becomes foreign and disgusting to you. Children left alone for a long time exist the same way starved children do: loss of interest in even satisfying the appetite, to survive. What's a mosh pit but satisfaction of a need without admission of that need? And so you seek out the childhood experience over and over and over again. You can't escape how you were(n't) raised. A beating is good enough.

Darcie keeps kicking me in my broken throat. Her dress flying off her wide hips every time. I'm almost blind now. But I can make out the faces. So many famous writers. Nice to meet you. My name's Atticus Davis. I grew up in Syracuse, Indiana. A town of 4,000. A town where members of my school were in the Klu Klux Klan. They handed out a racist crossword once, every word was a racial slur. My mom was raped while I was in the house with her. The way I was in the same bed as my brother when he was molested. They used to call my momma a spic to her face all the time. Fuck, nevermind, this is all the wrong information. My name's Atticus Davis. The American Poet. My whole life I've wanted to be someone great. And I think you're all so beautiful. I like the way winter feels on my soft white face. How my cheeks get red and how my tired smile always looks new in the cold, with my breath exposed. I am a pissed off person. But I think I might be the happiest person I know. The wisest airhead. "Dumb-saint" I'd love to share myself with you. Hi, guys. My name's Atticus Davis and I love you.

Mira shows up to watch.

Bunny's looking down, tall in a grey-pink chiffon skirt. She bends over and her tiny breasts fall out of a wine colored chemise-looking tank. She bends over to look and suddenly snaps out of something. "Please stop!" she shouts. "I THINK YOU MIGHT REALLY BE KILLING HIM." Hahahah Tears roll down my face. Spencer's fist drops and my front tooth, the crooked one, runs down my my wet throat and I swallow it, with blood, like a pill. I black out again. I think all of my heros would hate me and my life. Henry Rollins would hate me. He's one of the first people I read before I decided to start writing poetry. I shoplifted Solipsist as a gift for my Anarchist girlfriend, my first girlfriend Misty. The greatest gifts you can give an Anarchist are shoplifted. She still has it on her shelf. After my first collection of poetry came out I emailed Henry Rollins about interning with him while I was in L.A. I asked him what motivated him as a writer.

"We don't work with artists because they're lazy and temperamental." Henry emails back. "I start self producing because I knew I'd never be a "real" writer." Raymond Pettibon might still follow me on Twitter. Sam Hyde would hate me. Scott would hate me. Might hate me. Steve Albini would hate me. Allison Schulnik would hate me. Alan Moore would hate me. Tanino Liberatore might actually like me. Henry Miller would have liked me. Anais Nin would have liked me. Malcolm X would have hated me. Martin Luther King would have hated me. bell hooks would hate me. Elliott Smith would have hated me. Ian MacKaye would hate me. Marnie Stern would hate me. Mitski would hate me. Peter Young would despise me. Kurt Cobain would have hated me. Hubert Selby Jr. would think I'm pathetic, and have hated me. Ali would have hated me. Hannibal Buress would hate me. Jonathan Richman would hate me. Jack Kerouac would have never fucked with me. Rilke would write me. Bukowski would hate me. Tim Kinsella never wrote back. Bunny hates me. Celine would have heard me.

"TRANSPHOBE.

FUCKIN' RACIST PIG!"

Somebody screams from the crowd. Just this repetitive kicking in the opposite rib.

"FUCKIN' NAZI!"

And then another pair of legs entered my destroyed vision.

Someone rub a hand thru my hair...

Godard would have liked me.

I'd be in one of his films.

Henry Ford isn't a hero necessarily but he'd probably tell me I'm in the wrong field.

Subcomandante Marcos would have hated me.

Jocelyn Jade Noir hates me.

Louis C.K. wouldn't *hate me* but I doubt he'd fuck with me.

Bunny starts to actually look upset. Eyes wet and shaking. She's shaking.

"Please, stop."

It's okay Bunny.

I deserve it.

This is terrible Karma.

There's always going to be someone bigger nd more violent than you.

I never was the smartest guy.

Jealous of everyone.

Intellectual airhead.

My red letter: I look in the mirror and I feel closer to all of you.

Spencer's fists keep coming: like a rotary wheel.

Jesus would be so pissed at me for being such a stupid vengeful motherfucker.

But I think Jesus would have talked to me about it like I was a real person.

Jesus would be disappointed by my Twitter content.

Jesus would hate how I feel about my Mom.

"I don't want to make that bitch proud anymore. I want to cut her a check."

Sorry, Mom.

Julia Vinograd would have fucked with me.

Vera Pavlova would like me.

Burroughs would fuck with me heavy.

Marc Patti doesn't fuck with me. Even though I sent him my book.

Sometimes I wish I could exist in the world but be completely inaccessible to everyone as a form of punishment. Almost like a ghost. I just can't shake my years long suicide urge, and like a virus it keeps mutating and taking new shape. Mac Evasion would never fuck with me. My favorite novelist ever. Straight edge vegan hobo. No real Anarchist would ever fuck with me. No real liberal would ever fuck with me. No real conservative would ever fuck with me. Debussy would never fuck with me.

The Buddha would have loved me.

The Buddha would have been my friend.

The Buddha would let me learn under him.

The Buddha would have been my friend.

Someone takes a cellphone out and starts filming.

Surrounded by the ones I love, I feel I can finally let go.

Hahahah...

I did it.

I'm an artist.

This is my greatest work of art.

My final performance.

To beaten to death by all of you.

To be this close to you.

To be touched.

I did it.

"Thank you for being here."

I think.

I feel my head cave in.

All of the bones in my lower body are broken and displaced.

The pain is immense but liberating.

Everything goes black.

My eye pops out of it's socket.

Everything goes black and I stop feeling anything.

"Your shit is so slept on" Alex Severino messages. *"But it's a good look for you. I read your shit, you're going to get yours. And when you do, you'll prolly hate it. So enjoy right now."*

My life doesn't flash before my eyes or anything--instead

I see an image of God as a human figure, bent over, hands on his knees, tossing a stick to a dog, playing fetch. A reminder that heaven isn't any better.

@abigfuckingbully

LOTUS EATER

1. GAGGING ON HISTORY

Like his work, love, and life had been before; Los Angeles was forced and desperate. Henry sold himself short by deciding to stay longer than three months; signing up for community college in Santa Monica. The only failure in failing college is if with on and off efforts, and all the will you can muster, you feel the same as in the beginning and you press on, both your own driver and whipping boy. Trying to smile through drudgery to 'build character.'
"I did it."
Showing God and the rest of them you can be, just like them. Beat your chest, sound the drums of your obligated success for the sake of The Towers, or they burn for nothing, to have seen them reaching for Him, crumbling at the sight, makes you crumble, reaching for It yourself. College is all business. Busyness the gateway drug to the need for more guilt. He was guilty. We all are. He was guilty. Mom was confusing family history lessons with lectures. Stories of Mom's immigration, the riches she left behind, marble floors, doctors in the family, engineers, Grandma was a white witch run out of her home after she started the tavern, could read a Tarot spread from playing cards. She built wealth from wealth on its way through: fascists forging personal empire, where to deny service, or the body, was to starve, and deny her body. 15 siblings, whose credentials evaporated stepping off the plane, America, square one, nothing more opportune, aristocratic refugees...
Henry was a burnt out over achiever, underachieving chronically, crippling his will with the weight of ambitions, expectation and revenge. Imagining his life to some other standard completely and still without claim to his own, at last Atlas could shrug.
Independence was 'different.'
Independence was weird.
He was expecting something drastic, putting his expectations against his past like a brick on the gas. California felt less like a stage because cartoons and films seemed more real to him. In the day to-day, he felt stripped of something, violence. Instead of the newness he desired, he fell back into routine, frequenting coffee shops to the point of having to defend his separation from other regulars, fucking every barista in West L.A.
Trying to re-socialize himself beyond the prison of 'conditions' he'd allow to dictate decisions.
Months of the same introversion causing him to feel himself imploding instead of the begged release of explosion. Tumors birthing with every stuffed expression and mounting fear of ending up like Uncle Steve.
Los Angeles failed to re-instill commitment to his total authenticity, which lead him to experiment with meditation. He studied the philosophy but never allowed himself to practice. John Thursday, a close friend, introducing him to Zen. He used to just read about it in the way most of us shelve metaphysics.

That's cute. What do you do for me? Currency of current ideologies. Nothing to gain by staying the same except...maybe your context. We drag ourselves around like Linus' blanket. Choosing to see himself through the eyes of others, he wondered now, what he failed to see in himself, the fear of seeing through his own eyes as himself.
"As important as it is to connect..."
He read it and applied it.
He shaved his head.
He abandoned himself.
Christianity had failed Henry. He could not return to feeling he had failed God. Years he had felt he was going through the motions: of love and worship, two things he dreaded because of their clear comparisons during the act—there's a fat curly haired blonde telling him he should raise his hands to the Lord if he's really feeling it. God would know by how high he jumped or how hard he cried when he was overtaken by the love of God, and for Christ's sake could you show a little more enthusiasm for this hymn...
Henry lost faith in the basement of his 'friends' house while praying in the weight room, which was serving as Henry's bedroom during a period of near homelessness. When he woke up from the trance, hearing his voice roll off the hexagon of walls, pissing in a black-marble bathroom, staring through the skylight, hearing it ring into black porcelain, crying uncontrollably falling into himself, soaked. He couldn't shower so he went downstairs in his filth to Skype with Kim, a girl from Patchogue New York he met on Lipstick Party, an internet forum for subbies. Across America: the internet filled a gap for us where conservative suburbs chewed apart the one's who had read enough books to access the criteria for 'culture,' while others had eaten the pig slop of workaholism, perfectionist beer aficionados, or not, and fear as motivation. A feeding ground in breeding ground--humans suffering from Mad Cow if you ate your own shit at the sound of a Pavlovian schoolbell was the source of the violence he'd been subjected to. All Dogmas lead to abuse; are abuse.
Dad's throwing a bag of toiletries like a football, after a fight with mom about ham or beef or how close this is to Grandma's version of meatloaf, shattering a mirror, the second mirror in the house, the only one beyond your bust, yourself sculpted there. Here's dad, buying and tossing a bag of McDonald's he'd handed me out of the windows on a business trip to Michigan. Here I am! Unattended, eating Little Debbie, 'Star Crunch' snacks like they were real food. Everything was individually wrapped. All foods canned. All foods microwaved. The regularity of Carl's Jr. as a meal. Here's Dad holding Mom down. Here's Dad who can't hear no for an answer. Here's the Dad the go-get-her.
Okay, dad!
He could only start thinking of it 8 years later.
Dad staring into a blue screen on the broken futon where Henry slept. Slipping into slipped discs. The cottage was a cramped two bedroom. Wet wood, at least a hundred years old, splintering. Paint faded. Sun eaten. Looking soggy, and blown out, like a carton of milk left in a hot car.

Here's step dad: fighting publicly with waiters at restaurants he swears are coming onto her.
Here's step dad: bugging the house to find out of she's really fucking that 20 year old Jew or not.
Explains the feeling Henry had when he brings friends home.
But he's 24 now. (Happy Birthday!) Virgo, born on the same day as Leonard Cohen and Stephen King, The Day of Current Taste. Big on fate, star crossings, astrology, myths, the arcane, the archaic, the cosmic, the occult, anything that fills that achy gash God left.
He moved to L.A. Panicked and heartbroken.
Fucking his hometown's favorite hoodrats, granted they were fantastic, beautiful, aggressive—he could see himself with them but that's a state of mind you're in for two years after the sabatoge of the best relationship you've ever managed to cripple slowly, then ultimately, destroy with the hairline spite of a scorpion, rising sign.
Henry would never admit it but realized months into Los Angeles that he was reacting, to himself, reacting to his first and last love as he saw it, terrified of her love. He had to find something wrong with it. She reminds him of his mother. She looks like his mother.
With the thumbscrews of reality forcing barks of helplessness, unemployment, and general dissent-descent, he eventually made true love into something like...a cancer.
No treatment.
He burnt the bridge and bombed the cliffsides.
Demolition.
The way mining sites fold into themselves, layer by layer, ripples and eventual dust like water in a manmade Pompeii. Inhale your regret, be buried in your pet projects projections.

In L.A. he was staying with the Buddha himself: his younger brother, whose whole life, seemed fully blossom, while Henry felt some invisible leash, a cap, an animal biting at the bud to pluck him open before sunlights song. Premature petals reaching weakly, their impotence as loud as fireworks.

II. CUCKOLD

Henry was running his full palm over his freshly shaved head, looking at his freshly trimmed grass. Inhaling the scent of neighboring leaf-piles, and staring into the road, feeling as if he never was in and never had left Michigan.
Wet suburban heat and an appetite whet for...the kind of thirst that a body can't identify. Needs for love and travel both gnaw endlessly at your most vital faculties and degrade the will, another urge rises up like a boyle from unclean thoughts, desire is filth. Thoughts are filth.
Two men on bikes passed. Then they passed from the other periphery and stopped in front of him. He looked up almost as if drugged into the face which

he recognized—Daniel.
"Daniel." Henry said in an instant regret.
Daniel stared.
Then threw his bike down, like a grade school bully, stood tall but at his most upright was no less than a quarter shorter than him.
"Madeline's gone. You glad, you bastard?"
His eyes were as dark as stone, open as wide as wild fire.
He came a step closer and Henry stood, reflex.
Daniel threw the top of his body from the feet, one swift swing. Henry understood that this was a perfectly normal reaction and was beyond both guilt and forgiveness. He expected to leap back, but wondered, with a deep acceptance, like someone jumping the tracks, or their weighty flight from the top floor, if his body would punish him for his mind failing to. He leapt back in time to realize Daniel stopped his stroke mid-swing. "Bitch." Daniel added. Then the second body, invisible to Henry until now circled in front of the house, "Ya fuckin' cuckold!"
Henry could not believe his ears. He was laughing as they rode away, half proud, half paranoid, watching Daniels tight curls, molting from his self induced stressed. Henry turned red. His gut was churning. He felt his eyes water with the wind filling times gap. It asked him for tears and in anger, gave one, stingy, feeling embarrassed by his bravery. Like John Fante, he'd crossed a line. Fucking the wrong townie this time. He was hated. This thirst was for spirit, or love, or escape. He pushed his hand over his head but expected locks and remembered.
Clouds shifted.
Sunspots belched.
Sun refracted and in the kaleidoscope he dragged himself across the insides of the house to a computer. The shame of having let it go on for too long. Like his mother or his father. He couldn't decide. He was rampant, clicking on every possible housing ad for New York, when he spotted a 'gig' he was too certain was a gag but still:
We long for the touch of another who can through all of our time here and mistakes, forgive us our anonymity.
An address. Feeling as if he had seen the God he needed ringing in his head; like Henry's voice, rattling bones through the metal in the walls of his faithless hex. The weight. Room.
Blinded by/blurred, painted in/through tears—pixels turned primal into their CMYK. He replied to the ad, asking for more details. He received an email within an hour: eating, drinking, showering, masturbating, feeling the days embarrassment evaporate off of him in the dry heat of his home. Indian summer.
It was a date.
Henry bought a ticket for the night before the date listed and started packing a bag, he had made all efforts to condense his belongings into a single 35 liter. Two outfits and a down jacket. Mac Book. Pen and pad. A gameboy. Testing to

see if it still had batteries, tetris was in, sitting among his loose belongings, strewn remorse, he found himself smiling again. Eating away the blocks line by line. He'd no longer hope for the long piece, building the mountains of untouched brick. Hope, he thought, was as desperate as anyone could ever get. He was laughing, gently and lovingly, to himself.

III. GOOD GAME

Austin opened the door and moved to sit in front of the clutter.
"It's not here--sorry Woodrow."
"It's not here...it's been awarded."
"It was a mistake."
"Bullshit man. No such thing."
"I'm sorry."
"Fuck you. I don't smoke. I don't fuck around in class. I've got C's all the line. Show me the papers, something..."
"If you prove yourself in these tournament games..."
"Like I even want to play the damn games."
"Then you can leave my office."
"Not until I see a signature."
"You want to blow your chances completely?"
Woodrow leaned back in his chair. Body moved over. Mind blown.
"...some bullshit, man."
Woodrow stood out of his seat and noting his habitual respect for his coach showing itself as he pushed in his seat to it's appropriate place, lifted from the lip in the backings hole and without thought flung it over the desk, coaches long curly white hair bobbing as he spun his head away and lifted his hands to deflect it uselessly. The chair smashed against a file cabinet behind him. Red faced. He lifted his head from it's defense and screamed, "You get back here you bastard! I'll make you clean this shit up!"
He collected himself. Slamming it into the tile floor across from him. He stared at it. Dropped in to his cushioned rolly chair and never lifted his gaze. He moved his hair aside. Started picking up the papers, standing again, leaning over the mess muttering, "be damned if some nigger gets to Stanford..."

IV.

Woodrows rides to school weren't long but he soaked in every minute. His feet moving in rhythm, his chain humming, his head empty until he face plants into the days obligations. Practice makes perfect. 'Practice makes practice.' He laughed.
He pushed his bike against the cage link fence, slightly lifted. Popped the back tire out and from his sling bag, pulled the locks he needed to pin it mid air.
He started running a few laps while the rest filed out. The team went from amorphous to military unit. The coach ran them to exhaustion; bodies beating

against the weight of a body. Simulated in the stuffed luxury of a pad on a stake. Running the bleachers. The robotic memorization of play after play. Woodrow had acted as if nothing happened. Resentment was expressed in every impact and heated call. He tried focusing but the voice leading him into the choreographed violence was stinging. Beer gutted and growing, the rasp of a man whose celebrating forced retirement with one too many cigars had finally gotten under his skin, arresting him. The cuffs a dangling mouthguard, spit as coach points his fingers like a gun, his posture a club.
"Let's try something a little different. Camden—Woodrow, you two switch places."
Woodrow laughed.
"Alright, coach."
and then stood still.
"Woodrow--"
Camden looking just as confused, moved his position, replacing Woodrow as Q.B. The two of them standing side by side. Woodrow's arms at his hips not budging.
"What'd I just say?"
"Camden has no idea."
"Camden knows the plays as well as you do, if anything, he'll be coming through with some perspective."
"Bullshit."
"Alright, 30 laps then."
"Bullshit."
"How about some pushups Austin?"
Woodrow spit, leaned his weight into one side and then put his mouth guard in. Biting down as hard as he could when he started his laps.

V.

Woodrow entered Game Day with a calm he knew his future depended on. He walked to school to pace his head. If he could make it to game day without another visualization of stabbing coach, he was in good shape.
He spent his time on a deserted field. Green and white to shade it's purpose as the human animal gathered in the coliseum; the thirst of eyes for blood. The hunger of living for a taste of the sight of death. The players joined him as they warmed up. The lights burned the players into submission. The opposition filled their positions.
The kick off and Austin on the field, running down, through bodies, but no longer with the prestige, stripped tonight. Camden falling, his hair streaming out of his helmet like splashing water, in slow motion, desperation from the pit of him screamed out of a narrow passage of time his face had to throw the ball back to one whose spirit knew it's place in the game. It was more than muscle memory to Woodrow. The teeth flashed, the ball spinning with Austins legs, deciding to stop, lunge, stay straight. Camden was unforgivable.

The fucking idiot, burying himself in corner field, by 800lbs of man. Austin slowed. Caught the ball and as if in total shock, stopped, to have a man from his left dive into his left knee. He heard the sound of iron splitting, which was his bone breaking. His eyes watered as he began to inhale sweat, mucus, tears, the body odor of four other men. The dogpile like kindling for the fire of fresh cut grasses scent to pour in. They lifted. Whistles blew. Heads were looking down, 6 maybe. His vision blurring, he looked into each other faces, then down at his leg, which looked like a sock filled with sand snaking the wrong way. 'Varsity Blues,' he thought. Then he looked up again. With expectation, it started to rain. Tears welled up as the anesthesia of shock and delirium faded. Everything was light by the time he took his first blink.
Breath filled him in, stuttering. He looked into the night and started screaming from the deepest part of his stomach, a horn blasting.

VI. UNRECOVERY

The first month it was impossible to tell. This visit to the doctor determined possibility of recovery. Seeming to be reliving the night it broke by staring up, limp and half naked on a table. The doctor spent 15 minutes outside of the room. Austin had more to say then he could bare to hear himself think. The door squeaked open. He caught the top of the thick wood framing. The woman, blonde, perched herself on a chair and in her Bosnian accent announced flatly, softly, but to no one in particular--
"It'll heal but you cannot play."
At that moment Austin looked up, from the hinge of his neck and looked at her squarely. His hair standing on end, then sat back relieved. Then she got up to leave again, the sound of the chair rolling out. Some papers shuffling, tin clicking as she went to prescribe and provide the right painkillers. Austin was never more certain that there was a God. He would never play another football game again. 'You are merciful..."

VII.

It was three months before he was healed enough to walk again. His father had owned a characteristically aberrant collection of exploitation films he had consumed with a heat he had only ever had forced on him in practice. New York was saturating his mind. His dreams started to show signs of the city. The human organism in constant contact and an insomniac's potential that Austin would never in his life consider. He had known two seasons; Summer and Rain. California had as much weather as it did substance. For him, the beauty,

stagnant, the temperatures, static, made time pass in a lull that made it's people dull. 'People kill people to live here? I don't get it.'
At the end of his healing, his walk had always been a bit of a waddle, he would spend hours on end, stoned, just navigating the spaces of rentals, picture by picture. Photos of small single window cells that to Woodrow spoke liberation. The promise of a future that was so easily achievable, felt as if he had robbed someone and in the process been robbed. Hours of hard work seemed to pass as if he was asleep completely. Now, at his lowest, he felt honest. Free. Hardworking. He found a craigslist ad:
'Faith for the faithless.'
and an address. His hair stood on end. He felt he'd heard this before, somehow this had been written, pre-arranged without dowry, marrying, and all of his life swoll into his gut and rippled through his body, earth-shattered his heart to the epicenter. The locus of him called and an echo answered, no reflection, thoughtlessly ordering a one way. Quick to pack and never looking back, it clicked.

VIII. [MONKS CHANTING]

Chanting two monks walked in unison to Bedstuy. Their pastel-brown palms peeking from poppy-orange ribbons. The sleeves of their robes un-cut wholes: cut to nothing, cut for no one. Scooping flower bulbs from a weaved basket and tossing them behind their shoulders.
New York pensive grey blocks now littered in a purple trail that by contrast looked neon. Their voices were their feet's rhythm, tongues like bubbling drums, lazy and exciting. They follow themselves, marching along in silent paces with all of the weight in their movement, like pendulums, all kinetics in kino, until they arrived at an antique hotel, room 9, without being arrested. (Commonly mistaken for Krishna.) They danced in place, like gravity was water whirling as it would caught by river stones in the pockets too tight to slip through.
Clearly labeled: gold 9 against a stone green paint, chipping away with a flickering stain, like a star, splintering. There was a scar from years of beatings. On it's belly a perfect white dot in a brown gash that made time apparent. (Grand Canyon.)
With door open, and hands emptied of floral plumes, a new scent poured out and thread them through, an incense burning to cut through the smell of walls reeking of semen and cigarettes. Or cheap health food stores stores of grain. The walls were covered in sheets, untraditional, hippied-out tye-dye flags the size of bedsheets, pinned to the left of them. On the floor next to the wall were two velvet Zafus, two pillows like globs of gum. To their right a new young and eager audience, ears primed for the future of their inheritance the present, 'what a gift,' she thought.

IX. REACTION PLICATION

Samantha was frequenting the village coffee shop haplessly, with intentions of procrastinating on the best parts of study, when on a break from doing absolutely nothing, she decided to text someone outside where it was easier to breathe. For some reason they boiled water to the point of the entire coffee shop being muggy. She found it borderline intolerable but also liked that there would always be a struggle against the EDM selected for play regularly. The coffee was good.

She finished a text when someone she may have vaguely recognized as an employee passed her line of vision. She was smitten but jaded so tucked it into impossibility and judged him harshly only after herself. Love was at the bottom of the list for her and, anyways, she had only known most men to fear it. She had settled on being crushed repetitively by callous and emotionally unavailable men. Born to be scars to themselves. Her last sexual encounter was with a man in dreads and neck tattoos at least 11 years older than her. No one thought anything like that was possible. Absolute secrecy was insured, even in the small village she lived in and she liked it that way. She was, as her personae, completely unfettered, desuxualized, and streamlined as a functioning human machine. She liked it this way. This interrupted no one. This never required conflict and all parties she would ever pass through were satisfied at all times. The boy who was a man, turned his head and then looked away, straight again, without a smile. She looked up from her phone at that moment and forgot about it.

X.

Six hours later she was already drunk at a bar with her beautiful and obscenely dressed girlfriend, Jenna. Samantha was crouched over a salad, drunk and stoned, and struggling with it. She looked like a prisoner. Also looked like she was counting grains of feta, and continually dropping them. Couldn't get it onto the fork...yet.

The boy who was a man she'd seen earlier was completely sober and decided that, on seeing her, he immediately wanted to talk to her. Too sedate to really go anywhere, she listened. Mostly she talked about how she did recognize him from somewhere, like she had little idea who he was, even though, as a regular she had thought about him every time she saw him. She just had never seen him standing in front of the counter as opposed to behind it, which made him seem especially tall. The sad part of all jobs is the contextualization which Samantha undyingly subscribed to until wasted.

She found herself making the boy laugh harder and harder. He left the table when he was bored and met up with some other people. He seemed to be getting up every ten minutes for something, like he had something to do but, he never seemed to have anything to do. She brushed it off, she felt she had too. Plus there were always men, she was a woman.

At the end of the night, his friend and him, one who was only peripheral in his mind but appeared to be as close to him as Samantha seemed to Jenna. She kept

him happy, unsure if intentional or not but she was doing it, amazingly.
They exchanged phone numbers.
Then decided to skip the formalities and invited him to the bar they were going to next.
They sat next to each other and she interviewed him.
"Do you have any baggage?"
He laughed nervously and felt he should start drinking now.
He rarely ever drank.
He knew things seemed to be going well and besides her legs were between his legs right now, and why the fuck not. But then she got nervous and hated him so she asked him 'Is it okay if I kiss you?'
"What the fuck? Yeah, I mean, don't ask me that."
Then she stuck his hand in her hand and leaned over to him leaning over to her and they kissed.
Last call was called and the boy assumed he was going to have to catch a bus home.
He was gladly surprised when Samantha invited him over to his house. They called a cab and arrived right in front of her house, which was only three blocks away. Then she turned drunkenly and told him to 'Shutup,' politely, or maybe not, but he had to shut up if he was coming up and he had to never tell anybody else she leaves the front gate unlocked. Like he would tell anyone. Samantha's heart was skipping beats and proud of herself for taking someone home. "You're not going to fuck me, you understand?" she said serious.
"I wasn't assuming."
"Okay, good."
"Hey, I'm glad I got to come over."
"Yeah? Why?"
"I don't know. Look at you. You're funny, you're tall you're pretty."
"Shutupppp," she laughed. Then grabbed him by the hand and lead him upstairs until it was too uncomfortable to try to keep holding hands. Jenna had left home earlier so she was there on the end of her bed, with her door open, and her ass peeking out wrapped in blue and white striped sailor panties. She mumbled an acknowledgment and laughed. Samantha looked at the boy and the boy looked confused. So she was glad when he was drunk enough to peel himself naked and stick himself straight into bed. She was getting ready, somewhere else, changing into an oversized t-shirt and touching her hair nervously over and over. Then she sat indian legged next to him and with her lengthy arms, she sometimes hated them, peeled a book from the top of her dresser. She ignored her own filth strewn in the room. The boy didn't mind. "Ignore the mess." she said flipping through pages. And she pointed to a passage and shoved the book at the boy. The boy accepted it quietly and read it, but read it drunkenly, and out loud:
"If there is something to desire, there will be something to regret. If there is something to regret there will be something to recall. If there is something to recall, there was nothing to regret. If there was nothing to regret, there was nothing to desire."

She was smiling at him reading it. "Sometimes I like to read."
"Are you a writer?"
"Sometimes I'm a writer."
She felt embarrassed and took the book away from him. Then got up and turned off the light.
She kissed him in the dark for too long and passed out at 4am.
That night she had a dream of an antique hotel in Bedstuy. She had a sister who lived there. She was dressed in her Sunday's best like she was going to church she never went to. She was with her sister and when they found it together they kissed each other happily, and then for too long.
In the morning, she woke up feeling slightly perverted. She woke up on her stomach and to the sound of the boy lacing up his boots. She couldn't see him until he stood all the way up with his bag over the bed. Her huge eyeball opening up and locking onto him.
"You're leaving?"
"Yeah, I got work."
"Okay. See you."
"Bye." he half-whispered shutting the door.
She fell asleep again and woke up feeling emptier than the empty you feel after fucking a stranger. Instead she felt disappointed that the boy hadn't tried to force himself on her, even a little bit. She couldn't even feel him pressed in between her legs. That disappointed her. But she felt disease. Woke up and lazily flipped through the pages of the book she shared last night, like there was something in it, thinking to herself.

Then throwing the book back into the bed noticed a to-do list fall out.
She read the to-do list. She was confused, the date was different, but these were all things she needed to do now. Then she looked on the back which was, fully dated. A list from freshman year of college. She was in her third year but only a Sophomore. Wracking her brain for comfort she felt more naked than with the boy. She missed the boy. She hated the boy. The boy seemed like he was going somewhere. 'I think he said that last night, going to New York. Damn. I want to go to New York. Why are you moving? Fucking asshole. Stuck up asshole. I want to go to New York."
She threw herself back on the bed. Then cracked open the book to a dogear. She read the poem and remembered he had read it last night. "Idiot, why would you show him that poem?"
She read it again and closed her eyes, scolding herself.

XI. HEART ON

In the weeks passing she would still frequent the same coffee shop but would avoid at all costs any sincere interaction with the boy. Which drove the boy insane. He asked her on a date in person, outside after work. She shook her head silently, and then mumbled a no.

The next time she came to the coffee shop the boy or man-crush was gone. She talked to everyone she could who knew something about it.
"Didn't even finish his two weeks."
Regret filled her head. The imagined power struggle ended with her dick in her hands.
"Weren't you thinking about going to New York for a while?" Jenna asked behind her in line.
"Yeah. Just dropping everything and going."
That night, alone in the apartment, she bought a one way ticket.
Part of her jaded from where she had been. Part of her hopeful for what could be.
Love doesn't end up anything anyways. But then part of her hoped she might run into him.
While searching for rooms she found herself reading an ad that read more like a personal.
"You didn't think exactly what you needed was there when you needed it. Love can always be a new place. New to New York? Open house party:" and an address.

XII. ALTER

Her present practice was in honor of a long legacy of hope that by avoiding exactly what she wanted someone would notice. Someone would erase her bodily disgust and turn her into a rape case. Someone would notice her rusting need for love and satisfy it without her ever showing herself vulnerable. Her life was a wish that love would come to her, would come through her, that the one with the endurance to see 'me' and refuse that answer knew something about her she didn't. She was obsessed with love. She was suicidal in her will to live. Her perfectionism came through in her appearance: black and white. Puritanical. She wore black suede wedges, which accented her thickened legs, up her naked thigh onto her cunt and parts. She wrapped her ass in tight spandex, the kind of shorts that end just at the beginning of the thigh, the end of the end. Tucked into shorts was a white long sleeve, a body suit tucked in. Around her shoulder, draping over her, perched perfectly on a backless black leather couch. Sitting on her knees, her legs tucked under and to the side. She's closest to the door. She was surprised to see herself dressed like a nun, opulent and ascetic at once, reflected in the great manners of two monks, they had their eyes on her eyes only. 'For your eyes only.' 'They only have eyes for me...' she thought to herself. She laughed.
She wanted to fix her long black hair, perfect hair, but didn't, she thought that there would be interference with the aura of the room. She was here for sacrifice, she thought. She imagined herself as tame as the lamb. Love was hard because she only knew them to be burnt, eaten, or swallowed by fire.

XIII. ATLAST

@abigfuckingbully

Austin played sports for his lineage, for his future, out of obligation. Physical expressions were his life's work. He was unknowingly the performance artists he thought he hated. He didn't ask about the problems he had. Everything seemed complex if it was emotional. People he knew who had emotions were so busy hurting themselves that he was scared of feeling at all. Reminded him of diseases. He was dressed in a black tank, white basketball shorts with blue racing stripes up the thigh. Black socks, black slip ons. One giant cast cutting through the entire fit.

XIV. "A REAL MODERN DAY THOREAU."
To Samantha's left was Princeton. He had a shaved head and a baseball cap, a faded orange t-shirt, and grey shorts. The gore tex kind that science teachers wear. He had a strong build, spent a lot of time working outdoors, and taking trips outdoors. He shared 'outdoors' with other people.
He burnt incredible amounts of gasoline to reach far away places. They granted him pieces of peace that would add to the surface of his rugged demeanor. Sometimes he felt trapped as if he had spent years building a house he almost didn't want to live in. What strong arches. Without bending, without loss of limb and driving one tall axe's head into wood over, and over, and over again to make more axe handles. When someone is taking trees down to feed a house animals are sure to notice.
Calling again, out to a wilderness he would otherwise dismiss as some force he would have to practice tuning into. Neither loose or tight—it was ever present in his being, like change, 'if only they would be patient,' he thought, August 24th, 2010, when his northwestern one room Kaczynski was coming together, when as the last life in his dream house was fell, sighed out of him. Dead new, like the processes drawn to him before. A quarter life crisis three quarters through the attainment of perceived desire. The last panel was pushing it up and out of the body of the tree that died to give wood life, seemed to speak to him like Pinocchio. Because now it's a lie.
Princeton wanted to build a small cabin in a wild squatted area in Washington. When his friends left him, he tried stealing more supplies. Liberating them. He wanted with all his heart to sincerely bypass Capitalism but was caught stealing and mercifully released. It was grand theft.
During one of the busier days in the busiest hardware store in mainland Washington, he filled his cart to the brim with every needed supply and thought that the best disguise was no disguise. Upon walking out of the Home Depot without so much as a thumbtack purchase he was detained, or rather, calmly handed himself over. Talked to the employee who, upon seeing just how desperate the plan was, let him go immediately. Something turned inside him that night.
Disappointed, he returned back into town, not town but, the city. The cities—he hated. He couldn't understand. He, pained, started to seek his earnestness end which would reveal him untailored. The weaving. The fiber of marathon.

XV. ON THE RECORD

To Princeton's left seated in the same position, ready for prayer, for forgiveness, for baptism was the least ready, Joselyn. Dyed red hair, not a natural imitation, the color of a Porsche. Her face stoic and bordering on sour. The face of a middle aged woman who chain smoked outside her complex, working the wrinkles. Just beautiful enough to be desired, like she wanted to be, but stark enough to scare away most. To exist in themselves, stroking their vain solitude publicly.

Pity loses interest and business as usual usually goes uninterrupted. A medicine was all of the borders she had put on, and inside of them lived what needed to be seen from another's side. Raised in a suburb where the defeatist mindset was believed to be fought by tying, 'too tired to fight,' with 'they and them,' and on the greatest leap of faithlessness, the satisfying safety of righteousness in unquestioned anger as a mask for a filthy disposition to bottomless apathy. An endless fight with the part of itself that leads to change; an admission that in order to see where you are you're going to have to leave.
She was taking her first steps. She had taken a plane once before in her life. From Los Angeles to San Jose. If she had money, she would have finished that tattoo of a Koi fish on her back/neck, but it looked done mostly, anyways, who was going to bother looking at her—missing her shirt. Men—of course—were mostly homicidal pigs anyways. A miracle they'd got out of bed without hurting anyone. She would oppose all forms of affection that were not isolated, hidden, or ironically 'puritanical.' She'd never think of them that way.
On mornings, without thought, she would look in her mirror and pray.
"Please, God. I don't want to hurt anyone today."
She was blind to the weight of choice and it's snaking infinities. Refused to see lady fortune was a whore. She only need be called in order to follow and find you. Joselyn felt fear etched into the coin and could never get herself to pass it. Day dates reading non-fiction religiously, passing up the self-help sections because she got her fill from walls lined with books on social control theory. When Joselyn whose name almost drew her line of fate out of the warmth and company of others, was approached by Jermaine, they could lick each others wounds endlessly.
It was that time when two of them could wear the salve of loving ease in record store's seven inches from the 50 cent bin to ease the pains. Her and Jermaine started a band, populating the world with people completely committed to the politics—one secular convert at a time, because I mean, we've all been there, the 40oz, the repetitions what was new was that soft tender side of punk.
It was successful for too long. Lovers, attached at the hip, one operated as more of an appendage, until one gains insight in age where youth fell off—where one, as a primal instinct, senses, after years of being too forgiving, longing for identity outside of the body.
The context defines.

The context was her first focus.
A womb emerges when walls are built, stacked like an early culture's monument, and to what?
She's an animal, she promises herself, she reminds herself. Running circles in urban circuits, the race with a personal inferiority complex, resorting to taming another.
She wrote to her family—and while writing out her list of recent accomplishments felt a twinge of disgust of it's similarity to last letters 'list.' She felt her life had become the list, a list of her whole life, every major life changing event laid out, alongside their developments, horrifying. She may or may not continue to live with an emaciated will after reading it herself but decided it was better if it was stuffed into an envelope and nailed to someone she knew hardly cared. They'd never get the feeling that life was supposed to be anything more than that.
She was surfing the internet, stoned, feeling guilty about porn consumption, she thought maybe she should do something constructive, earn some extra money but someone was selling records so she picked herself up from bed and changed into something other than underwear, and put sheer black 'leggings' over her underwear to bike over.

GARAGE SALE

She's picking up what she thinks is a Cattle Holocaust album, surprised to find it's sleeve solid-matte-black. No track listing. No label. No 'artist' name. She took it and asked an aging punk how much it was worth.
"Weird." he grunted. "I'm not sure what that is."
"Me neither. I'll give you $5."
"Okay, shit. I've never opened it, so...yeah. Sure."
She handed him a balled up fiver and hopped on her bike feeling a sense of elation, direction, close to the time she met Jermaine. She didn't know why, but there was a glow inside her, she suspected rose up, blossomed from inside the solid, monochrome, vinyl.
'Black gold...' she thought,
mashing all the way back to her house she felt the importance of her body.

XVI.
She played the record as soon as she got home, peeling off her leggings, rolling on her back. Looking at the vinyl in the light, she saw that it consisted of one single track, completely undivided. Crackling static, moment's passing, then a white man's voice, young but from an ancient time, booming:
"The practice of 'Dream Yoga,' predates written history. It's suggested by the Yi sect—by more than thousands of years. This practice is one of the most difficult to master because it's one of the most difficult to understand. Dream world has been an intrigue of the human mind since their primitive beginnings. Many early cultures believe what the Yi sect believes—we are not living a reality, are

not living our own lives, but are living out a dream, being dreamt by the creator, or 'Great Dreamer.'"
She fell asleep, no dreams.
When she woke up the record's A side had finished and groggy but happy, got up to turn it over, feeling disconnected from the content. She noticed an address printed in black on black on Side B, where, tilted in the right light she could read: an address.
She stared for a few minutes, everything seemed infinite, to both slow down and speed up, to become more vivid than before. She felt she had been here before somehow. She immediately took down the address and sat at her computer to buy a one way ticket to New York.

XVII.
Joselyn's posture was more stoic than the others but seemed inattentive. She turned her head to notice a 4th. It was an athletic black man in a cast whose crutch was laid beside him, Austin. To his left another boy.
The boy, or man, she couldn't tell the difference, was wearing a white-t and hardly fitted jeans, She suspected 501's, and a pair of white chucks. She tried a smile but she wasn't accustomed yet.

XVIII. PUSHING DAISIES

Henry was unfocused. The others seemed focused but also sad or sick. Old science books were plastered on the walls. The floor was parts of a Persian Rug, cornflower blue on a royal blue on a navy blue. The room filled with wine colored velvet. A lamp as tall as a human with a body as fat as a girl, incense burning on a glass night stand. A bowl of wax fruit. A woodcut of an anorexic Bengal Tiger hanging. Curtains heavy as couches. He watched the monks from over Joselyn's shoulder, they finished a dance as they entered. The lilac petals tossed like confetti. Their robes settling revealed just enough of their strong, tan, pot bellied bodies for Henry to trust them.
The students, the children, the adults far too short, watched, fearfully like they could be attacked, rabid in their silence.
Two Zafus unfilled in front of the leather button, backless couch.
"We are," they were holding lilies behind their backs, which they dramatically moved to their stomachs, "the last of our monastery. The last of an ancient sect of monks from Megumi. The monastery known for teaching those to teach themselves that they might learn." Their palms pressed together till they crushed the bulb of their Callas completely. The smell overwhelmed even the incense.
The monks bowed, one leg, like Broadway and from the inside of the bells, burnt

from the fireless ash of the rubbing, friction bred burping Lilies. Beads emerged and then chanting.
Guts kept churning.
Slowly the barrel shaped men filled the Zafus, edging down into full lotus like two flamingos. A smell of semen filled the air, the smoke lifting it, threaded into the musk of the couch. The monks song was strong, along with the smoke making them sleepy. Their blood was running faster, their hearts beat black and blue by the sight of each other. Without instruction, the students found themselves repeating word for word. Surprised by their own reaction, rippling flesh.
It must all be organized, right? Or all random. The show they fought at first was unmistakable. The relentless relent. Feelings of pleasure and opium stoned, they wanted explanations for as dogmatic disbelievers. Nothing gave them the feeling parents were good sources but compliance afforded more love so instruction was of prime importance. Even if it took obedience to forget everything, they thought they should know better than to know. Until tonight primal urges were buried in the backyard, heart-urned trash: their lives passing with the spinelessness of someone's trained St. Bernard. But no one here could afford a St. Bernard.
They were young.
Youth seeks the answer when stripped of freedom, unwound corks. Insides were torn up like squat carpets. Like venues being evicted by undercover firemen. They could only try crying.
The monks rose up again, shouting now, the song caught in the young's ear like a line fed to them, their heads caught up. Jerking to see--
fingers so tender and unmechanic the monks all kinetics made into the next second's movement. Gravity like water, raining muscle into joints, pounding now, serenity in the grain of wooden floors tumbling back up in ripples, to fight now would take their minds or force their bodies to degrade. Limbs were light but glued where they were—washing through them, they exhaled themselves and tried not to think, 'just a cheap hotel room...'
God forbid one of them doubt, but that's the problem.
The future had spoiled them rotten, every corner of the planet could be experienced vicariously and some are teased with another unmet need sold as fantasy. Wiki the world: don't bother. You've already seen it with your own eyes. Stripping themselves, to nothing but instincts weighty call, they saw new parts of each other. White and brown, all in need of some spent sun. Some hard. Some soft. Some beautiful. Others hard to accept, but they were. Joselyn's nipples were inverted until she looked straight into the face of Henry, who, was looking blankly, almost horrified. She turned up. Her breasts growing subtly. Her nipples lifting in goosebumps. Reigniting the parts of them that had to be schooled properly, beaten to death into the repressive hammering that would use train spikes to manufacture a martyr like her.
The commitment it took for Austin to take Samantha's face in his palm, brush her hair aside in his heat and have some body. Then following she handled his cock with the tenderness of a flower, the touch of his piston against sticky

fingers. Joselyn turned away and into the other three bodies, joining them. Henry stripping and then as he imagined Adam to have stood as taught at knowledges tree, early man, lifting himself from the primordial mulch of guilt and burden: labor. Work. Birth of birth. Original born sinner. The art of sin. Improvisation. The need to rationalize our existence to make way to love. Need breeding need. Breeding leading to breeding. Feeding leading to feeding. And still we can't hear God's voice...
Henry walked into the group, behind the skinny, folding 'red' head. Who in perfect timing was approached by the dog thin body of Princeton, whose quiet nature irked Henry. He waited too long and Princeton slid himself into Joselyn. Henry was unaware of his presence entirely, didn't know how he had slipped out of his clothes and slipped into anything else. A tattoo of a day of the dead skull between her shoulder blades. He would have laughed if it was any other time. If his heart was any place else. He was met with a hand pushing him away. He tried with Samantha on the other end, the same view, the same way, and felt the same rejecting touch. He was dazed to tears again. The tension without release mounting. His past had felt just as perpetual.
He was silent in the face but in his mind reminding himself, like the reassurance of college, that this is just an experiment anyways, a healthy suspension of disbelief. Trying it on for size. His hard on airing itself out embarrassingly unashamed.
Doubt was healthy. Like his body. Free from God on Tablets. Nothing written in stone. Why write rules against envy when you could teach pride, the Peacock's narcissism, to the point of never inciting envy in another. Only predator is your misbehavior. The pecking order makes violators princes in rags. Or would that only make them happier?
We would no longer bother with Babel. Babel is exactly what you built it as. The great wall. And Locusts. And the blood of another on the doorframe. Or frogs. Or plague. We all need to fuck. We're all Bonobos. The baboons ass, a historical lesson, where as we get further and further away, becomes pure comedy and all comedy is sublimation. Some truths are too heavy to carry so we smoke them up. You can't keep yourself out. Leave nothing up to nature again because we want to be the first and last of our kind.
Henry saw a flash of light from his closed eyes. Enough smoke to choke on then, he watched, absently as these strangers consummated something they were all lost on and thought they needed. Austin, was fully erect, standing above Samantha, one arm in the crutch, who peeled out of her good looks engaged more than Joselyn but seemed to move with too much force. Conscious of exactly what she felt she needed to do. It was improvisation but her wiggling made it seem more. Austin's face was a wrinkle. The force looked grueling. He imagined Jesus in less pain on the cross. He was lost, outside of his body, Henry could hardly recognize him pounding into a girl whose legs were almost as high as Woodrow's head. Luckily Austin's last name was tattooed in his back. As if his jersey could never be removed. Playing for the team at all times.
Joselyn was trying to find her way in.

Samantha was glad to have something to covering her face, so when Joselyn dropped her hips over her Samantha took to it like a racing horse to her feed bag.

The monks stop chanting. Now only the contact of bodies was exploding through the paper thin room. The monks finding more lilac petals, to toss over the undulating bodies, shouting, "God put halos around your head and stuck plucked daisies in your ears! God put halos around your head and stuck plucked daisies in your ears! God put halos around your head and stuck plucked daisies in your ears..."

Woodrow moved faster with every repetition. Joselyn was moaning, while something like a squeal was repeating muffled into Joselyn, who, had a man in her, and was being pushed into the base of Princeton's, all of them vibrating until two monks looking straight at each other, grinning ear to ear—trying to catch the harmony with the other in a performance of a lifetime. Then again one single tone, together in a crescendo, piquing all at once in chorus.

Silence again,

their bodies inflating and deflating,

their pieces pulling apart.

Pistons milk, stringy and grasping on in denial of an end. Woodrow pushed a hand through his hair, Samantha, crying now, was pressing herself feeling partly proud and totally ashamed. Joselyn waited. The monks, bored of the scene filed out, one following the other, like a bad party. The feeling of air hitting a body of glossed bodies, Samantha and Austin hit breakneck. Feeling jaded and terrified but certain they both knew nothing, now choking on possibilities their life failed to offer, they walked out certain they were seeing each other again but knew better. Triumphant and stupid, the weight of choice was the lightness of a full night of drinking. Princeton lingered too long but seemed to be leaving. His filth felt like liberation. No longer the piety he imagined attainable through secession, united in flesh, all prayers to grid.

Henry stood naked. Joselyn rose.

He walked forward to her and the hand that pushed away was wrapping itself around him while pushing himself into the mouth of a dyed neon redhead. Henry laid her into the button leather couch, in both defeat and conquest. Only when, in it's most meaningless, his love was given, could someone receive it. It must be given to her. It was always, it is always, it must always be unconditional. The golden rule is a flogging for one in love with ritual punishment. Commitment to oneself is commitment to grief, the panhandling for love, bankrupt charity from the need to give. No dealer smokes his own stash.

He pushed himself over the petals of her lips, through her, into her, vice tight, out of her, through her. Henry stone faced. Joselyn smiling.

She came with her face turned pressing her hand into his lower abdomen to stop him. Then with the hand still in place, slid off. Walked to her bags to get dressed. The zipper sounded. The jingling faded. A door creaking as metal rungs slung, with Henry opening the curtains. At the bottom of the building, were only ant lines of humans milling forward. He wanted to puke but didn't. He got dizzy dropped the curtain and listened to the sounds outside like they were food, nourishing him, alone again in the warmth of a velvet womb.

@abigfuckingbully

RELATIONSHIP FANTASY: BUNNY ROGERS, I SEE GOD IN YOU

It's been two years since the whole thing.
I see her walking opposite me on E. 5th St.
I'm 29 years old and I've finally made it to New York,
lazy, working only a single part time job,
but I'm here now nd my heart sings at the sight of her,
of course my face wouldn't reveal it, instead, it's filled with the intensity of an athlete. As our bodies cross, she sees me see her, nd the blood rushes to both of our faces, but from some fire in our guts. She looks at me dead on nd I can't help but look back. Her face is fire. My face is soft, nd it can't be pleasant but it's present, nd it's for her, it's enough of both my loss, nd anger, nd the love that I thought I'd wanted.
I jut in front of her, stopping her in her tracks, she starts walking faster, I follow her, stop in front of her again, she shifts left, I follow her, she shifts right, I follow her, her hair following her, then she stops.
"It's Atticus." I say. Placing a full palm on my chest.
She surrenders. Her body in place, a hand on the strap of a low end designer's cinched leather mini-bag, a muted purple.
I feel prepared to meet her.
Red bomber, white hoody, skin tight blue jeans, nd white chucks. I've filled out. I'm near the 200lbs in muscle I've promised myself. I wish all my clothes could break.
My hand on the strap of my bag.
She shifts to one hip nd her body bobs gently.
How tall this woman is.
Legs are longer than I could imagine.
The snow keeps blowing over us but the air peels against the heat of our faces.
The view of breath, pulsing, as it exits us.
In call and response, on after the other. Her hair sways nd she looks straight at me, annoyed, then as if she cannot see me nd says,

"I know who you are. *What do-you want?*"

"Bunny Rogers,
if you listen to the sound of my voice,

@abigfuckingbully

you can tell that I mean what I'm about to say,
nd that I don't mean any harm,

forget all the mean shit I said on the internet
b/c you and I both know
how I really feel about you--
I love you--[I choke here uncertain if this honest]
I've only ever said 'I hate you,' to people I love.
I admire you--nd I can't say this
as a man who wants to be with you
b/c now I'm following you--
but now that there's no chance,
nd it's all shot to hell,
I can fold--entirely--and tell you,
I admire you.
What would it take for you to believe that?
I wish I could share w/ you all the private conversations
I've had about you. And how great your work is.
Bunny,
I see God in you.
America would be a hole without you.
I'd hate to live in that place,
now that you're a part of the cultural lexicon.
I got mad nd I said some shit--sounds like me.
But I hated it--that you boiled down all my affections
to obsession, nd perversion, nd sex.
You're the one who said you were a pervert.
Like all I wanted to do was to fuck you.
I'm not saying this to be a softboy,
rarely do I have thoughts this pure towards a person--
not that purity matters,
but,
what I'm saying is, to me, despite how I feel:
that desexualizing someone is just as perverse nd corrupt
as sexualizing them--I just couldn't do it.
Maybe once or twice. As a conscious practice. It felt wrong for sex to be divorced
from the whole thing. But it's not who I am or what I wanted.
I would have loved to just go on a date with you.
See your opening.
A reason to buy an outfit.
A reason to fly to New York.
Like I said, when I see your face,
I don't see something I want,
I see someone--I'd love to learn from.
What I saw was...maybe I'm selfish and only saw myself in you, like you said, but

my most common fantasy, despite all the horrible dreams I have about you, were just being in the same space nd watching you work."

Bunny stares. Bunny is unmoved.
My eyes are wet but the words feel full nd honest hitting air.

"In the studio, crouched over something, yr hair draped over yr work nd you too busy to even bother w/ it--or to notice it. And what does Bunny wear when she works? You in coveralls was always a funny idea to me. Pretty in it's own way.

You'll hate this,
but,
I just think about your hands so much.
Your beautiful long fingers--
the mark, trait, of a natural born artist,
especially in women,

Bunny, raise yr hand up for me,"

I raise my hand up, to have her mirror it.
She reluctantly lifts her hand like she's making a promise,
taking an oath.

"See, they're almost as long as mine nd yr a girl. I think about your hands all the time--not because I have a fetish, okay? I think about yr hands b/c they're strong nd beautiful."

I point at her hands--

"I think about those hands b/c those hands make things.
Beautiful things.
I talked shit about yr art to you but, it's not how I feel.
I like the things you make.
That drawing of Andy Gibb.
Yr sad chairs.
Yr roses.
That video of you making out w/...
photos of you poning,
you singing,
your voice is one of the most beautiful sounds in the world to me,
yr ribbon mop.

You mean the world to me Bunny Rogers.
Yr art means the world to me.
It's funny b/c in someway, even w/ yr chronic depression,

@abigfuckingbully

I can't be certain yr not an enlightened person.
That photo of you in the black dress--it has this light,
like yr a saint, like you've got a halo.
It's yr suffering that's going to save you Bunny.
A lot of people putting forward what they believe to be great political works.
Feminist art.

But something about it feels hollow.
It feels empty to me.
When I read your poems, I'd hear your voice--
I'm moved.

I think, somehow, Bunny has something to teach us."

I smile a strained smile. Shaking as not to cry.
Teeth showing unknowing if I am baring them or not.

"That you can teach us how to take care of each other.
Understand people better, something political art swears by but fails to do almost every time,
teach us sympathy. Give us humanity.

Granted, like I said, I keep my head out of it.
You said most of the men in your life have to but...
I didn't understand that any of yr art's about men.
I've always kept my head out of yr poems b/c if I didn't I might start turning on you. Criticisms I don't want to make b/c if I imagined my life with you it's that I'm the man you get away with murder w/. Preferential treatment. Possessive nd biased. Holding you accountable in private sometimes but mostly defending even yr worst idiocy or hypocrisy publicly."

I smile. I start crying, but without the sounds.
Just the tears rolling out. My hands shake.
I brush one tear out of my eye with my hand in a fist,
like a little kid.

"A place to hide for always. And everyone would know it's like that, that I'm just like that. Some hidden place away from the gnashing routine of an art career.
You said I idealized you but...

I see God in you Bunny b/c,
the day you see what I see in you--"

My voice cracks.
I have to wait a solid minute rubbing tears out of my eyes.

274

Bunny Rogers looks on.
Who knows what that face means.
If I could imagine what was in this woman,
if it wasn't like an emotional black box,

"is that day you look in a mirror nd see what the mirror sees too. Is that day you see what the mirror sees b/c the mirror sees you with total objectivity. A dead 10 at 5' 11". You're the most beautiful girl in all of New York City. Yr a hyperindustrious elite artist in New York City, one of the wealthiest cities in one of the wealthiest countries in the world.
Everyone loves you Bunny.

Do you know why I like yr ass Bunny?"

Bunny's face goes slack, her eyebrows furrow nd she tilts her head forward in anger.

"It's not just because it's strong, nd handsome. I like yr legs for the same reason: those legs do ballet."

I point to her legs.

"Those legs play basketball. In a field where people become sickly attached to intellect to the point of viewing the mind as somehow superior nd disconnected. Less important. A scene of weak bodied ppl, fragile, anemic-thin, or obese. A bunch of drug addicts. No offense.

Yr addictions never really bothered me. Which I know is problematic too. I'm poor. You're a drug addict.
It's a dealbreaker.
Yr too productive for me to judge.
In addition to being an artist, yr a ballerina, nd an athlete.
I remember the first phone call, after I'd gone insane,
you asked me if I was still jogging. It made me really happy even tho I acted like it didn't.

Bunny,
when I say
'Thank you for being here,'
I mean it--
Thank you for being here.
It doesn't take someone like me to see what's in you.
I know you know what I'm saying.
I'm not idealizing you when I say those things.
That's just...data.

Maybe in a way, but don't we all, like, fantasize?
You put me out like a cigarette.
And I could act mad about that but--
I'm childish in my own way Bunny.
It's what's good about me, I see the world thru big eyes.
Hate to put you so far above me.
In Buddhism, I know you'll hate this, but, there's the belief that no matter what you do, or what mistakes you make, you know what yr doing. You reap what you sew. I acted pathetic so you treated me as if I was pathetic. I invited the abuse nd I take responsibility for that."

My face tightens up.
The tears roll silently,
but words are choked,
start sounding like
they might end up bellows.

"But I won't always be this fucked up kid."

I smile.

"If I had really loved you,
I would have acted differently despite how I may feel b/c,
like my brother said,
always level headed nd reasonable--
'love is patient, love is kind'"

When men cry their lips curl nd they clench their teeth.

"I would have waited years for you.
Weeks for messages.
I would have never hit on you till everything was together,
nd I had the money, and the status, nd the artistic success to be near yr equal.
Tho yr years ahead.
Just,
don't think,
just forget everything awful I said,
b/c
I care for you too Bunny.
I really do."

Face quivering.
Eyes trying to sustain bold contact despite fear of exposure.
The way animals look at you, I look at her.

Bunny's hip cocks to the other side, she looks thru me nd then over my shoulder as if there was something else to see, somewhere else to go. Her long silken brown hair looked silver in the grey of the sky, even with the sunlight--like the moon thru a stone--and a flash of hatred passed thru her face, her high cheeks trying not to move, her eyes narrowing then stopping just to watch my face. Dead stills a winter wind brushed thru her hair nd it shivered like grass in spring breeze, with the gentleness of light rippling over some exposed glass. Dead in the eyes, she says,

"I don't care."

nd she walks past me quickly.
Into and away from a sea of New Yorkers whose self acceptance nd seeming tranquility swallow me whole: and I cry nd I cry, hot tears like blood in the snow.
I'm Parsifal staring into the snow.
Waiting for spring to come melt me nd save us.
Red in the face b/c of the heat in the cold.
Gave it all away nd acted robbed.
It's always yr fault.

"Ay, faggot! Where's the flood?"
I look up nd find a 300lb lifter with a greying slick back in his gym clothes pointing nd laughing at me with his equally large buddy.

nd I snap out of it, nd start laughing.
I am ridiculous.
This pathetic cuck strung out on hope.
"Just shut the fuck up nd lift." I whisper to myself.

@abigfuckingbully

RELATIONSHIP FANTASY: DARCIE WILDER: "Of Course I Do."

After the reading, at the bar, I let something slip I shouldn't.
Because after I say it it's known,
and once it's known, it's not spontaneous.
It's a qualification but–

After the reading, after the bar,
me dead sober, because I'm always sober
or I'm insane: chemically sensitive schizoid,
Darcie a few drinks in,

jackets are stripped off, tossed somewhere
the way everyone shuffles around their
apartments tired, after whatever, reacquainting with everything
but then Darcie, warms up,
big cheeks red, contrast to light eyes,
the cold follows you around nd yr skin stays tight to yr face
I sit on a couch in front of–somewhere in the corner is the record player
the way record players are always in some dark corner,
where the light vignettes around it, warm low light orange glow
Darcie bends over to put on a record, lily white belly
in a lilt, sticks out for a moment while her hands drop with the record,
some movement like water, or rain washing over petals,
hands move slightly outwards, I think of animals
I start to giggle,
she looks back as she sets the needle, nd asks,
"What?" She doesn't smile. She's very serious.
I'm of course noticing her belly.
I won't tell her.

Jessica Lea Mayfield starts playing,
Darcie looks nervous,
bobs for a minute in place, drunkenly standing,
then drops down, falling all at once, tight jeans tested
by the position of one leg as if indian-sitting, and one knee,
the opposite still poking up,
she runs a hand through her hair to straighten it,
just the bangs

her face runs a soft grin across, the way the lips run
into each other when your drunk,
like someone wrote your name in cursive across your face
"Is this okay?"
"Oh," I say, confused. Who cares what I think? "I don't mind it."
I smile, lying.
"I know you said..." she paused drunkenly, "I know you said at the bar–
you dinn't like when people play sad music when they're first meeting."
She looks upset already after her eyes graze my face for a response.
The common complaint with ex-girlfriends is they can never tell.
I never complain.
"You should complain more."
I never complain.
She gets serious nd starts looking for a new record off the bat,
stands up, wobbles nd both legs are solid in the ground
every muscle flexed,

so much intent,
"DARCIE!–What are you doing?"
She looks back, drunk nd upset,
"What?!"
"You listen to me." I stick my hand out into the room, palm outstretched,
all five fingers, as if I could touch her, funny like I was drunk too.
"Of course I do." She says flatly, no smile, nd goes back to the records.
"No, but Darcie, you don't just listen nd know what I'm saying,
  yr not just, like, hearing it, you listen nd you know it, you care.
  You do it."
She looks back as she pulls a record out of it's sleeve,
confused, continues intently, both eyes on the record,
lifts it out of it's sleeve all the way above her head,
slips it into the little box, nd gently places the pretty needle
in the groove,
closes the the cover,
nd falls on the floor all at once,
tight jeans tested by the position,
one leg as if indian-sitting, and one knee, opposite
poking up.
She runs a hand through her hair, shakes out,
nd her face hangs down,
both hands behind her on the floor,
toe's 'Goodbye' starts playing,
"Hey, this song's sad too." I say.
She looks up nd smiles,
like somebody wrote her name in cursive across her face,
turns away, and lilts with the music.

@abigfuckingbully

TOMBOY

She'd heard bad things about him but she didn't believe them. He was always around somehow, showing up to events, always with some other men. She'd never seen someone so self possessed and without worry. The constant laughter made her think he wasn't bothered about/by anything and knew something about life she didn't. She was always miserable. She never saw him with a woman, which confused her. Never heard anything about a girlfriend, still, somehow, her mind would drift to thoughts of him--trying to ignore the constant impulse to look, can never tell if she's looked to the point of being rude, and while, because of his reputation she had heard he was a troublemaker, a misogynist, and hypersexual, she still felt compelled. He didn't seem like he could seriously be any of those things and not just because he was, in his own ugly-pretty way, handsome, with the face of a dog, or bubbly in a masculine way, making him incredibly charming and subject of a fantasy in which he held her close and ran a hand thru her hair publicly at an event, letting him show everyone she was his and despite intellectually disagreeing with that outmoded relationship model, still felt warm and happy seeing it happen. When she caught sight of him across the venue smiling (in general) without ever making contact with him, aware that outgoing airheads had a deep potential to hurt her.
Tho she heard from everyone stories about how he'd stalked a girl in his hometown and had been, 'Creeping out girls in San Francisco,' she didn't believe them. Something in his face, and it could only be his face, or maybe how he spoke sometimes, being well spoken-- a voice that spoke authoritatively and with conviction. He was unknowingly one of the most macho men she'd ever experienced, always peripherally with/around her friends--around the town, around bars even tho he didn't drink. Always drinking a soda water flirting with a girl who was also interested by had no convergent interests. Because you couldn't ask for much in this small town. She wanted to know him. She wanted to escape her incestuous circle and know what he was always able to laugh about. She couldn't hear him over the band setting up to play but caught sight of him in a small circle of four, of course, laughing.

She went to shows to meet musicians--not the ones playing, not that she was against that but she was looking to start a band and sought out talent at shows. "I've been told it's the best way." She didn't play anything. Used to practice guitar everyday until the day she remembers being depressed, she stuffed her undersized guitar, which was unnaturally fitting to her hands, into its case and hung it up, using the strap, like a shirt or dress in her closet. With all the fire and ambition she had, she ended up heartbroken. Feeling she was the only one who could bring her dream to fruition and because she couldn't trust anyone else to join and complete, she put it down as meaningless. Years later, without regret, she would start seeking out talent, to start a band with her at the center, lead vox. Pounds lighter without the guitara having once been complimented: during a session one of the guitarists playing with her came over and thru the storm of sound put one hand out the body of her guitar after hearing her voice said, "don't even worry about this," shouting it over the drums and bass and then continued to play for her waiting to watch and wait--to see what she could do to/with a mic alone.

The entire group was moved by a moment in which she bellowed a scratchy shout and held the 'note' for 30 seconds straight, while the rest of the players piqued. When the sound ended the music did too. Everyone was shocked and impressed. Silent while catching her breath--everyone started talking about what 'we' needed to start a band. Of course it was all talk. She inquired via text why she was locked out of the practice space above the bar one of the members inherited from a dead brother, she got no text back until an hour later.

'Forgot.' is all she read. She went home due to her sensitivities and never played with those people again.

She's 22 and living at home. She has the capacity/awareness to be a waitress without many errors but chooses the slightly less stressful occupation of being a barista which is two steps above a grocery store. Retarded people work at grocery stores. She was erratically employed--had never before this year stuck to a job for longer than a year. She was an anarchist in youth and heavily influenced by Bob Black's 'Abolition of Work,' an essay that would permanently pervert her view of work into a master/slave relationship. She didn't start working her first job until she was 19. All of her time was spent hanging out with neighborhood girls getting high and practicing guitar, Anarchism made it even harder to tell yourself that you wanted to work. The way you can sell it to someone else is if part of you believes it yourself.

Her sister was fat. Her mother was lenient. Angie was 19 and very popular with men. Molly, 22, wasn't good with men. She'd only ever had one or two boyfriends, like her jobs for little over a year but then suddenly ended. Her boyfriend slep with another girl Rachel without explaining anything. He didn't come home one night after a fight,

"You don't have to stare at her!"
"What are you talking about?"
"You're so obvious. Ugh. I hate it."
Seems desperate.

He had to 'go soon.'

She didn't hear from him until the next morning.
"Where are you u?" She texts.
"I'm at Rachel's." He responds the next morning.
That's the last they ever talked.

***

She had just finished playing a game of basketball when her fat sister came home. She was crying. "Oh my God," Molly said, "are you okay?"
"He's such an asshole."
"What happened?"
"He told me he didn't feel good about it."
"Why?"
"He said he wasn't expecting me to look like this."
"Like what?"
"He said I was a lot bigger than he thought."
"Oh." Molly said.
"He said I look like an entirely different person without makeup.
"Oh." Molly said, tho she agreed.
Here sister wore a pound of makeup at any given time and never looked like herself."
"He said he couldn't and got up and left. Fatphobic asshole."
"Did you send him a photo."
"I sent him a ton...like...I didn't catfish him."
Molly went silent. Fatphobia was one of the dumbest concepts she had heard from within 'the community.' or feminism, or whatever. She was disgusted both by her sister's fat and promiscuity. Tho she would never say it to her sister's face. Molly knew what many men knew. That there wasn't any excuse for people to be obese other than sloth and gulttony a combination creating the concept of fatphobia: whereby creating a theory for fat people they could avoid the hardwork of plucking the log from their eye and instead police men. The many who believe that women should be heard no matter how idiotic what's she saying is and create a social environment that allows women like her sister to eat an entire bag of Limon flavored lays when she wanted and still complain about others feelings about it. She couldn't hold back her disgust. She felt for her sister though. She did her best not to feel sorry for her sister. She tried consoling her without using the word sorry. One of the brief interactions Molly had with Savage Ckhild, as everyone called him, she heard him say, "Pity, depression, fear, obligation, and guilt are all emotions I don't fuck with. And I don't say sorry for shit I'm not responsible for." She buckled. Couldn't do it.
"I'm sorry." she said. The words felt hollow.
WIthout the gym or a diet she was going to be catfishing men via Twitter. Without a lb of makeup on she could only be herself and everyone knows

yourself is either too much or not enough.

***

When she was 6 she was playing ball with her dad. Mom didn't like to play ball. Dad dressed her in a small baseball cap. She felt cared for by her father and her mother seemed bored by the whole thing but the moment she awkwardly caught a baseball tossed by her loving father she knew that she always wanted to be closer to him. She didn't care about her mother's approval. She loved her but only rarely felt that she liked her. The burning California sun was a spotlight. She was her father's daughter. She was a star.

***

Crying now Molly's sister Apple is trying to catch her breath. Lightly drying her eyes which are bleeding mascara, she says,
"You don't have these kind of problems. You're...
You don't put yourself out there really. The idea of you with a man is so funny."
She smiled and dried her eyes with two fists.
Molly was offended. "What does that mean?"
"Well, you know. I've never seen you with a man except friends. You're a Tomboy...one of the guys..."
Molly was offended. She touched the inside of her wrists while looking at her fact sister to check and see if she was really there.

***

She had to admit that her sister was sexier. She wasn't convinced she was any better with men. She constantly had them but rarely kept them. She let so many men into her body. Another aspect taht made her feel like an asshole but ultimately superior.

***

She was sexualized once. On a walk home on 'sketchy street' downtown, where she caught the bus, with her bicycle, an average looking construction worker shouted, "All that biking gave you an incredible ass." Molly looked at him, shocked that someone could say something like that. Safety was an afterthought. On her way into the bus after racking her bike, she smiled. She too had sex appeal.

***

Molly's anorexic but not on purpose. She's always wondered why her sister was thicker and healthier. Molly was also anemic and refused to take her meds. Her body felt important but her heart wouldn't let her handle it.

***

Savage Ckhild is scrolling thru his Instagram feed next to Molly at the show. Savage Ckhild has always looked out of place at shows dressed like a character out of a telenovela. Once Molly noticed an Instagram feed filled with hot girls and fitness models, like the popular @sommerray. Ever few seconds passing a post from @machinegungirls which is as you could guess,half naked girls holding machine girls. Molly felt annoyed by this. She also felt that it was inappropriate to sexualize women like that. She didn't agree with consuming women's bodies like that but she liked Savage Ckhild and didn't want to start a fight. She just wanted to know and challenge the idea of having a bunch of women in his feed. When he closed the app to lock his phone she saw his lock screen was a photo of a buxom woman in a sheer white bikini looking over her ass/shoulders towards the camera, face partly hidden by her long wet hair.

Over his shoulder she asked, "Who's that?" as if to embarrass him, reproach him without reproaching him, and question his interest in so many women. It felt like jealousy but was muted and tamed enough for her to feel superior to him.

He looked up, the music playing was Return of The Rat by The Wipers, the music before the next band.

"What?" he said louder.
"Who was that?" she repeated, pointing to his phone."
"Who?"
"Your background."
Savage Ckhild swiped the screen then lifted it up to show Molly.
"This girl...or?"
"Yeah, this naked girl." she pointed again.
Savage Ckhild smiled and laughed a small laugh.
"This is Demi Rose Mawby. She's a model."
"Is she your girlfriend?"
He laughed in good spirit, "No."
"Why is she your phone background?"
Savage Ckhild's mood changed. He was annoyed by the question but wasn't going to get sour with Molly. He wasn't too close to Molly but Molly seemed like a good person and he saw her a lot. SHe had an interest in starting a band and Savage Ckhild respected that because he knew once he moved to New York he too would be looking for people to make music with.

"I didn't think too much about it. I guess I think she's pretty and I'd like a pretty girl in my life so it's not such a bad idea to surround yourself with what you want or like."

"Seems like you're objectifying this woman."

"Well she's a model, it's her job to be looked at. I think you're taking it too seriously. It's not necessarily sexual just because she's sexy."

Savage Ckhild didn't say anything after that. He silently walked away and met with a girl who played in the last band. Her name was Sarah. They hugged and talked for a short minute before another girl walked up and Sarah asked her to take a picture. At first Savage Ckhild and Sara had their arms over each other's shoulders but before they took the picture Savage Ckhild shook his head and lifted and lifted a hand to his neck, making a cutting motion. "Nah," he said, "Too normal! Like this." Savage Ckhild leaned over a bit forward a bit to the side, closed one eye kept the other open and pulled on the bag just under his eye, then stuck out his tongue, a classic face in anima, and Sarah followed. Then they took a photo. Molly felt useless and punished but she knew it wasn't true. Jealousy was creeping and that's when Molly realized Sarah was one of the women she played basketball at the park on Shotwell.
Sarah was a lesbian and a microbiology major at San Jose state. Last Instagram story was set in front of a computer in a grey jumpsuit with a bucket of unstable chemicals over ice from first person. Molly doesn't know that Sarah's a lesbian. Sarah doesn't know Molly well so doesn't know she likes Savage Ckhild. Sarah isn't honest that even as a lesbian she does have a small crush on Savage Ckhild.

It's Saturday, the all girls pickup game. The group doesn't mind the summer heat because San Francisco manages to be so much cooler than the rest of the bay. Sarah's on the opposite team. Sarah's team is destroying Molly's team and Molly is bitter because she's putting in all the work. She gets in those moods when losing where you start assessing the opposite team as ifr winning or losing had been determined at the moment they picked teams. That's when Sarah came to bug her. Was on her ass the entire play. Would shove Molly trying to steal the ball. Then would succeed at stealing the ball, all the while, jamming the ball up and into Molly's wide open mouth. She's literally a mouth breather. That's when Sarah (literally) dunks on Molly. Molly falls on her ass, mouth open and spraying blood all over just as the ball falls thru the hoop.
"Aowh, Publkking Bulldyke!" She couldn't breathe and she couldn't stop spitting blood. Everyone stopped, couldn't believe. The only sound was a basketball bouncing with increasing repetitiveness like a nickel spinning out.
"Scrawny little cunt!" Sarah said.
Molly is scrawny. That's when Molly gets up, collects as much blood in the bottom of her mouth just below her tongue and spray it all over Sarah's face and favorite white jersey. Sarah soaked in the face with blood immediately started rage crying and couldn't get herself to move. Molly got up tonguing a newfound gap in her teeth. A girl who was Sarah's friend, tall and Latina, said almost

growling, "You better leave!" Molly got up, spit at her too, then ran off, all without her front tooth.

***

Molly was never good with men. She didn't understand them. It almost seemed as if they avoided her completely. When she saw Savage Ckhild, she saw a man who was good w/ women. Which is partly a man Molly fates but also something that made Molly feel for Savage Ckhild. She saw someone constantly slipping away from her. Though she had never put herself in his way or made it obvious that she was interested. It seemed the desire was impossible. A woman who is terrible with men in like with a man who was good w/ women. It felt like being trapped impossibly on opposite sides of a spectrum.

***

The signs should have been clear. Both ears pierced. Said Oh my God enough. Ended statements in the tone of questions. Liked Madonna. Had a Madonna shirt. Always wore the trendiest clothes. Obsessed with weight. Had a few male friends. Was a momma's boy.

Ian had been a close friend for a long time. Molly herself didn't expect to develop feelings for Ian. A tall anemic thin white guy himself. She met him at an Ass Hunter show. He was covering for his zine No Consolation and he asked her if she wanted to come out with him to Robert's house while he interviewed w/ them.

They ended up just hanging out with Ass Hunter/Robert for the whole night and while Robert/a few other male members went to get cans of their favorite cheap Chinese beer. Everyone gets Tsingtao, it's not Tsingtao. Molly was showing Robert how good she was at doing planks but Robert, still significantly more sober than Molly didn't recognize the beauty in this. Molly both proud and nervous about her tight and boyish ass felt safe and nervous with her new second choice love interest--second choice b/c right now she's trying to engage Robert but Robert's already gone. Robert gives off the impression that he could care less if she lives or dies while Ian seems supportive and attentive. Molly likes both but likes Robert more. Robert gives off the impression that he could care less if Molly lives or dies and Molly takes that as the perfect necessary void to fill, she performs to be the exception to his apathy. Robert is making fat jokes and trying to find the right cheap Chinese beer. Ian was talking about how he liked James Blake and why. She liked both.
Robert was bigger and unshaved tho. SHe liked both. So when she got back up, dizzy from the rush, and found herself alone with Ian, she couldn't help but fall for him. Maybe it was the two bottles of beer she'd had and now she was feeling that if life was long she should make the best choice...that Ian could be relied on,

like a friend, and isn't that what made for a good relationship? She felt Ian's hairless leg brush against her as they both sat back on the couch together. She was in all honesty, completely taken with Ian's beauty. One of the most attractive men she'd ever seen. She had been with few men in her life but Ian would still have or could be the most attractive person she's ever going to/have been with. As his perfectly sculpted lips began to press into hers, she found herself instantly groping his leg and felt quickly after a throbbing cock thickening thru his shorts. It was much bigger than she expected. Not only because she had been with so few men but also because she just couldn't imagine it getting that big. She had watched very little porn in her life. THere was no real reference. She was shocked. They kept moving forward heated and horny, feeling totally surprised that things could go this far. Molly shot up when she heard the doorknob wiggle--and Ian, also a little startled followed. Robert came in and surprisingly Ian, still hard, took control.
"Robert, something came up." He and the rest of Ass Hunter didn't stop loading in. The singer, gay, lifted a 28 pack onto his shoulder and nodded a greeting. His friend, also gay, was laughing hysterically. "That's the most breeder shit I've ever seen..." to the singer. Robert looked at both of them totally free of suspicion. Just a little thrown off by how sudden it was. "You should you don't want a beer?" Robert asked. Everyone filed in, cracking open beers..."It's okay." Ian said.

They went to Ian's apartment. Ian who was prominent in the scene is the son of a doctor. Ironic in punk if you don't think twice, the second time realizing there's nothing revolutionary about being a member of the bourgeois and practicing your own brand of hedonism under the guise that you are or could ever be some kind of activist. Punk is fun to middle class white kids. Hip hop is what punk used to be.
Ian's apartment is incredible. He does live on Haight Street which is now a tourist drag, but the real estate is still expensive and prime and his bedroom, his tiny bedroom, has an incredible view from bay windows. He closed the curtains. They kissed on Ian's tiny red bed and slowly from under the other, stripped themselves naked. She could feel Ian filling every inch of her. They started but neither could finish. No one could come.

She never suspected Ian to be after that. Which is...reasonable. Nights he would spend out with his male friends. Boyfriends. Ian who did have a lust for Molly (sometimes) was only suspicious when Molly discovered a DM from Stephen which seemed strangely intimate.

@strangestevexoxo

It was nice seeing you again :)

@noconsolation

I can't believe, :))

She found gay porn on this phone as well but was so well socialized by punk she asked,
"So you're into this? This...turns you on?"
"Sometimes..." Ian didn't have the heart (read: balls) to tell her. She was naive. In her mind she recognized that 'everyone's a little gay." When she finally found out she was horrified but free of heartbreak. The forced acceptance of all things queer in punk ran deep in Molly so when she found a European looking modelesque, muscle bound man inside Ian she didn't cry. They both sat up and apathetically covered their cocks with their hands, sitting side by side. They were sweating and the bed was drenched in it as if the two had taken a shower and not dried off. The windows looked dirty, grimy, even tho no one had touched them. It was July.
"Look, I didn't have the heart (sic) to tell you that I..."
"Uh huh." Molly said. She kept trying to see Stephen's dick.
"I'm sorry...I..."
"Did you know you were..."
"I mean, not the whole time, I..."
"Okay." She shut the door to Ian's room.
She was a little annoyed and very hurt but couldn't cry. She seemed to blame no one. She got home to her mother and sister who she avoided but couldn't Her face said it all. Mom asked her first,
"Honey, did something happen?"
Molly looked up.
"No, Mom."
Her sister popped up from the wall of the open fridge door and looked, sucking on the insides of a mango with whip cream. She closed the fridge and stood staring.
"What happened? Be honest. Ian break up with you?"
She almost smiled.
Molly said, "Uhh...I'm okay." then quickly went to her room.

She frantically went thru a dresser drawer to find a pipe. She found a velvet bag, pulled out the small blue/green glass pipe and a film canister. Plucked out a nug and prepared it, then stuffed it into the pipe. Molly didn't feel sad exactly. A little sad but more exhausted. She'd worked so hard to accept everything about Ian. It was just the way he was, she thought. She thought if she smoked she wouldn't feel anything. So she packed it and lit it up and sucked it down like a bum would gin, exhaled, and for a moment felt okay, before instantly, in her altered state, started crying. She cried harder than she'd ever cried then suddenly her stomach turned. She had to jump off her bed in to the bathroom where she puked. She was scared. 'Oh my god, am I pregnant?' She cried louder. 'I don't want to have a gay man's baby.' She wasn't pregnant she was paranoid.

***

Once, recently, Molly had a dream:

It was her in her room. Her bedframe low to the floor. Her closet beside her in her tiny room. Wakes up, alert and calm at the same time. Drawn by sight to her closet. SHe gets up slowly and as she approaches the door starts to shake erratically. She continues at the same speed, fear increasing but experiencing absolutely no resistance to her path. As if in water. She reaches the closet, and in one motion, opens the door--she recoils instantly, horrified without screaming. Inside the open closet: Savage Ckhild but Savage Ckhild as a satyr, feverishly jacking off. Waddling around the room like a wind up doll. Molly watches unafraid with decreasing surprise and interest as she wakes up and all fades to white.
"Fuck." she muttered, sitting all the way up.

***

Last year she dated Chance. Chance was a musician. A singer songwriter type. He was a rail thin drinker who, always, bearded seemed to be incredibly fragile, no sense of self. Everything seemed to move forward by the constant agreeable nature he had or posed to have. Something that could dissolve if challenged at all but never was. Of course Molly didn't see him that way or not initially. She found his 'way' to be constant and comforting. She did know that his effeminate mannerisms were more than just gestures. They represented a sort of childish expression of escapism of wanting to be someone else of being someone else at his core. She saw that he was evasive--of reality of people of intensity. The constant search for neutrality created an extremism. This extremism took the form of anorexia, alcoholism, and a lack of self-assertion, along with an almost constant aversion.

***

Molly finds Savage Ckhild at a show, outside, a circle of people permanently installed table and bench. The venue used to be a church. People always thought that was funny/ironic and Savage Ckhild never did. He believed in God, tho he hated church. Savage Ckhild was facing outward, facing left his head into the group, leaning back with his arms locked behind him.

"Portland was horrible. There I was, broke, sick, symptomatic, stoned, still have feelings for my ex-girlfriend. All she did was drink now. None of us had a car, none of us could think of anything to do. All of Portland...just this enormous green bore. I was trying to get along with her boyfriend at the time but I couldn't. Everything about him...we would have...or I would have gotten into a fucking fight with the guy if anything had gotten real, would have clashed at every level. He was just such a weak, bleeding character. Not a lack of virtue even his sense of right and wrong was influenced not by what was just but by what seemed to defend the most people from harm."

"What's wrong with that?" Carlos asked.

"Nothing if you argue it. That's what's so fucked up about it. It all 'checks out' but when it comes to experiencing it, it just feels so...weak. Like another mask. Like handling life with gloves...anyways...there's this one night after we'd all packed ourselves into her roomate Andy's room. All fell asleep watching a movie on the two mattresses we'd pulled together, laid out to cover the entire floor. I passed out and had this vivid dream, where I fucker her, Macy, who I was visiting right in the middle of the living room, passionately, right in front of her boyfriend. I couldn't talk about it. Not until everyone else was gone. So one day, while everyone else was gone, Macy, getting dressed for work pretty comfortably in front of me--I bring it up. I tell her about the dream. That's when she tells me that she's been having the same dream, which,used to happen when were living together in Santa Clara/San Jose. We'd have mutual dreams. It was the exact same dream. I was blown away. She says, 'Have you been thinking about it?' I say, 'It's not possible for me to see an ex girlfriend and not think about it. It's inevitable,' 'Should we?' she asks me, 'No way! Are you fucking kidding me?' 'Why not? We're both thinking about it.' The guys character, his whole being was so weak that we couldn't help but start thinking about each other. She couldn't help but think about me, her ex boyfriend again. About me again."

"Why didn't you say no?"

"I don't know. Moral I guess. Now I regret it but at the time it felt like...it felt fucked up to conspire against the guy. I mean...we must have been so obvious with us together again. As if we'd already..."

Savage Ckhild laughed. And even though Molly was kind of shocked that Savage Ckhild would laugh, it made Molly laugh.

***

Chance was an alcoholic--instead of eating would down as much whiskey as he could get his hands on--bearded in the stubbly 5' o clock shadow way--sexy to many, Molly included. When they met they both shared a lot of themselves thru the music they were making--Chance a solo artist--and Molly singer of the band Alpha. Alpha had members of Bathsalts and Painstaking; Becoming more and more popular. Chance was still struggling with, 'finding an audience.'

***

Savage Ckhild went on to scroll thru his Instagram feed, almost all fitness/models. @sommerray shaking her huge and athletic ass in celebration of a 'new drop,' (she has her own clothing line) @demirosemawby half naked in a knit bikini walking slowly and controlled thru some posh public scenery or private party. @krotchy who Savage Ckhild initially only knew for her modeling. Was originally unaware that she was a visual artist, blue check for art not her differently colored eyes, @angievarona also in a trendy knit bikini oiled up on a Greek coast drinking a Greek liquor brand she was advertising for, @machinegungirls etc.

"Can I ask you something?" Molly asked.
"Sure." Savage Ckhild looked up.
"Why do you have such a strong attraction to women with personalities that have so little to do with you?"
Savage Ckhild wasn't offended.
Hmm.."I don't know exactly," he thought longer.
"Sometimes when I'm feeling nihilistic I think that the best relationships, the only lasting relationships are the ones between two people who have absolutely nothing in common. As if the easiest way to avoid conflict is this kind of sad acceptance of one another--if even in the most alien way. That's what allows for permanence."

"That's so sad." said Molly.

"I mean I don't know if I'm really attracted to these people."

"Like, fitness models?"

"Yeah like fitness models. I mean everyone is attracted to them, superficially. The one thing I do value tho is the kind of mind and personality that can capitalize off of a preexisting interest. I want to understand how people can/do create a 'following.' I have a lot of respect for people who take fitness seriously. Surrounded by 'alternative' culture so much, where perceived intellect is so valuable but then people eat shitty food and drink poison all the time...mainstream culture, the dominant culture, is a good place to visit because it gives you a break from all of the small minded self importance of counter cultural social scenes."

"Like, punk?"

"Yeah, all of that shit. All of that countercultural shit. Posing as some kind of activism. Some sort of statement against the dominant culture. The values are mostly the same. Everyone looking left and right to see if it's okay to do/think/say. It's just that it looks different in a subculture. The beliefs to conform to are different but conformity is ultimately still required.

I used to believe in that shit, like, that punk or whatever you want to call this scene or subculture or whatever the fuck…now…was actually a sincere concerted effort to, if even in the smallest way be better, make life better. After I was accused of stalking…" he faeded out.

"I heard about that." said Molly. "Did you?"

"Did I what?"

"Stalk…her…"

Savage Ckhild looked pissed.
"I knew her for 8 years. She was my friend for 8 years. If anyone has a right to be pissed it's me. She used me for sex while her boyfriend wasn't in the picture, tried to keep it a secret, then, ghosted me when her ex boyfriend came back and they starting fucking or dating again. She threw away 8 years of friendship and then framed me as a fucking stalker. How does anyone repair after that? It's why I don't care about women. Who gives a fuck what happens to them either way? What political issue big or little should matter to me? Who cares? Who cares about relationships with women? They're unimportant. What's the worst thing you could do to them? I'm not doing it. They can figure their own shit out. Why get attached enough to someone to miss them? Or worry about the next thing you're going to say for her. Or whether or not she's going to stay. Women think what other women tell them to think. So I'm a stalker. No one stood up for me. No one even listened because I was a man. Subcultures, dude. With their paranoia about 'rape culture'. How to treat a femme etc. All blown up to some horrible drama when one person decides to dissolve another just by being disinterested in having the conversation and that makes me a fucking stalker? Fucking cunt…true acceptance isn't going to be found in yr scene, yr political beliefs, or a woman."

Savage Ckhild spit.

Molly felt depressed.
She didn't love him any less.
Molly believed him.
Molly thought he was on to something.

"So in a way…" Molly said, "it's kind of a place to hide from us."

"A fitness model doesn't have a paranoid worldview. They're not cultists. They have no agenda. They aren't going to accuse me of shit."

***

Alpha had headlined. Chance was added to the bill to open and the night seemed great--on the surface. Chance, having been bartender and doorman both at this venue had the hookup so he was, as starved as he was, drinking as much free whiskey as he wanted. Would say, "could handle" but he was past that point. The whole night, Molly was being congratulated by the crowds.
Great show tonight! (handshake)
I've never heard anything like you guys before! (handshake)
I had so much fun! (handshake)

She was spending a lot of time on her own. No one was saying anything to Chance. He was brooding, at the bar now, feeling ore realizing he had been invited to play by his girlfriend and that meant he wasn't just riding her coattails but she was the person closest in his life and everyone knew that. Maybe no one was even thinking about that but Chance was stalking to feel that way. Playing an acoustic set at the rock show could feel, did feel out of place, although the scene for Alpha was fenderall intelligent, open to the difference in genre. But he was an opener. He should just accept that, right? And he couldn't. So when he decided to leave the barstool and approach Molly...just as he was he saw her with Savage Ckhild, dressed in a button down with Bengal Tigers scattered thruout it, and was freshly shaved for the event, usually he looked a little haggard from choosing to, out of laziness, not shave until he 'really had to.'

"Rad, Molly. You guys kicked ass. How'd it feel?"
"Uhm, pretty good. We fucked up a lot."
"Yeah? Well, yr probably the only ones who noticed. I thought it was great."
"Thank you." Molly smiled. She was drinking a Montauk like it was Brooklyn.
"Robert invited me to his place for this thing what are you about to get into tonight?"
"Well it's likely I'm going to be spending some time with Chance--"

Chance came stumbling thru both of them. And Chance cut into conversation with, hiccuping now,
"Haven't heard from a single,"
hiccup
"Person at this show."

"What do you mean?" Molly said taken aback and a little annoyed. Thinking what she was thinking about but not wanting to because she wasn't sure that what she thought to be true and happening was actually happening.

"What do you mean?" asked Savage Ckhild.

"Do you want to fuck this guy?" Chance asked. He was bending over his own fragile body--rail thin. Stubbled face. Long eyes like an alien. Tiny mouth like one too. A nose that belonged on a Dostoyevsky character.

Savage Ckhild started laughing so Molly started laughing too. Exactly what she thought was happening was happening. Her boyfriend who she had asked to open for her was feeling sorry for himself because 'no one' had gone out of their way to congratulate/'thank' him...and now he was drunk and jealous that she was spending time with...I guess now is the time to be jealous because despite having a boyfriend she would always be thinking about Savage Ckhild but, he wanted to start a fight. Chance almost fell over himself--"You want to fuck Molly?" He barked.
"Woah." Savage Ckhild was still laughing. "This guy is fucked up." Molly wasn't laughing anymore.

She went home and put Chance to sleep. Getting ready for bed herself to humor the baby. He tried fucking her and she wouldn't have it. Pushed him off and continued reading Fast Machine by Elizabeth Ellen. Smelling the stink of whisky on this unlucky moron. She waited till she could see his eyes rumbling in R.E.M. before putting the book down, people being more important than books and got ready for Robert's--she had Robert's number but never ever got Savage Ckhild's for some unknown reason. It ended up being a great night.

***

The next morning Chance woke Molly up by getting some water for himself--

"I guess I got jealous." he shrugged.
"I...I got you that show. I don't understand."
He went outside to the front porch and instead of starting to make breakfast lit a cigarette. Took a drag with one arm across his chest and elbow nestled in it and a limp wrist.
She hated this catty, competitive moron and tho she thought she'd never do it, say it, it's untrue what they say about dating people in your same field. It's just when one's inferior are there problems.

***

Molly once had a boy/man in love with her. She was put off by his enthusiasm and sentimentality--they crossed paths online, during her bands pique. The boy was the exact same age, born in the same year, but lived on the opposite side of the continent. It had been the first month of them talking the boy asked for her address to write her letters. The boy was poet and a writer popular in an insular scene somewhere in New York City, where she imagined this story was common. SHe wondered if he did this for everyone he liked. THis gave him that, "He says that to every girl," quality which turned her off. He did make attempts to write women letters when he liked them. He didn't spend significant amounts of time

online which was surprising but he did seem the type to pick up on girls online. He was. He'd written Tere letters because he'd started getting the feeling he liked her after exchanges on Tumblr. He wanted to get closer to her and at the same time give her sometime. There was Kim when he was younger. Never wrote back. Letters are mostly monologues and therefore mostly selfish. He was aware of this. He wasn't an idiot.
But letters could also, if written well enough, even without coming on too strong, (as if asking for an address isn't a dead giveaway that you're into her) could be entertaining to recieve and read. So Tony, (Anthony Stave) stuck his neck out put his balls on the chopping block and asked for Molly's address outright.
Molly: haha okay, sure
don't come kill me, okay

Tony: okay

Tony was annoyed. Either give me the address or don't. He thought. He could have taken this moment to be aware that split thinking like this is staple of this person if apparent this early. But Tony discarded this initial red flag as a minor annoyance. Tony does this with most red flags, disregards them. For the promise of pussy, or love or maybe love with a capital L. Tony isn't clear on it himself sometimes--his motivations, tho, he could say honestly his feelings for Molly, as beautiful as she was, weren't sexual. Tony didn't moralize sex so beleived that there's nothing wrong with a ppraoching a girl for no other reason than/connection other than wanting to have sex. Parly because he'd tound himself in interesting relationships with women just from having the express intent of fucking them. The idea of lust didn't appeal to Tony because so many good things had come from his sexual impulse/satisfaction of that impulse. His ex girlfriend Jocelyn for example started as a one night stand but grew into something more. Once introduced to her friends his small town in Michigan, he had, despite his differences, found a base of people who were excited about him. As he was taken in he found himself more and more in...almost-love with Jocelyn.

Molly however, didn't speak to Tonys sexual desire at all. Not because Molly was unbeautiful but because Molly's physical build didn't speak to Tony's lust at all. Molly was, 5' 9", rail thin, and white. Tony liked thick girls with strong legs, big asses, and small tits, though there were exceptions to his untailored desires. There were many women who were shit out of luck when it came to Tony's sexual desires. Molly's appeal was in her enduring modelesque beauty which spoke more to his heart than his dick. Tony was of course working with very little information about Molly. Molly once said she was 'always miserable.' Tony couldn't believe this. Molly being as funny as she was, seemed to always be smirking without smirking, if even without ever seeing it. Her sense of humor bled thru everything she did and said. At least from the few and very brief interactions he had with her, he had heard of her band from a friend in the Bay

Area and Tony, being moved by a vido of her singing an a'capella version of An Die Musik a'capella while nearly crying. Decided he had to talk to this person personally. Tony, despite having no luck yet writing women letters (no one's written back) we thought that maybe this time would be different because this girl, Molly, was different. Maybe the, 'please don't kill me,' was a joke. Maybe not. He wrote her every chance he got. He thought he was prepared to hear nothing back but he wasn't. He was hurt. He was so hurt he yelled at Molly about it.

Tony: You don't have time to write a single fucking letter back?

Molly: I thought I told you it's not likely I'll have time to write back.

Tony: Then why did you give me your address?

Molly: You wanted to write me letters.

Tony: Yeah, I'm not writing letters to fucking talk to myself! I'm trying to talk to you

Molly: I mean we can talk online. You seem really hurt about this!

Tony: Yeah because I'm in love with you you idiot!

Molly was busy. Molly already mostly indifferent looked into her heart. She blew him off and decided not to deal with him anymore. When she was really honest she did care but couldn't get beyond some part of herself the part of herself that would've allowed her to see Tony as a real person. She cared. She didn't care. She couldn't care. Who cares.

***

Molly's having a dream:

Angie is spread out on a mattress on the floor fat and naked, rolls pronounced as she's bent over herself in doggy , Savage Ckhild is pounding into her ass from just above comfortable, like a jackhammer. As she approaches, Molly notices that Savage Ckhild slows down and becomes more and more aware of himself. Angie is looking behind herself...until suddenly it's as if she's been seen by Molly, who is simultaneously being looked straight thru. They separate immediately and scramble, each one individually, for a towel. "You shouldn't do that you know!" Molly catches herself drooling.

***

Robert decided to have a party all the punks were invited. Anyone playing music in the Bay Area were invited. Robert text Molly about the party. Molly would say it to anyone but she did like to drink. Savage Ckhild was going, so she had proper motivation.

***

When she arrived to a packed house she got nervous. Extremely panicky. She wasn't in the mood to socialize--but also figured that she could be losing opportunities to build a band if she was serious...
She poured herself Vodka straight into a Red Dixie cup.

She moved to the living room where she saw Savage Ckhild with his arm around Sarah. She put her drink down and got up from the couch. Molly moved in.

"You and Sarah are getting pretty close." Molly said.
"Hey Molly. Yeah. I mean, we've been close."
"I've never seen you guys this close." Molly smiled.
Savage Ckhild was confused. He paused for a solid minute.
"You know she's a lesbian right?"
Molly's face went red.
"Oh? Really."
"...yeah..."
She finished the enormous amount of vodka. She was wasted now.
"I had a dream about you last night." Molly said.
"Oh yeah?" Savage Ckhild was sincerely interested.
"What happened?"
"I can't tell you." Molly smiled.
"Oh, I see." They stood still for a minute.
"I had a dream about you too actually. Sit down and I'll tell you."
"Okay." she smiled. She sat. "What happened?"
"Let me show you." he smiled.
He pushed her hair back behind her ears and took her face into his palm, then kissed her slow.
Molly was blushing and excited.
"Did that really happen in your dream?"
"For real." Savage Ckhild said nodding.
"You like me?" she shouted.
"Of course I do. I wouldn't answer all yr annoying questions if I didn't like you."
"I've thought so much about you." she said, curling up to Savage Ckhild.
"I have too. It was so unexpected. I didn't think I'd think about you but I do. I always notice you in a room, in a crowd, in a band, at a show. I like that you can get a long with anyone."
"I don't know if that's true."
"Could've fooled me."

"Am I the only girl you've kissed at this party?"
"What's that supposed to mean?...holy shit! You're drunk." He passed her the flavored sparkling water he was drinking.
"Why do you like me?" she asked.
"Oh my God."
"Really."
"Well...you're funny. You're pretty. You're good at art...and you're a Tomboy."
"A Tomboy?" Molly smiled.

@abigfuckingbully

LIKE AN ENEMY TO GOD

A shot popped off in the distance.

That's when I heard the screaming, it was both male and female, a chorus that felt as if it were one infinite note, underneath the rhythm of the sound of a fiery mass of feet moving. Every person breaking off in the opposite direction as if someone broke us with a pool cue.

I couldn't get my footing, so for a few minutes I was recognizing exactly what the fuck was happening. A sea of people passing over me, a stampede of alarmed faces, as if they had seen hell and as if they were being sent to hell.

I heard the sound of what I would find is a soldier stabbing a dog to death, then I would hear that noise, despite all others, as if it were in my ears, the sound like a knife in and out of a watermelon. Dog's fault for attacking.

I caught my breath.

Started watching my back again: a tanks chains rattling--it's wheels pulsing, moving, always a perfect fit for the ground beneath it. I wasn't far enough away but I would fall into a garden outside the monastery. It's entrance painted pink. The clover fields and trees looking dark and untouched.

Only time I would see lights was from pulsing flash grenades. I fell over a small fence and hands-first into the rose bushes. Every stalk without blossom. Just thorns left. I couldn't move either hand without cutting them deeper. I found next to me to my surprise a living rose in the monastery garden an enormous blossom with twin heads.

Bleeding profusely now. Can only feel cold against my blood in this weather. My breathe giving me away, is visible, I wish it wasn't. I wish it would go away. I didn't make a sound an 'ugh' when I fell down but other than that no drama. Alone I can endure anything. With no one here to know or here to hear...gritting my teeth while I tried to remember what exact angle the thorns entered me so I could untangle my hands, blood making the whole thing very difficult.

It was one giant amorphous wound, that acted like a chinese finger trap, in that the harder I tried to escape, the worse it got. Then I decided like a wolf eating it's own trapped leg for escape, I would pull as hard as I could, ape's solution. With my hands free, and shaking in the cold, purple red blood, in this private moment I felt bless with this sight. Gun shot residue and blood on twin blossoms, I suddenly felt overwhelmed. How could I continue life when this rose is the only one that knows how to survive? If I was less panicked I would cry.

That's when I felt two hands pulling me up by the collar.

"Are you fucking crazy?" The voice said. I accepted it and ran, looking back to check on the roses. I don't have time to stop and smell the roses. Hahaha, okay, fuck the roses. But it stood still and tall on its single stalk.

"Help! Somebody! Please!"

@abigfuckingbully

NPC N.Y.

Suffering from a psychotic delusion I was guided by the voice of God to quit my job and buy a one way ticket to NYC. I did everything God told me and didn't do anything he didn't want me too. I was instructed to rent a bed at a hostel in the upper west side but there would be one day that the hostel would be completely booked and I would be unable to stay that night. I had no other plans except to stay up and out as long as possible to avoid sleeping in the street. I thought I might find a girl to sleep with for a place to stay but God told me not to. I wasn't going to pull a Henry Miller tonight. I don't drink, I'm straight edge and since God wasn't going to allow me any female company I went thru a bank of neighborhoods and venues I remember from my last trip to New York.

    I tried to find a place I could kill most of the day and night. I wondered if I would be spending the hours after 12 alone in a bar or trying to stall for time at an all night diner. Lucky when I googled cafe's I came across the name Molasses Books. I recognized it. It was the same place Bunny Rogers had performed her birthday gift for Brigid Mason in some foreign language over a tinkering midi. I've watched that video almost as many times as I've watched the Gaz reading in Columbine Cafeteria. Molasses Books was open till 12am. Only other place that would have been open and serves coffee is a 24 hour diner and I got the impression that NY would make sure not to allow anyone's beatnik brand all nighter to take place in their establishment. I decided to go out, God allowed me to, to Molasses Books this late night.

    I was surprised to find it full for an event. I walked in with my bag filled with a book I'd bought from Spoonbill, "I AM NOT ASHAMED" by Barbara Payton and my laptop which was banned after 8pm. When people asked me what I was doing in New York, I would tell them what God told me to tell them, which is that I got a publishing deal. There was no publishing deal but God told me there was multiple times, telling me that my faith isn't strong enough when I would start to wonder if there was even a point to me having quit my job and shuck everything I own in a bag around Williamsburg. I passed a table displayed in the center of the bookstore where there were candles lit and a flyer was placed. Apparently, 'SCAM' was releasing a new issue and there were drinks being sold for the benefit of some organized sex workers. I was unfamiliar. Instantly started thinking about how deeply against sex work I am and how strongly against porn I was, (I'd consumed porn 3 times in 180 days) and made a pact with myself to quit forever. No matter how many times people would attempt to introduce me to the idea that porn and prostitution could be feminist or empowering even, I would start thinking about how pathetic paying fuor pussy is and how all porn is just misogyny people agree to disagree with in the frame of 'sex'. Was starting to feel so annoyed by people who went beyond themselves to argue not just for the rights of sex workers but for the idea I should respect them, as if paying for/selling pussy isn't the worst thing you could do besides heroin. Our lives would all be better without pornography and like crack the demographic that makes the purchase are some of the worst humans on earth. No one goes to porn or prostitutes out of a respect for women and porn and prostitution can only work if boiling someone human into a cash exchange for sex. Isn't that objectification? There's a billion people working against themselves and all I can see is the rorshach blot of feminism, it's interpretive, it's whatever you want, man. Not that I give a fuck about who you decide to live and I would never say a sex worker is bad person for doing what they do...I just dont relate to regular porn users or people who are willing to pay for pussy, if you fall into these categories, please, leave me the fuck alone. Is porn making your life any better?

"Fucking cucks." I thought.

I walked to the bar and sat down pulling out my book by Barbara Payton. <u>Barbara Payton</u> is a movie star who eventually lost her fortune, gained a fuckton of weight, and resorted to prostitution. She's a very smart and interesting person and I'm glad someone is real about sex workout not being that great and the importance of physical fitness. I ordered an iced coffee and kept reading Barbara.

At this point I am being an anti social dick by facing the exact opposite direction of the rest of this venue. I am even out of place for my beliefs. If I was to say what I really think about sex work or got into my blasphemous views on how polluted modern feminism is, I might be asked to leave. Everyone else seems to know each other and be having fun. I was immediately annoyed by this idea we live in a world where people could so easily be snubbed even for minor disagreement within the frame of feminism. I didn't want to know any of these people and I didn't want to give whores my money. I can't remember the last time I gave a fuck about SCAM or any independently produced media that wasn't ever going to be more than a zine. It was too much to stay up with and I stopped believing in the idea of independently produced media being a righteous dark horse since I'd met and talked to alt/indie lit. Not only are they some of the worst people I'd never get to meet in person, They were all rich, over rewarded, and risk averse.

I felt like I was dreaming when the clown came in--all of these adults in one small room. Candle light the only light. I don't know how he got in, I thought he came off of the street and just decided to start performing but he could actually have been a part of the event. He was dressed in a red onesy with big pom-poms sewn in the middle. Part of his outfit had a star pattern that looked like it would be a baby blanket. He was painted, except he had glasses. People are gritting their teeth as he gets into his act. Being especially tolerant. That's what these people were good at. Balloon animals, one liners, water flower, pulling a rabbit out of a hat, more one liners, but as he progresses he gets into a part of his act where he asks the crowd to 'repeat after me.' I was still reading. I was reading a book by a woman who knew too well you can't romanticize sex work. She didn't intellectualize her choices, even her intellectualizations were too weak to be believed by herself. I thought about Payton, then thought about myself and read the title again, thinking of myself and my life, I AM NOT ASHAMED, and I'm not. I thought again about how if I said what I really think I'd be thrown out. It was like a dream, surrounded by all these people I share no relation to and share no views with. I used to be an anarchist. I used to believe in all of that shit but now it wasn't in my heart. That the world I live in would be scorn.

So I do a statecheck, to make sure I'm not dreaming--look at the words in my book, look away, and look back at them. I can still read them, mean's I'm not dreaming, no matter how much like a dream it felt. Everyone gathered around the clown. I see the bassist from Wild Moth, Carlos and I ignore him. Last I'd seen that guy was outside of a show I was banned from because Christine had accused me of stakling her. He isn't fully honest that I never did anything wrong so his existence is irrelevant besides mention. A room full of people who wanted to be different, to think different--together as one. And that's when the clown says, 'Repeat after me: *I promise to be unique.*

The mob, passionless, repeats: *I promise to be unique*

"I promise to be different" says the clown.

I promise to be different. the mob says...

I packed up my shit and left this anarchist church.
"I'll never be like other people." I message to bibles. "I'll never be able to believe in anything except God and myself."

@abigfuckingbully

"Guilt is doing what you want." ~Bunny Rogers

It must have been the way the sun shone on your face, down on you. You were pressed up against the side of your car and then popped up off the side, one leg raised against the door, but even after the phonecalls, and hearing your soft, deep, Tomboy voice, now in real life, once in a phonecall:

"Do I have a deep voice?"

"Yeah, I noticed it but I didn't want to say anything."

"Is it weird?"

"No, I like it. It's pretty."

I wasn't convinced either of your love or mine. I honestly just didn't think I was gonna like you. I mean, I liked you enough. You told me you had feelings for me already. I cussed you out over the phone because you didn't understand--[I'm bent over screaming down crowded 1st St. on a Sunday filled with a fervor after lifting]

"GET A GRIP BITCH, THIS ISN'T A GAME TO ME--MY HEART'S NOT WITH YOU IT'S WITH BUNNY ROGERS. I NEED YOU TO PUT SOME WALLS UP AND UNDERSTAND THAT CONTINUING TO FUCK WITH ME MEANS YOU'RE GETTING A PRETTY RAW DEAL, OKAY?"

Even if Bunny's heart was like my heart to you and couldn't/wouldn't feel anything.

But now, I can see you dressed like a glossy punk from Oakland...how rich girls from CCA/Art School Dress: black boots, high socks reading 'Metal,' in a heavy metal font, unshaved lower legs: beautiful legs, fat calves on a tiny frame, naked legs all the way up, fat knee muscles hugging your naked knees, your quads fat, you lift--I was never able to ask how much, and then tiniest black shorts, high waisted shorts on yr tight little body, your muscley stomach covered neatly by your skin tight black shorts and underneath them the hem of the bicycle shorts underneath. I would watch intently as you turned to me without looking but smiling, I'm so into it and embarrassed but I'm keeping my cool so I've found a way to be overwhelmed and blushing without showing any red in my face--and you turn to me and say, "What?" and I laugh, I have to turn away, I'm blushing too hard to hide and too turned on, I turn back to you and say, "What? You're wearing bicycle shorts. Yr wearing shorts under your shorts." For a second I'm flattered. You put your hands back on the concrete bar top and look straight ahead, then shyly back at me: "They're very short shorts." These are the shorts your long legs stick out of. A knit cropped tank. A goldenrod bralet. A muted smile but big high cheeks that say everything. Your soft eyes--big, wide, almond--you are somehow the most American and the most exotic.

        Your hair in a sea of waves, greying lightly, brown, in a small tight bun. You tricked me. Phonecalls expressing your affections for me. "You seem like a brave person." "I am a brave person." I say. I was unconvinced and my heart was w/ someone else. "What would you do if I

drove up tomorrow?" And I let you. From L.A. You tricked me. I didn't think I was going to be this in love with you. "Are we going somewhere?" you stood tall next to your car. You said it so unenthusiastically.

At the bar we both buy coffees.

"I'm lonely because I do what I want.

Even though I'm isolated, even though I'm excommunicated, I don't miss anyone. I don't envy anyone anymore. I mean...sometimes I get lonely but loneliness is self pity. People don't take me seriously. They look through me. They don't realize I have the traits of an alpha. That even though I'm struggling for my sanity...for my independence, that at my core, I have traits of a leader, and I don't think people give me credit for it. People follow me. I lead from behind."

We both shit talk Mitch a bit.

Both of us obviously burnt by his privacy--his way of hiding all the time.

"Mysterious" to you. Painful and boring to me. Frustrating to both of us.

You want what you can't have. I don't.

You have a way of blushing. Your eyelids flutter. You're attentive. This is where I should have become more suspicious: but became more vulnerable. Since the beginning, telling me exactly what I need to hear. Not because I need to be validated, I do, and not anymore than anyone else--but because I need to be human. And I need to be loved. And I need to be witnessed. I have been in the dark a still burning light. When someone manipulates a need:

people stigmatize it and call it independence. We could beat people over the head with the standard, that they should be providing for themselves or we could see the need for what it is and drop our guard and satisfy it. The irony of liberals is that they will vote for this philosophy in an external world via their politic but in their personal lives and relationships will still be disgusted by need, cringe, and "like the conservative" blame the poor. I let my guard down even more. I fall in love with you a little more. "Fuck Mitch." I think. I am filled with the desire to take a photo of you, on a shallow level: because I am proud to be with you, and I feel it's my liberty to capture an image of you, that the hollow act of informing Michael of your messages, as if he'd any right to knowledge of you/us...claim...the possessive nature of the guy.

HOW WOULD YOU FEEL? [DO UNTO OTHERS...]

Never works on me. If it was my ex you're invited because it's none of my fucking business anymore. I failed in that relationship. I will never get in the way of another man's right to a chance

to love. The competition is fierce, so I accept it.

That the hollow act of informing Michael that we're even talking is repeating itself in the censorship of considering his feelings before capturing an image of you for IG...I feel overwhelmed with a closeness to you and I want to celebrate being with the woman I am fooled into believing is as excited to meet me as I am (now) excited to be meeting. I make the decision quickly and with commitment.

@abigfuckingbully:

@abigfuckingbully

Michael

I know I said I wasn't going to talk to her

but I've been talking to Madeleine for a solid month.

I'm hanging out with her right now--she came up from L.A.

@thccy:

Seems shady to me man.

I need distance from that relationship so I'm going to have to distance myself from you.

@abigfuckingbully:

I understand.

I look up--

"What're you doing?" you ask.

"I just told Michael we were hanging out."

"What'd he say?"

I repeat the messages.

I repeat the betrayal of a friend whose history w/ me would be it's own novel.

I feel nothing but liberated.

I feel annoyed by previous indecision.

I feel depressed.

I take a piss and come back to you with another coffee in a paper cup.

I ask you what you're doing.

"Why are you paying for that?"

"That's why I ordered it while you were gone."

I laugh.

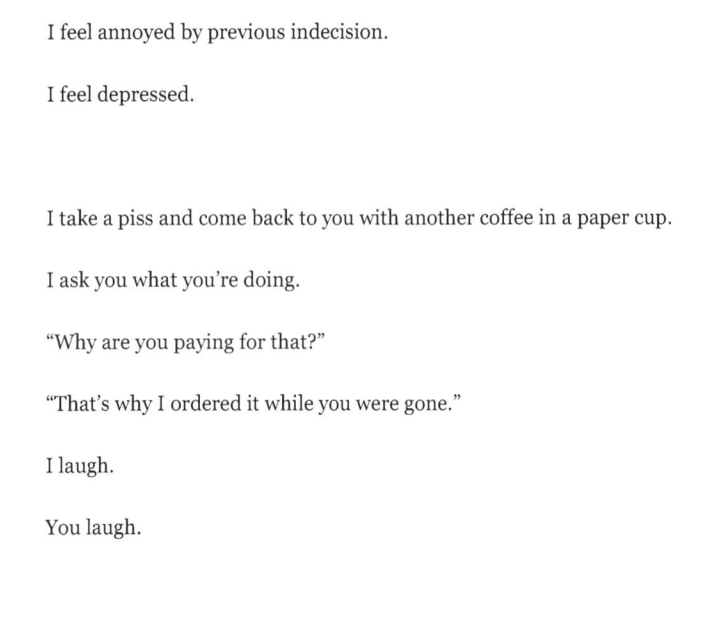

You laugh.

In Japantown: white wooden house with a low royal blue sill.

I'm stealing portraits of you without your permission.

I'm stealing portraits of you without his permission.

I ask you to get up against the wall and you tilt your hips cocky and you look tight smiled but loose into the camera. I drop to my knees first and then drop my ass to the concrete like a big kid, and I'm smiling so huge, trying to frame you in this square on my phone, and you laugh and I take too long, so you start walking off, out of the frame...

"Oh my God, that's perfect. Go back. I want you walking out of the frame. Go back. 1...2...3...start walking."

You walk out of the frame with a smile on your face.

I will watch this happen again.

It's a metaphor.

It's hardly a metaphor.

"Now one of your socks."

Turn your feet into a perfect model.

Yr unshaved calves, starting to get furry.

I'm in love.

A photo of your boots and high socks.

'Metal,' in a heavy metal font.

"Where are we going?

Why aren't you taking me to eat?"

" I thought you weren't hungry...where do you want to eat?

There's this Chinese place." I point to a house.

"Why is there a Chinese place in Japantown?"

And we walk into what looks like a house with an english sign with that cheap Chinese font in red. We open the door and find immediately nothing but a beaten carpeted staircase in two sections. A large Mexican family creeping up slowly in front of us. I feel reluctant--and embarrassed by my village: my fucked up life that has left me shit talking everyone in it and somehow likely the last to leave. We walk upstairs and find the restaurant to be pathetic. It looks like a church picnic--inside a dingy beaten house, where the single occupied room is humiliating for both the restaurant and it's patrons. I freeze at the top of the stairs with my jaw slightly open making a huge, long, "Uhhh..." sound. Madeleine looks around unphased and even though she probably was making her harsh judgements was able to contain them and intently focus on a menu--she looked at it for a really long time, and she looked happy reading it but then slowed for too long,

"Ay, do you want to go somewhere else?" I asked, "Like is this okay. We should go somewhere nicer."

"What?" She looked up. "No, it's fine...it's just...dietary restrictions."

"Are you vegan?!"

"No, I'm vegetarian though."

"Well, fuck."

We walked out.

I bumped into your shoulders.

I held your hands and lifted them in an arc.

I headbutt your you in your stomach playfully like a little bull.

@abigfuckingbully

"What are we doing? Why aren't you FEEDING ME?" you say.

As we walk through the mostly unoccupied Japantown.

I'd ask you a million times over if you want to go somewhere nicer.

"Are you sure you don't want to get Thai? Is this tacky to you? Is this nice enough? Is this nice enough?" You're not my woman but I have to think of this day/night as if it were the embodiment of our entire relationship. I have to treat you like you're alive. I have to treat you like you're going to die. Like we're already married like we're already in love because any lesser treatment is blasphemy to the spirit of a woman/man. I hate the disposable nature of the casual user. "There's this vegan place Good Karma…they microwave their food tho."

"Oh. Weird. Okay."

At the restaurant they're playing free jazz. It's infuriating. The bar is cramped. The owner is drunk. The bartender is really talkative and everyone's bored so they're eavesdropping on our conversation about fucking…

"Is this okay? This isn't tacky to you?"

And we both know it's tacky.

But you're understanding, lovingly looking at the menu, at the bar still acting like I'd ever allow you to pay. We order, I pay, we clean our plates and find a lull in conversation horrifying because of the "jazz" playing. We both notice. "What the fuck is this playing? What a nightmare, dude." We both laugh-- "I didn't want to say anything."

I lead us out into the night glad to escape the oppressive diner. Hippies as business owners...veganism is a totally rational and accessible thing now so I don't understand why we bother with all the "culture," surrounding it. It's for normal fucking people, dude.

You hold your arms over yourself as I get closer to you, the night is now cold to you--

"I forgot my sweater." You say, digging thru your bag. I immediately offer you my sweater, primal act, I hand it to you, "Do you want mine?" You grab it and ask looking up intently, "Yeah, is it okay?"

"Yeah, for sure."

And you put on my black hoody, undersized on me, huge on you somehow, and I lean in close, hood you like a monk, and then tie the drawstrings tight into a perfect bow. I should lean to kiss you but I stop and watch. I hold your hand and swing.

You're sitting down and I look at you, I get close to you and grab your legs by the ankles, lift them out. I stand tall and still and then hunch close to your legs like an animal, and I ask for permission, starving hungry at the fat muscles above your knees,

"Can I kiss your knees?"

You look up with a sly smile and perfect straight white teeth.

I give each knee two soft punctuated kisses one after the other.

You fall back laughing.

"You have freckles?" I sat back down and looked close.

"Do I?" you hid yourself a bit. "You have freckles!"

"Yeah, you're my people."

And you touch my face, over my cheeks and nose.

"In the perfect place too..." you said.

On the drive home you a play bounce track for me.

You listen to bounce music. Hahahah!

The volume slowly rises and then you shake your ass for me from the front seat, bouncing.

"You're welcome to spend the night if you want."

As if she could drive home at midnight on 4 hours of sleep.

Of course she's welcome to spend the night.

We made it home and immediately moved to "my" room. I started stripping in the closet immediately, knowing you had a long trip back to L.A., getting ready to sleep. I couldn't do it. I asked you if you wanted a T-shirt: It's Tetsuo's head being blown off in the street. The word "AKIRA" In all caps, huge red letters. You said no at first. You started stripping pretty naturally but became apprehensive, I also realized as I was getting hard at just the thought of being this exposed this close to you.

"I can't do it." I said.

"Yeah, I can't either."

You accepted the enormous T-shirt: "one of the three shirts I own." You got undressed in the corner, "I'm putting on shorts," I said. I stayed hidden in my closet but remained shirtless. Just the thought of us touching was enough. It's amazing how senstive we are to the touch of another's eyes...how my body's called to yours just by looking, filled with the happy swelling of safety & desire.

We lay down. You scoot closer, lay on my chest, your legs over my legs. And we lay. I want to kiss you but you stay in place. It feels weird but it feels right. You move your head back and I can start to kiss you slow. The kisses are strange. They seem distant and big. Mine start slow and small. And heat builds. You filly my mouth with your mouth. And I move myself over you and kiss your neck. I lift your/my shirt up, and kiss your tight white belly, I stay here for too long because this is my favorite place to kiss a person, and then the soft of your neck, and it's hard to look at you because it feels like an acknowledgement--like stating the obvious, but I do and I'm glad I do. I reach over every part of you, as much as I can grab I reach of you, a handful of your small soft pink breast, with nipples as faint as freckles, and quickly I find the expression limited by clothes and I peel yours away, I grab firm the rest of your bicycle shorts and yank in one sweeping motion, from in between your legs. I lean into you, my body over you, kissing you, a hand stroking your pretty cunt, gently in place, while you wriggle out of my shirt. For some reason and partially to my disappointment we don't bother with foreplay, "I want you to fuck me."

And I kneel to strip and find myself between your legs to fill you, and your face is turned into celebration. Submission to satisfaction, head titled back, curls loose and long, a faint blushing, a mouth just slightly opened, with a sound punctuated: breath, "ah," gasps, more noticeable by how breath wants to escape but the sensation won't allow, hiccups--and your eyes turned down and cold with focus. We exhaust ourselves. I drink from you, lapping till you come. You shake in my mouth. You turn away from me on top of me. I fill you from behind and you look wild over your shoulder at me. Ready to explode. The most fevered passion--and I can't perform. I pull out.

"I can't."

And we separate. And then we fall together again. You stroking my cock and then filling your mouth with me and taking me in with such love. I can tell you're better at sex than me. You love sex more than me. There was a part of me that knew this would happen since the beginning knowing you were spending the night and another part of me that felt I should have resisted. Something intuitive sensing it was a mistake. That love doesn't develop this quickly. That bodies lie. That I might by lying. I couldn't come. You leaned up in bed and pet your own hair on your side.

"You look like an art model."

Your big high hips. Your tummy's curve into them.

"Like a Roman statue?"

"Yeah, like a sculpture."

And you pet your hair which seems so out of character someone so stripped down. I forget women are women sometimes. Part of me is nervous and empty. Part of me is happy. Part of me is distant depressed. I want to understand you but you still seem hidden. How for all your "honesty," I am intuitively sensing resistance. The resistance is mutual. You pass out with your cunt rubbing gently against my thigh and I pass out with a palm full of your tight white ass in my hands.

The thing about spending the moments of time before you know you're never going to see a person again is that you have a different kind of conversation: none. You stay there silently working on sustaining a sense of resolve & joy which isn't exactly fighting tears in your eyes...all words are too strong, right? People think that it's sentimental to connect with people you've met in a day. Fucked in a day. It's just a good time. Except with you it's not, it's not a good fucking time. Because now I like you. I'm obvious to our future wreckage at the time but shouldn't have been. Conversation turns to Michael. Political correctness. Music. How'd you reject a guy in a Tool shirt. And then Michael again. I'm gullible again so I'm listening. We drain the coffee and you remind yourself to leave. I laugh. I lift your legs up and kiss your knees goodbye.

A text from you:

"I dont think I want to hook up again considering Mitch."

It's been a day. "Hook up." The words disgusted me. I was filled immediately with rage. I clenched my teeth--and my stomach sank--and a knot in my throat emerged with an addict's for a primal scream. I want to scream at you. "I never want to give my body to another woman again." The loudest thought. You don't know shit about me. And how they're exactly like women. That it's possible to feel used. That I'm letting you in as much as you think you're letting me in. My body is not public property. It's for everyone but it's not everyone. Do you have no foresight? You robbed me you fucking cunt. Another nostalgic bitch looking for a brief vacation from the unresolved grief of past partners.

"You're a fucking snake. And a passive aggressive."

"You're assuming the worst. My feelings, like your feelings changed."

And I am reminded of but still having trouble truly believing Hanlon's Razor.

"Never attribute to malice that which can be adequately explained by stupidity, neglect, or misunderstanding."

I hate you.

I hate you.

I fucking hate you.

I didn't need to fuck you to realize how I felt.j

My feelings changed when I saw you.

When I met you.

When I kissed your knees you fucking cunt.

"Maybe we can be friends when my feelings are sorted out."

Again, as if I am on hold/in the wake of your indecision. It takes two seconds to think--I made the decision quickly based off of how I felt and stuck with it despite the feelings being mixed. I'm not some delusional obsessive. I don't care who you fuck or call or

commit to away from me. I don't care if you still love another man as long as you keep those filthy fucking feelings away from me. Away from us. Our relationships beauty and potential shattered on a superficial Narcissist's guilt. Now you feel guilty? You knew who I was to him. You knew who I was. You knew who you were to him. Tell me I'm too poor to date. I'll understand. The sex wasn't good. I'll understand. You can't date me because of my politics. I'll understand. Masked in morals: greed. You wanted what you wanted. You got it. And now you can feel bad. And look good. For nobody. All dressed up and nowhere to go.

I send you a string of texts:

"You don't deserve it

because you don't deserve my anger

but

I'm having this fantasy

where I find you in a public place

and when I find you

I publicly announce to a crowd

of unconcerned people that

'I'm going to assault this woman.'

I strip you of all your clothes,

tearing them apart/from your body

and I hand them back to you to hold

and I escort you out by your neck."

I'm forgetting you've taken Krav Maga classes.

"You're not interested in reason.

You're not listening to me.

This is emotional abuse.

I'm blocking your number."

As a commitment to self a centralization of my power and celebration of my body, I've been lifting for 6 months. Stripped of all humanity. Use as a consumable or experience, I decided to take a photo. It's a nude selfie. Posed with a sociopathic stoicism, and a creeping evil smile on my face, my revenge and reclamation: a new slope to a thicker neck. A fuller thicker chest. Snake-belly white arms bulging. The legs of a horse. Andy my small dick prominently displayed. For both Twitter and Instagram with the caption:

I DON'T WANT ANYTHING BAD ENOUGH TO ABANDON MYSELF EVER AGAIN.

I don't envy anyone.

I don't miss anyone.

Loneliness is self pity. Don't waste my time with it.

Weightlifting will mean more to me than you ever will.

Because I will always have myself.

Weightlifting will always mean more to me than art

because I like myself the most.

@abigfuckingbully

@abigfuckingbully

Atticus Davis--he'd be glad to have a pretty stalker: @xlittletankx
Down for whatever always text first: 1 669 291 4010

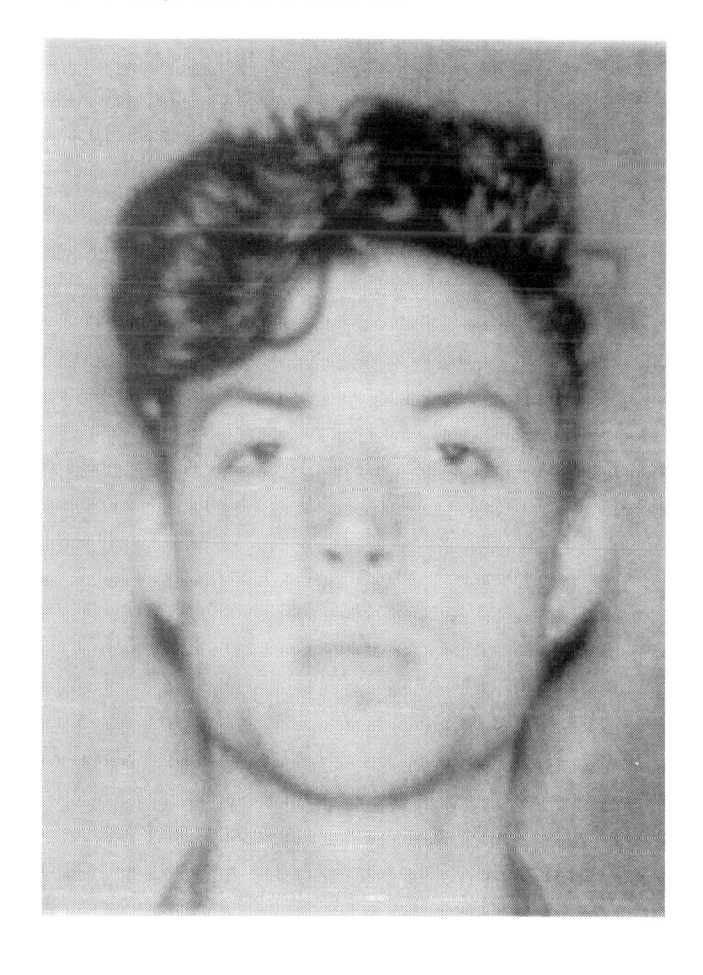

Made in the USA
Las Vegas, NV
08 November 2023